W0254548

THE DISMANTLING OF INDIA

ALSO BY T.J.S. GEORGE

Biography

Askew: A Short Biography of Bangalore
M.S. Subbalakshmi: A Life in Music
The Life and Times of Nargis
Lee Kuan Yew's Singapore
Krishna Menon, A Biography
Pothan Joseph's India
Jawaharlal Nehru

Journalism

The Goenka Letters: Behind the Scenes at the Indian Express
The Provincial Press in India
Editing: A Handbook for Journalists
Moments

Reference

The Enquire Dictionary: Ideas, Issues, Innovations
The Enquire Dictionary of Quotations

Politics

The First Refuge of Scoundrels: Politics in Modern India
Revolt in Mindanao: The Rise of Islam in Philippine Politics
Revolt in Bihar: A Study of the August 1965 Uprising

In Malayalam

Ghosha Yatra (Procession)
Nadodi Kappalil Nalu Masam (Four Months on a Cargo Ship)
Ho Chi Minte Nattil (In the Land of Ho Chi Minh)
Malayaliyude Swathu: Bashir mudal Mohanlal vere (Malayali Wealth: From Bashir to Mohanlal)

THE DISMANTLING OF INDIA

in 35 Portraits

T.J.S. GEORGE

Illustrations by

Tapas Ranjan and Soumydip Sinha

SIMON &
SCHUSTER

London · New York · Sydney · Toronto · New Delhi

First published in India by Simon & Schuster India, 2022

Copyright © T.J.S. George, 2022

The rights of T.J.S. George to be identified as author of this work has been asserted by him in accordance with Section 57 of the Copyright Act, 1957.

1 3 5 7 9 10 8 6 4 2

Simon & Schuster India
818, Indraprakash Building,
21, Barakhamba Road,
New Delhi 110001
www.simonandschuster.co.in

HB ISBN: 978-93-92099-15-1
eBook ISBN: 978-93-92099-16-8

Typeset in India by SÜRYA, New Delhi

Printed and bound in India by Replika Press Pvt. Ltd.

Simon & Schuster India is committed to sourcing paper that is made from wood grown in sustainable forests and support the Forest Stewardship Council, the leading international forest certification organisation. Our books displaying the FSC logo are printed on FSC certified paper.

No part of this publication may be reproduced, transmitted or stored in a retrieval system, in any form or by any means, electronic, mechanical, photocopying, recording or otherwise, without the prior permission of the publisher.

This book is sold subject to the condition that it shall not, by way of trade or otherwise, be lent, resold, hired out, or otherwise circulated, without the publisher's prior consent, in any form of binding or cover other than that in which it is published.

CONTENTS

FOREWORD

In 1997, fifty years after Indian Independence, I began writing a column titled 'Point of View' for the *Indian Express*. It appeared without a break for a quarter century, that is, until June of 2022. A year's 52 weeks multiplied by 25 tells me I wrote a staggering 1,300 columns in all. Some of the pieces were profiles—of artists, politicians, entrepreneurs, criminals and thinkers. The idea then came to me that it would be possible to construct a history of India by looking at a selection of the personalities that have dominated the nation's attention for 75 years. This book is the fruition of that idea.

Special thanks to Simar Puneet, for editing and steering the book, Sayantan Ghosh for providing the harbour, and to my son Jeet Thayil for everything else.

INTRODUCTION

Is journalism history's first draft? Much of journalism is reportage, which is understood as the style in which news is reported. This can be factual or biased—and if expert hands are handling the bias, you won't even notice it. Evidently, what matters is not the journalist but what he reports and how he reports it. Martin Luther King Jr. was enough of a realist to say: 'We are not makers of history; we are made by history.' Most politicians in power will say, openly or through their actions, that they are the makers of history. Outwardly, it would appear to be so. Who can deny that Narendra Modi is a maker of current history? The history he makes is a different issue. The logic of power surpasses individual quirks.

But political leaders are a transient phenomenon. Even Jawaharlal Nehru, India's most venerated prime minister, had his innings and was then put in a corner. Karl Marx got it right when he said: 'Men make their own history, but they do not make it as they please; they do not make it under self-selected circumstances, but under circumstances existing already, given and transmitted from the past. The tradition of all dead generations weighs like a nightmare on the brains of the living. And just as they seem to be occupied with revolutionising themselves and things, creating something that did not exist before, precisely in such epochs of revolutionary crisis they anxiously conjure up the spirits of the past to their service, borrowing from them names, battle slogans and costumes in order to present this new scene in world history in time-honoured disguise and borrowed language.'

Marx had his own view of India as he lived in an age when

India was a synonym for Hinduism. And his view of 'the religion of Hindostan' was typical of his times. He saw Hinduism as 'at once a religion of sensualist exuberance and a religion of self-torturing asceticism; a religion of the Lingam and of the juggernaut; a religion of the Monk and of the Bayadere (a female temple dancer).'

That was a rather crude way of saying that Hindustan had a non-religious concept of Hinduism. It was always a surprise to the uninitiated that Hinduism could be a culture more than a religion. The culture encompassed everything, from the Brahman who was formless, all-inclusive and eternal, to the Atman, the universal self, identified with the external core of personality. The essence of the message is that the individual is basically a soul that uses its body and mind as instruments to gain experience. The experience so gained is used for the well-being of all. The individual working for the common good—that is a civilisational dictum.

This book examines certain individuals who made themselves special by working for the common good. Sometimes their concept of the common good wasn't very good at all. But that did not reduce their historical significance. What, after all, is the significance history gives to events? Marx gives us food for thought when he says, in the course of an article he wrote for the *New York Herald Tribune* in June 1853: 'England has broken down the entire framework of Indian society. This meant loss of the old world, with no gain of a new one. It imparts a particular kind of melancholy to the present misery of the Hindu and separates Hindostan from the whole of its past history.'

The story of the individual helps us to understand melancholy as well.

T.J.S. George
July 2022

1

J.R.D. TATA

Public Trust, Public Good

In mid-2012, out of the blue as it was, reports appeared saying that Air India was preparing to sell its art collection, one of the most valuable in the world. This was when the national carrier, mishandled by national leaders for long, had run up a debt of ₹43,777 crore and accumulated losses (in the previous five years) of ₹27,700 crore. Fortunately, the family jewels were not sold at that time. Six years later, in mid-2018, again unexpectedly, came an announcement that the government was open to the idea of putting up the Air India collection as a permanent art exhibition under the custody of the National Gallery of Modern Art. This followed a proposal by an Air India chairman to set up a museum at the airline's own headquarters in Mumbai's Nariman Point. A tender was floated, estimating the museum's cost at ₹3.5 crore. It came to naught when the government decided in mid-2017 to privatise the national carrier. It is another matter that there were no takers for the privatisation idea. What was at stake was a unique collection of about 8,000 artistic treasures. Nearly 4,000 were paintings by masters of Indian art, from M.F. Husain and K.H. Ara to S.H. Raza and V.S. Gaitonde. There were sculptures and woodwork, antique clocks and memorabilia, some of them going back to the 9th century. There were ash trays designed by Salvador Dali, which were meant to be gifted to first class passengers. Air India's menu cards were famous for the paintings reproduced on them. These too were faithfully collected and listed among the treasures.

What was an airline doing with paintings and sculptures? That is a question that will take us to the magnificence that was Air India in its early days and the shame it became later. It was a proud national flag carrier in every sense of the term until it turned into a national embarrassment following nationalisation. Across the board, nationalisation meant the replacement of visionaries by shortsighted politicians and bureaucrats. It denuded the country of its aesthetics, its joie de vivre, its buoyant liberalism, converting even the cheerful cosmopolitanism of Bombay into the arbitrary micro-culturalism of Mumbai. Air India withered in that climate. But that did not affect either the reputation or the leadership position of 'the Tatas', a name that had come to represent all that was good and noble. Behind that reputation were the insights that guided the conglomerate's founding father, Jamsetji Nusserwanji Tata. When he set out on his mission in the mid-19th century, Jamsetji laid down two principles—keep social responsibilities in mind while pursuing business success, and uphold nationalism in the era of colonialism. The dreams he had developed could not all be realised during his lifetime. But the standards he set helped Tata enterprises develop a character and a social standing that were unequalled. That standing won fresh laurels under J.R.D. Tata whose principle 'Live life a little dangerously' gave his persona a touch of glamour. J.R.D. took Jamsetji's mission to new horizons by building on the humanism that had guided the founder.

It was the Tata approach to life and business that made Air India different from other airlines. Its contributions to the prestige of India were incomparable, significant, and visible. To J.R.D., the founder, Air India was not just an airline. It was a national symbol consciously developed as such when India was beginning to emerge on the world scene. Tata Airlines, founded in 1932, changed into Air India on the eve of independence when there were few airlines in the world and fewer flying across continents. Going abroad was an exceptional experience for ordinary Indians until the 1960s. When Air India's first flight to London took off from Bombay in June 1948, it had to stop at Cairo and Geneva en route. In a universe still waiting to be opened up, Air India set out to project to the world the wonder that was India. It did so with such dedication and imagination that the world marvelled at the colours of India, the warmth of its hospitality, the variety of its cuisine, and the richness of its art.

The inspiration for all that came from one man. The standards J.R.D. set were high and he would personally check things out from time to time—the cleanliness of the pantry, the freshness of the window curtains, the spotlessness of the toilets. If he wanted improvement somewhere, he would send a polite note to the managers. If Air India's greatest asset in its formative years was J.R.D.'s vision, J.R.D.'s winning asset was the creative genius of a staffer named S.K. Kooka. He carried a humdrum job title, commercial director, but it was Bobby Kooka who made Air India a household name, and a beloved one at that. He invented the Maharaja as the airline's mascot, named the flights the Magic Carpet services, and introduced an inflight booklet with the title 'Foolishy Yours'. The publicity hoardings he put up always made an impact, although one that said 'We do business in three languages; English, English and English' rubbed some patriots the wrong way. Kooka not only shared J.R.D. Tata's ambitions for Air India; he enlarged on them as he translated ideas into action. He wanted Air India offices, especially those abroad, to project India's cultural splendour. Art became a tool for him. Such was his attention to detail that he put emphasis on the exterior walls of Air India's offices in Europe's premier cities. Colourful murals on Indian themes by Indian artists were mounted on the walls making them points of attraction for the locals passing by. The world got a close-up view of India, a colourful one that caused excitement. To realise the dreams he had on the art front, Kooka enlisted the services of Jal Cowasji, officially Air India's publicity chief, but in reality a connoisseur of modern art respected by aficionados for his knowledge and for the high standards he set for himself. Cowasji was allowed to do what he thought fit. He could buy and commission art. This was at a time when buying art was not common in India, and buying it as an investment was unknown. It was also a time when there were no stellar names in the field. Husain and Ara and B. Prabha and other stalwarts of the Bombay Progressive Group were around, struggling to get some attention and considering themselves lucky if someone bought a painting for three- or four-hundred rupees. Often, Air India paid artists in the form of free tickets. That was the milieu in which Jal Cowasji was able to put together an impressive collection of antiques, jewellery, studio photography, as well as paintings. The general public got a taste of the treasure in 2008 when Air India brought out a coffee table book (Mapin Publishing) with 201 colour illustrations and analyses by four experts.

Interestingly, Air India was not alone in collecting and patronising art in those halcyon days. An unlikely rival was the Tata Institute of Fundamental Research (TIFR). Air India at least had a rationale for its ventures into art; it was a commercial undertaking and projecting the right image was useful for business. TIFR could not possibly come up with any such explanations; it was a government-sponsored science organisation with nuclear physics as its main line of activity. But the man who headed it was Homi Bhabha. If J.R.D. Tata was a visionary, Homi Bhabha was a visionary and an artist. His pencil sketches and pen portraits proclaimed talent of a high order. At a Nagpur conference in 1941, C.V. Raman introduced Bhabha as 'a modern equivalent of Leonardo Da Vinci'. Another man who appreciated Bhabha's Leonardo-like double talent in science and art was Jawaharlal Nehru. It was not difficult for Bhabha to persuade the prime minister to let him spend on art acquisition 1 per cent of the funding TIFR received from the government. With this, a collection of about 300 works reached TIFR, including a mural that covered an entire wall in the main building, considered one of the great works of Husain. There were paintings from Tyeb Mehta, Raza, and Gaitonde, and one specially drawn for TIFR by Jamini Roy, a large one by Roy's standards.

Tata and Bhabha, Kooka and Cowasji—the contributions made by Parsis to the industrial and aesthetic richness of India are astonishing in comparison with the smallness of their numbers. Many of them were international in their training and outlook. J.R.D. Tata was born in Paris to a Parsi father and a French mother and remained a French citizen until his twenties, even serving in the French army as was required of citizens. He later became an Indian citizen. In the 1920s, he was caught speeding on Bombay's Marine Drive in his Bugatti. He was defended in court by a colourful lawyer of the day, Jack Vicaji, and J.R.D. ended up marrying Jack's niece Thelma. His long innings as the head of the Tata group saw new marquees coming up: Tata Consultancy Services, Tata Motors, Titan Industries, Voltas, Air India. 'I don't want India to be an economic superpower,' he once said. 'I want India to be a happy country.' He was not happy about democracy descending into license. Many were surprised when he made statements that supported Indira Gandhi's emergency rule on the ground that discipline was essential for a democracy's health. He was certainly not enamoured by the populism of the Gareebi Hatao kind. He was an admirer of Sardar Vallabhbhai Patel rather than of Jawaharlal Nehru. His explanation of this is included in *Keynote: J.R.D. Tata—Excerpts from His Speeches and Chairman's Statements to Shareholders.* He said: 'While I usually come back from meeting Gandhiji elated and inspired but always a bit sceptical, and from talks with Jawaharlal, fired with emotional zeal but often confused and unconvinced, meetings with Vallabhbhai were a joy from which I returned with renewed confidence in the future of our country. I have often thought that if fate had decreed that he, instead of Jawaharlal, would be younger of the two, India would have followed a very different path and would be in better economic shape than it is today.' That was a viewpoint commonly heard in business circles. While J.R.D. was frank in making his position clear, he handled his group with shrewdness and acumen.

When he assumed charge, the Tatas had 14 enterprises under its umbrella. When he retired, it had 95.

All this belong to a hardly remembered past. India has changed. There are no Tatas and Kookas giving an extra dimension of value to public undertakings and business organisations. Art too nosedived with government favourites taking control. The scandals that overtook the Lalit Kala Akademi from 2013 showed the extent of corruption and self-aggrandisement among bureaucrats appointed as secretaries and administrators. Repeated attempts by successive chairmen to get a secretary removed failed because the minister sided with the secretary. Finally, the minister himself found it impossible to back him. Meanwhile, major artworks disappeared and no one was held accountable.

Political standards had not reached so low when Air India was nationalised in 1953. But it was clear that control by ministers would be different from control by Tata and Kooka. The change was visible even under early civil aviation ministers like Arif Mohammad Khan, Madhavrao Scindia, and Ghulam Nabi Azad, although no major scandals rocked the carrier during their term. Then C.M. Ibrahim got the portfolio for 1997–1998. His landmark decision was to disallow a Tata–Singapore Airlines joint venture for a domestic airline. He said he was ideologically opposed to a foreign carrier operating in Indian skies. Published reports suggested that he was shielding a preferred Indian carrier from strong competition. Sometime after Ibrahim disappeared into political no-man's-land, Ratan Tata made a public statement that 'a minister' had asked for a bribe of ₹15 crore to clear the Singapore Airlines Plan. Ibrahim was followed by Karnataka's Ananth Kumar (1998–1999). It was his first stint as a minister and it coincided with the determined efforts of a lobbyist for the French aircraft manufacturer Airbus to get an entry into India. The lobbyist was Niira Radia who was to become famous soon as a lobbyist for the Tatas and Reliance among others. Radia's friendship with the aviation minister paid off and India changed its aircraft acquisition policy in favour of Airbus. Criminal lawyer

R.K. Anand discussed this and other issues in a sleazy book he wrote in 2011, under the title *Close Encounters with Niira Radia*.

Ibrahim and Ananth Kumar were rookies compared to Praful Patel who became civil aviation minister in 2004 and stayed on till 2011. Those seven years are remembered by chroniclers as the years that destroyed Air India. The recklessness of his decisions was so evident that it was surprising that he got away with them. Consider just three. He raised Air India's order for new aircrafts from 28 to a staggering 68. There was no development plan or revenue scheme backing the decision. The result was that a company with ₹7,000 crore revenue was loaded with a debt of ₹50,000 crore. In another suicidal move, he cancelled the Kozhikode–Doha–Bahrain service. This was the most lucrative of Air India's sectors. Jet Airways and Etihad quickly moved in to rake in the revenue abandoned by Air India. In the most absurd move of all, he merged Air India with Indian Airlines, virtually killing both birds with one stone. Praful Patel is a shrewd businessman, belonging to a family that became one of the richest in Maharashtra through the beedi business. He could not have been blind to the fatal blows he was dealing to Air India. It had all the signs of a planned sabotage from within to help friends who stood to gain from Air India's collapse. Jitender Bhargava, a retired executive director of Air India, chronicled the events. No sooner was his book *The Descent of Air India* out in 2013 than Praful Patel filed a criminal defamation case. This alarmed his publishers, Bloomsbury, who quickly pulped the book and publicly apologised to Patel. Bhargava stood his ground and not only made his study available as an e-book, but brought out a self-published print version in 2016.

After Praful Patel, it was a miracle that Air India survived. Then again, it was no miracle because the survival was solely on account of public money being pumped into it by the government. The real miracle was that the bulk of the art collection was still there in a godown in Bombay. 'These paintings moved around a lot and it is very difficult to keep track of them,' said Meera Das, an art historian. *The Hindu* quoted her in June 2019, saying that officials were wary of participating in any procedure lest they face charges of mishandling or theft. It must be the punya earned by the Tatas that kept Air India's priceless art collection safe from the government pilferer-rich Akademis. That punya must have started accumulating from the first generation of Tatas who floated the idea that assets should be kept in public trusts run for the public good. Many Tata initiatives were born from that insight.

Perhaps the notion of public good seeped into the Tatas' collective psyche from the priesthood they pursued as a family tradition. Administering to the spiritual needs of the Persian Zoroastrians in Western India, the early Tatas became respected community elders. Nusserwanji Tata, Jamsetji's father, was the first to strike out on a new path. Born in Navsari in 1822, he moved to Bombay and started a small export trading firm. Jamsetji joined him as soon as he finished his graduation at Elphinstone College. A succession of travels followed. That exposure to the world became a turning point in the career of Jamsetji, aged 20 then. He understood that industrialisation was the key to the future of the country. He noticed how British companies had monopolised the textile industry, taking advantage of the abundance of cotton in India. He bought a bankrupt oil factory in Bombay, converted it into what he called the Alexandra Textile Mill and later sold it at a profit. He went to England again, this time to study how Manchester had acquired leadership status in the textile industry on the strength of Indian cotton. This led to him starting the Central India Mills at Nagpur, chosen for its strategic location with easy access to cotton-growing areas and convenient railway connections. He renamed it Empress Mills when Queen Victoria was proclaimed Empress of India in 1877.

Jamsetji's principal asset was his ability to see ahead. His reputation as the first Indian to take the country towards industrialisation rests on his identification of two businesses and two backup projects as keys to the future. Steel production and hydroelectric power were the industries, science education and a hotel that would attract investors the backups. Only the hotel materialised during his lifetime. The other three, conceptualised by him in detail, were pursued by his sons Dorabji and Ratanji and their successors. The steel plant in Jamshedpur became a pace-setter of India's economic growth. Hydroelectric projects, beginning with the Khopoli plant in Maharashtra, became a lifeline for industrial centres like Bombay and Pune. The Institute of Science in Bangalore acquired a uniqueness that remains unchallenged to this day.

The hotel project cast a spell of its own. There are many folk tales about how Jamsetji Tata happened to build the majestic Taj Mahal Hotel on Bombay's inner seafront close to the Gateway of India. The most widely circulated story is that it was his response to being refused entry to the city's Watson's Hotel with its 'Whites only' policy. The more credible story links the hotel to Jamsetji's ideas of developing the Indian economy. The British editor of a British-owned newspaper in the city apparently urged Tata to build a hotel that would be 'worthy of Bombay'. What finally emerged was an iconic masterpiece in Saracenic style that became an instant Bombay landmark and continues to be so to this day. In 2017, it became the first building in the country to acquire a trademark status with its architectural design protected under the intellectual property right. The Taj, built as a symbol of India, did not hesitate to take the best from across the world in the course of its construction. When it opened in 1903, it was the first building in Bombay to use electricity and the first hotel in the country to have German elevators, American fans, Turkish baths, and English butlers. It also became the first hotel to have a licensed bar, the first all-day restaurant and the first discotheque in the country. The total construction cost in those days as the 19th century fused into the 20th was ₹4.21 crore, a fraction of the market price of an MLA in 21st century India. The Taj shared its luck with its guests. The cost of the room with attached bath was ₹13 a day, with full board, ₹20.

Rates at the Taj might have been a reflection of the temper as well as the standards of the time. They certainly fitted into Jamsetji's philosophy of responsible management. What made the founder of the Tata empire different was the importance he attached to social responsibility. Integral to the plans he drew up for the steel plant in Jamshedpur was a settlement for the plant's workers complete with schooling for their children. He also left instructions on how broad the roads in the township should be, what shady trees must be planted and how generous should be the space allotted to football fields. He also provided for dispensaries, one for men and a separate one for women. Ideas like provident fund and gratuity were introduced when they were virtually unknown to employers and employees alike. This approach would explain an article of faith that J.R.D. Tata developed in his time. 'To lead men,' he said, 'you have to lead them by affection.'

There is no disputing the fact that the Tata name acquired a prestige that no other business house could match. This was a distinction that had an adverse side as well. In 2008, when terrorists attacked Bombay, they picked the recognisably seminal Taj Mahal Hotel as their main target. Gun battles raged in the hotel's lobbies and corridors for three days and a portion of the building was set on fire. As many as 167 people were killed in the hotel, including staff and guests. With a determination rarely seen in the corporate world, the owners of the hotel set out to restore the property to its familiar glory, the employees playing an exemplary role in the effort. The first foreign head of state who chose to stay at the Taj after the terror attack, Barack Obama, said in 2010: 'The Taj has been the symbol of the strength and the resilience of the Indian people.' The House of Tatas as a whole has been a symbol of India's heritage, its potential, and its inner greatness. The legacy of Jamsetji Tata shines bright, illuminating the best of India.

2

SUBHAS CHANDRA BOSE

The Mystery of the Mauni Baba

The thrill effect of the Subhas Chandra Bose saga never fades. His escape from India, his two-month submarine voyage from Germany to Sumatra, his alliance with British India's wartime enemies, Germany and Japan, the magic of the Indian National Army and its near-capture of Imphal—the Netaji story can be re-read again and again with undiminished excitement. The irony is that, despite the involvement of world powers and successive Indian governments, there is still no certainty about what happened to Bose in the end. Did he die in an air crash? Was he shot dead by the Russians in Siberia? Did he make his way to India? Was he the Mauni Baba who lived for several years in Faizabad? There are many questions, but answers are also in plenty. In 2016, the Narendra Modi government released what was described as the first set of 100 declassified files pertaining to Bose. There were plans, officials said, to release 25 such files each month. The first set provided no new information and public interest diminished, leaving the questions raised from 1945 onwards unanswered.

This is strange, to say the least. It is difficult to believe that the Government of India, and perhaps the governments of Japan, Russia, Britain, and the US, do not have the information necessary to close the Bose file. The Modi government's talk about declassified files means that classified files still exist. What could be the reason to keep them classified after more than seven decades? Obviously, political interests are involved. It is no secret that Jawaharlal Nehru had animosity towards Subhas Bose. That goes back to the days of the independence movement when Mahatma Gandhi resented the election of Bose as Congress president in 1938. (Bose was forced to resign the following year.) As prime minister, Nehru was reported to have kept a spy-watch on the Bose family. Officially, Nehru accepted the Japanese announcement that Bose died in the 1945 air crash. But did Nehru know more, persuading him to keep an eye on what was happening in the family? India's viceroy at the time, Archibald Wavell, dismissed the Japanese announcement. 'I suspect it very much,' he noted in his diary, and asked his principal assistant to start preparing for the trial of Bose and his associates for war crimes. The colonial government's Intelligence Bureau submitted a report in October 1945 that said: 'The general opinion among Indians here [Bangkok] is that Bose is not dead but... has made his way to some place occupied by the Russians.' Two theories gained ground: that the Japanese conspired with Bose to fake the air crash so that the British would not capture him and put him on trial, and that Bose worked in the prison camps of Stalin's Siberia.

Other theories strengthened the impression that politics had seeped into the issue. There were reports that files marked 'Whereabouts of Subhas Chandra Bose' had disappeared from the Internal Security Division's desk in the 1970s. What was known as Nehru's master file on Bose was said to have been destroyed during Indira Gandhi's rule. Who will confirm such reports irrefutably—or deny them irrefutably? The absence of a final word led to a clutch of books on the subject. Among them are two by Lt Manwati Arya who was born in Burma and joined the INA's women's wing, the Rani Jhansi Regiment, in the early 1920s. Arya's *Patriot* published in 2007 under the imprint of Lotus Press is a 'personalised biography' of Netaji. It is written in flowery language and is replete with exaggerations: Bose's marriage to Emile Schenkl is described as 'the divine wedlock'. This approach of the author cast doubt on her credibility. But her second book, *Judgment: No Air Crash, No Death*, published in 2010, is a compendium of records and stories about Netaji's disappearance. The burden of the book is that, with Japan collapsing in the war and the British planning to arrest him, Bose wanted to avoid landing in Japan and faked the crash in Formosa (Taiwan) instead. He then escaped to Russia and from there to India. These are not books as understood in the modern idiom. They are amateurish to the core. But some of the records quoted in *Judgment* have not been denied by the authorities. Therefore, attention needs to be paid to her proposition that Netaji lived as 'Pardewala Baba' in Naimisharanya in UP and then as Gumnami Baba in Faizabad and Ayodhya until he died on 16 September 1985. She says that Netaji flew from Saigon to Diren in Manchuria in August 1945 in a Japanese bomber, then drove in a waiting jeep towards Russian territory. There is also a letter purportedly written by Nehru to British Prime Minister Attlee, saying 'Subhas Chandra Bose, your war criminal, has been allowed to enter Russian territory by Stalin... a clear treachery by the Russians.'

According to Arya, Gumnami Baba in Faizabad would talk at length to visitors from behind a curtain. He would refer to little-known roads and localities in Berlin, Tokyo, Kabul, Singapore. He would mention details about world leaders. For example: 'Churchill could not pronounce the sound S.' Among papers catalogued after his death were photocopies of letters written and received by Netaji. Photographs of Netaji's parents were said to have been in the Baba's rooms. The book reminds us that it was Hitler who suggested that Netaji travel from Germany to Asia in a submarine to avoid the risk of air travel. The Japanese naval command objected, saying civilians could not travel in a warship in wartime. The Germans said that Bose was 'by no means a private person, but commander-in-chief of the Indian Liberation Army'. In a risky rendezvous off Madagascar, Bose was transferred to a Japanese Sub.

Two years after Manwati Arya's book, a journalist came up with the same thesis. Anuj Dhar had worked as a journalist but was so taken up with the Subhas Bose case that he set up the non-profit Mission Netaji Trust and brought out more than one book on the Bose mystery, such as *India's Biggest Cover-Up* (Vitasta Publishing, 2012) and *What Happened to Netaji* (Repro, 2015). He supports the view that Gumnami Baba was Bose. Quoting documents, some of which are said to be classified, he argues that the Congress Party and its senior leader, Pranab Mukherjee, wanted the truth to be kept hidden. Three inquiry commissions examined the issue in detail. Those, too, got mixed up with politics if informed gossip is to be taken into account. The first two commissions were appointed when the Congress Party was in power and they ruled in favour of the air crash death theory. The third commission, headed by Justice M.K. Mukherjee, was appointed by the A.B. Vajpayee government. Although that government did not last, Justice Mukherjee's inquiry went ahead without any hindrance. After a seven-year investigation, he rejected the theory that Bose had died in a plane crash. The government for its part rejected the commission's report. Justice Mukherjee made observations that cannot be easily dismissed. He examined 40 trunks with Gumnami Baba's belongings. Among the contents were documents about the freedom struggle, books in Bengali as well as English, and old photographs of Bose's family members. He said the handwritings of the sanyasi and Bose 'matched perfectly' as certified by the National Institute of Criminology and Forensic science. Off the record, he said, 'I am one hundred per cent sure that [the sanyasi] was Netaji.'

In 2016, a public interest litigation prompted the Allahabad High Court to set up the Justice Vishnu Sahai Commission to look specifically into the Gumnami Baba issue. It spoke of the problems created by the passage of time. The 'conclusion' it reached was that, 'A majority of the witnesses said that Gumnami Baba was Netaji or may have been Netaji.' If that sounds non-committal, certainty characterised the thesis put forward by a book that came out a year later, *Gumnami Baba: A Case History* by Adheer Som (Eastern Book Company). It provided more chapter-and-verse evidence to show that the silent sanyasi was no 'small-time standard-issue godman' but a man whose papers included notes about his links with Vietnam and Chinese commanders in the eastern theatre of war.

It would be naive to assume that the Government of India was not aware of the truth about the mysterious Baba. In fact, the Saha Commission reports one of the witnesses saying that he had helped a visitor to meet the Baba in 1981–82, and later discovered that the visitor was Pranab Mukherjee. Manwati Arya's *Judgment* says that Indira and Rajiv Gandhi were aware of the identity of the Baba and saw to it that the district administration took discreet steps to ensure his privacy. For any rational citizen these records and assertions should be sufficient to conclude that Subhas Bose returned to his country at war's end and chose to lead a secluded life as a matter of prudence. That was perhaps the wisest decision Netaji took in his life. If he had revealed his identity and entered public life in newly independent India, we can imagine the mayhem that would have followed. If he had upstaged Nehru and become prime minister, the mayhem could well have developed into a turmoil; Netaji's concept was that free India should have a dictatorship for at least 20 years. For insights of that kind we need to scan a different set of books.

Among Netaji's associates during the INA days and early operations in and around Singapore and Thailand was a handful of journalists. Prominent among them were S.A. Ayer, Reuters correspondent in Bangkok, and M. Sivaram, Reuters staffer who became editor of the *Bangkok Chronicle*. Ayer became minister for publicity in the provisional government-in-exile of Azad Hind that Netaji set up. Sivaram was appointed chief of propaganda. Ayer wrote *Unto Him a Witness* (1951), a definitive account of Bose's work in East Asia. Sivaram's *The Road to Delhi* (1966) did not receive the academic acceptance that Ayer's book did, but it provided details that either Ayer was unaware of or did not want to write about. While Ayer hero-worshipped Bose, Sivaram brought in a measure of journalistic scepticism in his portrayal. Long out of print, Sivaram's book was brought out in a new edition in 2012 by the Institute of Southeast Asian Studies in Singapore. It is a mystery that no Indian publisher kept in circulation this essential telling of an important episode in the history of India.

Sivaram sets the background by providing a thumbnail sketch of Rash Behari Bose, an old revolutionary who had exiled himself to Tokyo and become 'a thorough-going Japanese, [who] spoke Japanese with an ease and dignity that amazed most Japanese'. He also introduces Rash Behari's man Friday, Nair-san, a Trivandrum boy who went to Japan, graduated in electrical engineering and then stayed on as a participant in local politics, doing 'undefined political work in China, Manchuria, Mongolia and Tibet, playing many parts, from camel dealer to Living Buddha'. (Sivaram does not include Nair-san's evolution in post-war Japan as the owner of Tokyo's legendary Indian restaurant, Nair Hotel. Newcomers from India were entitled to a free meal there. He married a Japanese lady but changed her name to Janaki Amma).

One of the highlights of the book is Sivaram's meeting with Abid Hasan, a college dropout who joined Gandhi's Sabarmati Ashram, then chose to work with revolutionaries who believed in armed struggle against the British. He later went to Germany for engineering studies and became an assistant to Subhas Chandra Bose. He was with Bose in the German U-boat that took him to the east. Sivaram quotes Abid Hasan to reveal that many ideas and phrases that were to become part of history were born during that long voyage underwater. Among the new coinages were 'Azad Hind' as the name of liberated India, 'Jai Hind' as the mode of salutation and 'Netaji' as the designation for Bose. The phrases were dreamed up by Abid Hasan, scion of a nationalist family from Hyderabad. (After Independence, Nehru gave him diplomatic postings in China and the Middle East. He died in Hyderabad in 1984, aged 73.)

Sivaram had long conversations not only with Hasan. Almost every day he and S.A. Ayer would have extended chats with Netaji at his seaside bungalow in Singapore. Consultations scheduled to begin 'after seven o'clock' often began sometime after 1:00 a.m. Netaji needed only three or four hours of sleep a day. Sivaram writes about Bose's fearlessness even in the worst of circumstances. He was full of confidence in himself and the victory of his cause. He insisted on maintaining the style and pageantry of a head of state. Sivaram says that the average Indian's heart swelled with pride when 'Subhas travelled in state and insisted on putting on the biggest show possible... Two Japanese military trucks, with mounted machine guns, and a fleet of cars carrying his personal staff, all flying the Indian tricolour, escorted Subhas Bose on his tours. He travelled by the fastest Japanese bomber.'

For all his admiration for Subhas Bose's courage and charisma, Sivaram had differences of opinion with him. The night-time consultations were often littered with Bose's criticism of Gandhi and Nehru in pretty strong words. Sivaram found it difficult to agree with this. Nor did he find it easy to accept Bose's vision of the India he would lead. A small-time magistrate from Bengal named A.N. Sarkar was appointed legal adviser by Netaji and asked to draw up a plan for the reconstruction and unification of liberated India. A comprehensive plan emerged. The plan envisaged, as Sivaram described it, an arrangement under which 'Politically, India would be welded into one grand dictatorship. There would be dress regulations, food regulations. Khaki shirt and pants for work, white shirt and pants for leisure, spoon and fork to eat with and, if hand was used, no more than three fingers to touch the food.' The Japanese, says Sivaram, took a dim view of this post-war plan for India, but Netaji was adamant and the plan was broadcast. Fortunately, it remained a plan, leaving India free to develop into a functioning anarchy, free to use all ten fingers while eating.

3

MOHANDAS GANDHI

Much too Human

Who and what was Gandhi? That is, Mohandas Karamchand, not the spelling manipulator Feroze Ghandy who altered his Parsi name and thereby created a succession of faux Gandhis, from Indira to Rajiv to Sonia to Rahul. Feroze said he changed the spelling as he got involved in the independence movement and became a worshipper of the Mahatma. In the process, he created a convenient confusion about the Ghandies-turned-Gandhis being blood relations of the Porbandar Gandhi.

Mohandas Karamchand was pure Gujarati with no trace of Parsi blood in him. It can be said that he stopped being a Gujarati and became an Indian, something many political leaders claim without the beatific conviction the Mahatma inspires. The rise to virtual sainthood was not easy. He let his wife feel unwanted. When he did recognise her presence, he treated her as though she was the house servant. He wasn't a responsible father either. Although as M.K. Gandhi he went to London and qualified as a barrister, as the Mahatma he took the view that formal education was not good. This meant that his children were 'educated' at the Phoenix Settlement and Tolstoy Farm he set up in South Africa. Manilal was one of the first 'experimental students'. The subjects taught at the farms were manual labour and character building. Clearly the Mahatma had put his new-found idealism above the realities that he himself benefited from. Was his idealism hurt by overkill?

Eldest son Harilal felt so neglected that he rebelled, became a drunkard, and, in a final defiance of father, converted to Islam. He also took to selling foreign goods just because his father had appealed for their boycott in favour of Swadeshi. He died a broken man. Second son Manilal saved himself by staying in South Africa to do social work. Nelson Mandela once said that Manilal's 'gentle demeanour seemed the personification of non-violence'. He became the editor of *Indian Opinion*, a Gujarati-English weekly published from Durban. He died in 1956 after a stroke.

Ramdas Gandhi was not all that enamoured of his father's self-denying asceticism. But he lived up to the name, participating in civil protests and going to jail many times. It was the youngest son, Devdas, who achieved distinction by carving out a career for himself. He did become active in the Gandhian movement, but he drifted to journalism and became editor of the *Hindustan Times* in Delhi. In his personal life, too, Devdas showed he was different. His marriage became as famous as his career because he fell in love with a girl who was not only from the south of India but was only 15 at the time—13 years younger than him. She was from a distinguished political family, being the daughter of ranking nationalist leader C. Rajagopalachari. The Mahatma and C.R. shared the view that Lakshmi was too young to marry. Thinking of a democratic solution to the problem, the fathers suggested that Devdas and Lakshmi wait it out for five years without seeing each other. The lovebugs agreed. It took unusually long for five years to pass, but at the end of it they were married.

Such was the halo that surrounded Gandhi that even his unloving approach to his family was applauded as a sacrifice in the service of the nation. It was from the depths of admiration that the title of Mahatma emerged as a people's tribute. The popular belief is that the title was bestowed on him by Rabindranath Tagore. However, Narayan Desai, son of Gandhi's secretary Mahadev Desai, held the view that the title was coined by an anonymous journalist in Jetpur, a town in Rajkot district.

Perhaps people in his home district were the first to notice that Gandhi had a mission that extended beyond their jurisdiction and indeed their country to embrace the whole world. Gandhi's mission covered not just politics but also people's way of life, their food habits, their dress, their attention to matters of health, their morals. Gandhi was no orator, but his themes and the passion with which he promoted them gave historic importance to some of his speeches—his 1931 speech on the eve of the Dandi March to break the salt laws, his 1942 speech that added two immortal phrases to the annals of history, 'Quit India' and 'Do or die'.

What can only be described as an astonishing speech was delivered in court in 1922. An article he had published in *Young India* had led to a trial over the charge of 'bringing or attempting to excite disaffection towards His Majesty's Government'. Called upon to plead to the charges, Gandhi endorsed the charges against him because '...it is very true that to preach disaffection towards the existing system of government has become almost a passion with me... I do not ask for mercy. I am here to invite and cheerfully submit to the highest penalty that can be inflicted upon me for what in law is a deliberate crime, and what appears to me to be the highest duty of a citizen.' The judge, an ICS Englishman, was shaken. He sentenced Gandhi to six years in prison but said, 'Even those who differ from you in politics look upon you as a man of high ideals and of noble and even saintly life.'

Circumstances led to Gandhi writing what became an autobiography. But the title he chose reflected his outlook on life. *The Story of My Experiments with Truth* was originally written for serialisation in *Navajivan* and *Young India*. He explained that it was not his purpose to attempt a 'real' autobiography. 'I simply want to tell the story of my experiments with truth, and as my life consists of nothing but experiments, it is true that the story will take the shape of an autobiography. But I shall not mind if every page of it speaks only of my experiments.' Appearing in 166 instalments between 1925 and 1929, Gandhi's narrative was lauded both for its linguistic style and for its transparent honesty. He acknowledged three men whose writings had influenced him—Leo Tolstoy, especially his *The Kingdom of God is Within You*, John Ruskin and his *Unto This Last* and the poet Shrimad Rajchandra.

Inspired by ethically evolved personalities, Gandhi became one of the most influential persons of the 20th century. But all his achievements came under critical scrutiny in the course of time. That a Gandhi statue was removed from a university campus in Ghana told its own tale. African activists even devised a hashtag #GandhiMustFall to show their anger at some of Gandhi's early writings. They saw Gandhi as a racist who considered white people in south Africa as 'the predominating race' and blacks as 'troublesome and dirty'. Jawaharlal Nehru apparently told Richard Attenborough, director of the film *Gandhi*, not to ignore Gandhi's 'weaknesses, his moods and his failings'. The Mahatma is 'much too human,' Nehru said.

Gandhi's experiments with celibacy also led to considerable disaffection among his close associates. He was in his seventies when, in 1946, he asked Manu, his niece aged 19, to sleep in his bed for him to test his sexual urge and celibacy vows. Later, he would ask his great-nephew's wife Abha also to participate in this experiment. His doctor, Sushila Nayar, was said to have bathed with him. Many of his associates openly criticised this attitude of Gandhi. A stenographer even resigned in protest.

Gandhi's overall views on women reflected the male chauvinist in him. Referring to rape, he once wrote: 'It is physically impossible to violate a woman against her will. The outrage takes place only when she gives way to fear or does not realise her moral strength. If she cannot meet the assailant's physical might, her purity will give her the strength to die before he succeeds in violating her. However beastly the man, he will bow in shame before the flame of her dazzling purity.'* Chauvinism mixed with highfalutin moralism persuaded Gandhi to make such overblown declamations.

---

* *Harijan*, 1 September 1940, p. 266.

Many saw Gandhi as a supporter of the caste system. Of course, he denounced the concept of untouchability, but he also believed that the caste system helped to keep the social order harmonious. Critics have said that Gandhi was keen not to alienate the upper castes. Apoorvanand, a professor at Delhi University, said in October 2019 that Gandhi had been reduced to '...a ritualistic presence in our collective life. He has been made a lifestyle guru, a feel-good presence—something he never was.' Rajmohan Gandhi, the Mahatma's grandson, has been a prolific writer on his grandfather. He once said: 'There is a stubborn core of people who have understood him and know that Gandhi represents the better angels of the Indian nature.' But just as stubborn are those who think of him as a devil.

In an article in *The Atlantic* in July 1922, when Gandhi was but 53, Edmund Candler showed how complex a personality Gandhi was, '...in turn patriot, martyr, high-souled idealist, and arch-traitor; evangelist, pacific quietist, and truculent tub-thumber and revolutionist; subverter of empires and founder of creeds, a man of tortuous wiles and stratagems, or, to use his own phrase, "a single-minded seeker after truth"; generally, in the eyes of the tolerant who are without prejudice, a well-meaning but misguided politician. Certainly a complex figure.' He concluded in dismay: 'Probably very few, even of the Anglo-Indian community on whom his personality impinges directly, a very substantial incubus, have made up their minds which of these things he is.'

A student of the Bible, Gandhi once wrote: 'Supposing I was deprived of the Gita and forgot all its contents, but had a copy of the Sermon on the Mount, I should derive the same joy from it as I do from the Gita.' But he also wrote: 'If a person wants to believe in the Bible, let him say so, but why should he discard his own religion? This proselytization will mean no peace in the world.'

Gandhi was in his time a new voice and a new force influencing the minds of people in his country and beyond. His ideas were as bold as they were novel. The concept of non-violence was something that elicited grudging admiration even from critics. Civil disobedience, even more so; the very suggestion that disobedience to the government could be civil roused curiosity. Gandhian ideas provided humanity with alternatives to war and rebellion. They turned into ideas that shaped the world.

4

NATHURAM GODSE

Murder as Duty

January is cold in Delhi. But that never interrupted Mohandas Karamchand Gandhi's prayer meetings in the green compound of the Birla family. In 1948, barely six months after independence, he conducted his usual prayers with the usual followers in attendance. One man among them was not usual, though. He attended the meeting not to pray or to be part of the Gandhian movement. He waited until the prayers were over, and as Gandhi made his way out through the crowd, the man took out his revolver and shot the Mahatma three times at point-blank range. Gandhi had no chance. He fell to the ground forward and soon was dead. The assassin, Nathuram Vinayak Godse, was unmoved. Even when arrested and tried and sentenced to death, no emotion showed on his face. There was only the contentment of a committed ideologue who had served his ideology with stunning success. Godse was hanged. He must have died with the satisfaction of a life spent for the good of his country, his people, and his articles of faith.

The relationship between power and ideology is a vastly discussed topic with a great deal of research and theories providing the background. Generally uncontested is the postulation that intellectual and technological elites play a vital role in the success or otherwise of government policies. It is also accepted that intellectual exertion can lead one into negativity and self-destruction. John

Wilkes Booth was very much a thinker. His thoughts led him to the conclusion that the abolition of slavery in the United States was a mistake, and so he assassinated Abraham Lincoln. His conviction gave him the courage to commit a crime. It did not justify the crime because his conviction was contrary to the common good.

Booth did realise that he was doing something wrong and had made elaborate arrangements to escape from law enforcers. Nathuram Godse did nothing of the kind. He was convinced that it was his duty to kill Gandhi for spreading 'anti-Hindu' ideas. He couldn't stomach the partition of India, which he described as an 'abject surrender to Jinnah'. He said it was wrong to call Gandhi the father of the nation; he was the Father of Pakistan. Godse put up a powerful, remorseless defence of himself, reflecting his ideological conviction about the non-rights of Muslims. Saying that he did not desire any mercy from the authorities, he made it clear that 'my confidence about the moral side of my action has not been shaken even by the criticism levelled against it on all sides'.

In a newspaper article in 2016, Tushar Gandhi made the point that Godse was inept and incapable of succeeding without the support of an organisation. 'There were two organisations with whom all the accused were closely associated—the RSS and the Hindu Mahasabha. For some strange reason, despite clues and confessions, these two organisations were never investigated.'* (Actually they were, but perfunctorily.)

According to Manohar Malgonkar who wrote the acclaimed book *The Men Who Killed Gandhi*, Godse and Apte were adventurists who liked to brag about their capabilities. They would impress Vinayak Savarkar, the messiah of Hindutva militancy, with proposals of daring action against Muslims, the Muslim League and the Nizam of Hyderabad. Once Savarkar blessed them, they would get the necessary finance from members of the RSS and the Hindu

---

* Tushar A. Gandhi, 'Nathuram Godse pulled the trigger, but who really killed Gandhi', *Economic Times*, 11 September 2016.

Mahasabha. For a proposed raid on the Nizam's revenue agencies, they asked an affluent family for one of their large limousines. As Tushar Gandhi puts it: 'Three weeks went by. When no news of raids on the Nizam was reported, the car's owner came looking for his vehicle and found Apte romancing his girlfriend in the car.'

Decades after the murder of Gandhi, Godse is not short of admirers. Pragya Thakur, a BJP Member of Parliament, described Godse as a 'desh bhakt', a patriot. Pragya is considered an extremist even by many BJP leaders, so her praise of Godse surprised no one. Narendra Modi disowned Thakur by saying, 'I'd never be able to forgive her fully.' Did he mean that he could forgive her partially? A prominent party MP, Sakshi Maharaj, went on record with his statement that, 'Godse was a patriot just like Mahatma Gandhi.' He was echoing RSS chief Mohan Bhagwat's view.

Once again problems rose from seeing politics through a religious viewfinder. For Mohan Bhagwat, 'Every Hindu is a patriot.' So Godse was as much a patriot as Gandhi. By the same yardstick, non-Hindus are not patriotic, period. This approach is unhelpful even for the majority of Hindus who consider themselves Indians first. That is why the RSS remains an extremist platform unacceptable to vast numbers of Hindu citizens. But extremists are heroes for many. Hitler was seen by large numbers of his people as a patriot, ready to die for his country. The mass killings he carried out were in the name of his country. Reginald Dyer became the 'butcher of Amritsar' by opening fire on unarmed civilians in the closed area that was Jallianwala Bagh. Even Winston Churchill, the Grand Imperialist, called the massacre a 'monstrous event'. But his countrymen collected upwards of £26,000 for Dyer in appreciation of his work. Rudyard Kipling called him 'the man who saved India'. Godse's countrymen have done better. In 2015, the Hindu Mahasabha released a film titled *Deshbhakt Nathuram Godse*. Bhumi Pujan for a Godse temple was performed in Meerut in 2014. A statue of Godse was unveiled in that city on Gandhi Jayanti day in 2016. Chief Minister Yogi Adityanath even proposed that Meerut's name be changed to Godse

City. The *New York Times* reported (February 2020) that more than a dozen statues of Gandhi's killer have been erected across the country and that 'several Hindu temples are being converted into Godse temples'. At the same time, several Gandhi memorials have been defaced, at least one statue decapitated and the word 'traitor' scrawled on his pictures.* The reason given for hating Gandhi is that he betrayed Hindus by being too conciliatory to Muslims and by allowing Pakistan to break off. There is a move from some Hindu nationalists in Uttar Pradesh to persuade the government to insert a special chapter in school textbooks presenting Godse as a visionary who championed the creation of a Hindu nation, the same philosophy to which the Narendra Modi government subscribes. The Meerut chapter of the Hindu Mahasabha holds prayer meetings in temples across Uttar Pradesh and promotes the line that this is the time, under Narendra Modi, to turn India into a Hindu nation.

New generation BJP leaders speak in modern parliamentary idiom. Experienced Lok Sabha member that he is, Rajnath Singh condemns 'any philosophy that describes Godse as a patriot'. He said: 'If someone considers Nathuram Godse as a desh bhakt, then our party condemns it. Mahatma Gandhi is an idol for us, he was our guiding light and will remain so.'

Idols and guiding lights are as good or as bad as their interpreters. The interpretation of Gandhi as the creator of Pakistan and therefore a destroyer of India is too deep-rooted in the Hindutva mentality to be ignored. Godse, let it not be forgotten, found inspiration in the intellectual giants of history. He was steeped in readings of Marxism, socialism, Dadabhai Naoroji, Gandhi, Savarkar, Vivekananda, Gokhale. After reading them, Godse said, 'Thinking led me to believe it was my first duty to serve Hinduism and Hindus both as a patriot and as a world citizen.' Vivekananda and Gokhale, let alone Naoroji and Gandhi and Marx, never propagated a religion-based patriotism.

* Sameer Yasir, 'Gandhi's Killer Evokes Admiration as Never Before', *New York Times*, 4 February 2020.

Godse was only proving that an activist could always find heroes who could be used to justify whatever needed to be justified. Godse said: 'In condemning history's towering warriors like Shivaji, Rana Pratap and Guru Gobind Singh as misguided patriots, Gandhiji has merely exposed his self-conceit.' He twisted the knife by asserting that Gandhi was 'a violent pacifist who brought untold calamities on the country in the name of truth and nonviolence, while Rana Pratap, Shivaji and the Guru will remain enshrined in the hearts of their countrymen forever for the freedom they brought to them'.

That was not enough for Godse. He had to go further and find a specific reason to justify murder. He put it as strongly as he could. 'The accumulated provocation of thirty-two years, culminating in his last pro-Muslim fasts, at last goaded me to the conclusion that the existence of Gandhi should be brought to an end immediately.'

All countries have citizens who turn against those in power, seeing them either as under-performers or as performing in the wrong direction. That is why even in democracies, presidents and prime ministers are surrounded by multiple security rings—as though people's elected representatives are in dire need of protection from the people. This is one of the ironies of democracy. Narendra Modi is flanked by soldiers with their fingers on the trigger of their guns. That is what is seen. What is unseen is scarier. When the prime minister steps out of his house, traffic on the whole route is blocked for ten minutes. Two vehicles of the Delhi police patrol the route with their sirens on. More than 500 commandos of the SPG are permanently stationed around the PM's residence. The convoy that invariably follows the PM has two armoured BMW sedans, one Mercedes Benz ambulance and a Tata Safari jammer besides Delhi police vehicles. The jammer vehicle is conspicuous with the forest of antennas they carry. These antennas can diffuse bombs on either side of the road. Altogether there are about a hundred trained specialists who accompany the prime minister on his outings. And his car is very special. If the tyres are punctured, for example, the car can still run 320 km at a speed of 90 km an hour. The SPG protection for the prime minister has a budget of close to ₹600 crore. Not too high when we realise that the PM's residence in the country's most expensive area, Lutyens' Delhi, spreads over 12 acres comprising five bungalows. A two-kilometre-long underground tunnel connects the residence to Safdarjung Airport.

It can be argued that Gandhi fell to the assassin's bullet because he did not have the security cover latter-day leaders take for granted. Compared to the 21st century, 1947 was a year of innocence. By the time the folly of that assumption became obvious, Gandhi was gone. India saw quite a few political killings in the years that followed, from Indira Gandhi (1984) to Chief of Army Staff A.S. Vaidya (1986), from Punjab Chief Minister Beant Singh (1995) to Abdul Ghani Lone, moderate Kashmiri separatist leader (2002), from bandit-turned-politician Phoolan Devi (2001) to political bridge builder Pramod Mahajan (2006). What did the assassins achieve? That of course is a question the killers never ask. Elimination of a hate figure of the moment is achievement enough for them. When *The Satanic Verses* was published, Ayatollah Khomeini publicly called upon Muslims of the world to kill author Salman Rushdie. It was the efficiency of the British secret service that kept him safe. The book's Japanese translator, Hitoshi Igarashi, was stabbed to death in Tokyo. The Italian translator, Ettore Capriolo, was also stabbed, but he survived. What did the Ayatollah achieve? Some lives were lost, some strains of hatred were strengthened, but *The Satanic Verses* received wider publicity and attracted more readers. Books cannot be fought with fatwas.

Nor can fanatics be softened with reason. From his point of view, Godse was a man of reason, his ideas and lifestyle reflecting what he considered the best model a reasonable man could follow. An ordinary man cannot bring himself to kill. The act of murder requires a stern will and a belief system that allows such an extreme step. Godse did not kill Gandhi on a spur-of-the-moment emotion. It was a carefully planned act, performed by a man who had an ideology he considered patriotic. Such men are not open to debate because they see their ideology as faultless, not requiring further examination. That Godse is considered by many Indians as worthy of worship, in temples dedicated to him, conveys a message that is important and needs to be understood as disturbing. But how many see it that way? Politics transcends rationality. In India, politics has often been associated with the emotional impact of political leaders. Why did the politics of the Gandhi–Nehru era change when Vajpayee and L.K. Advani had their innings? Why did politics change again under Narendra Modi and become an arena for the glorification of individual eminence?

It is difficult to avoid the conclusion that the power of the individual is a determining factor in the politics of power. Narendra Modi used the power of the individual more directly and more effectively than any BJP leader before him. The result was that he became more important than his party. Nehru had a similar position in the early years of independence. Vajpayee, too, was more important than his party, until he tried to correct that impression for his own reasons. The Nehrus and the Vajpayees were disciplined political leaders. Although they were bigger than their party, they acted as if the party was bigger than them. Narendra Modi is different in that he not only saw himself as bigger than the party but also ensured that the party agreed with his vision without reservation. Essentially, it is a difference in culture. Nehru, and to some extent Vajpayee, belonged to a culture that put the country first. That culture changed radically under Modi.

Values changed. What was considered unacceptable now became acceptable. What could not be said or done could now be said and done without causing eyebrows to rise. Maybe Mohan Bhagwat was right: every Hindu is a patriot. Maybe Pragya Thakur was right: Godse was a desh bhakt. May be WYSIWYG is mankind's ultimate philosophy—what you see is what you get. Perhaps we should add WYWIWYS to complete the philosophy—what you want is what you see. Godse might have been hanged, but he hasn't died.

5

V.D. SAVARKAR

The Discovery of Hindutva

If you look for the dictionary meaning of the word 'veer', misdirection and confusion will result. Literally, the English word means 'change direction'. But in Sanskrit-influenced languages it also means a brave warrior. As part of the term Swatantra Veer, it means a brave warrior of freedom. Vinayak Damodar Savarkar was qualified by his numerous admirers as Swatantrya Veer Savarkar, shortened for everyday use to Veer Savarkar. What made him Veer was his invention of Hindutva as distinct from Hinduism. He argued that Hindutva was Hinduness, encompassing a wide range of cultures including 'Sikhs, Aryas, Marathas, Madrasis, Brahmins, and Panchamas'. A cohesive nation, he said, could be built only by those for whom the country is not only the land of their forefathers but also 'the land of their gods and angels, seers and prophets'. The love and loyalty of Muslims 'is and must necessarily be divided between the land of their birth and the land of their prophets... Mohammedans would naturally set the interests of their holy land above those of their motherland'.

Those words suggest a logical flow of thought. He organised them in book form in 1923 under the title *Essentials of Hindutva* (reprinted five years later as *Hindutva: Who is a Hindu?*) The appearance of Hindutva as a philosophy was not an overnight phenomenon. Savarkar had been moving in that direction from his student days. He was politically active even in high school. An atheist from early on, he cherished the philosophy of Hinduism. In Fergusson College, Pune, he joined the Hindu Mahasabha to show his aversion to the Muslim League. As students, he and his brother Ganesh founded a secret fellowship named Abhinav Bharat Society. The need for secrecy arose from the activities the society envisaged. Several hundred revolutionaries and political activists were recruited and branches sprouted in different parts of India. After Savarkar went to London to study law, a branch took shape there too. The society managed to assassinate some British officials. Soon, the Savarkar brothers were imprisoned and the society disbanded in 1952. When in London, Savarkar had managed to send 20 Browning pistols to India. One of these was used to kill the district magistrate of Nashik, an Englishman named A.M.T. Jackson in 1909. This murder led to Savarkar receiving what was considered the heaviest punishment in those days—imprisonment in the Andaman's Cellular Jail, also known as Kala Paani.

We do not know whether it was a calculated manoeuvre by the cunning British, but within a month of life in the Andamans, Savarkar started sending mercy petitions begging for his release. He made repeated assurances of good behaviour and made it clear he was a changed man: 'If the government in their manifold beneficence and mercy release me, I for one cannot but be the staunchest advocate of loyalty to the English government... I am ready to serve the government in any capacity they like, for my conversion is conscientious.' In the fourth mercy petition, he wrote: 'Every intelligent lover of India would heartily and loyally cooperate with the British people in the interests of India herself.' He went on to extol the British empire. 'Such an empire as is foreshadowed in the proclamation wins my hearty adherence.' He also said that he was willing to pay whatever security or pledge the government wanted from him. Any condition would be 'gladly accepted' was the unembarrassed promise. Eventually he was released and he became, as promised in his petitions, an active collaborator with the British.

Savarkar obviously had a side to his character not evident at first sight. An unusual manifestation of this was the publication in 1926 of a book titled *Life of Barrister Sarvarkar* written by Chitragupta. It glorified its subject in flowery prose. One passage said 'Sarvarkar is a born hero' who possessed 'distinctive marks of character such as an amazing presence of mind, indomitable courage, unconquerable confidence in his capacity to achieve great things'. When a second edition came out two decades after Savarkar's death, the preface revealed that Chitragupta was Savarkar himself. Which explained his unconquerable confidence in self-praise.

It is clear that Savarkar tried, often successfully, to protect himself while pushing his followers into crime. Worse, he had no compunctions about betraying his comrades. Perhaps the most notorious betrayal was that of Nathuram Godse. Savarkar was accused in court of being the mastermind behind the Gandhi assassination. Godse was hanged, but Savarkar, though arrested, was acquitted for lack of evidence. In a *Mint* article in 2019, author Manu Joseph wrote: 'Considering the circumstantial evidence against Savarkar and how modern Indian Courts have reacted to this type of evidence, it is unlikely he would have been freed if he were tried today.'

It is just as unlikely that he would have faced any opposition in the India that is governed by the Bharatiya Janata Party. Long before the BJP rose as a claimant to political power, Savarkar put out the call: Hinduise all politics and militarise Hindudom. This was during World War II when he was President of the Hindu Mahasabha. Prime Minister Narendra Modi would have recalled this when, on Savarkar's birth anniversary, he bowed before the late hero's portrait and praised him for 'his indomitable spirit and invaluable contributions to India's history'. Vallabhbhai Patel, a hero of Modi, thought otherwise. His view was that, although the technicalities of law had acquitted him, Savarkar was 'morally' a murderer (Manu Joseph, *Mint*, 2019). Interestingly, Savarkar called Subhas Bose a Hindu Jihadi. Recalling this, Subhashini Ali, daughter of Lakshmi Sahgal of INA fame, said that, 'Bose was a staunch critic of Savarkar.'

Among those who were seminally influenced by Savarkar, was a disillusioned Congressman named K.B. Hedgewar. The idea of Hindutva appealed to him and he managed to discuss the subject at length with Savarkar in 1925, focussing on ways to create a Hindu Rashtra. He further sharpened the ideas that evolved during the discussions and founded an all-new organisation, the RSS, Rashtriya Swayamsevak Sangh. This created a fissure in the freedom movement led by Gandhi and Nehru. That pleased the British. But neither Savarkar nor Hedgewar became instruments the British could use to tighten colonial control of India.

Savarkar was a realist who accepted historical developments that he was unhappy about. He wanted the national flag to be saffron. When the time came, he had no hesitation in hoisting the tricolour in front of his home in Mumbai. In an article advocating social reforms, he lauded Buddha, Jesus, and Mohammed as 'reformers who rocked the boat' and were ready to face the consequences. It is no surprise that Savarkar's heroes were Joseph Mazzini, the revolutionary who worked for the integration of Italy, Kemal Ataturk who modernised Turkey by taking it away from conventional Islam, and, perhaps surprisingly, Vladimir Lenin, the revolutionary who restructured Russia into the Soviet Union. Evidently, his intellectual bent enabled him to see achievers as such, whether or not he agreed with what was achieved.

Vinayak Chaturvedi, author of 'Violence as Civility: V.D. Savarkar and the Mahatma's Assassination' examined the proposition that violence was central to the epitome of Hindu thought.* Advocates of this theory argued that violence was an ethical mode of conduct. The average person will find it difficult to see violence

* Vinayak Chaturvedi, 'Violence as Civility: V.D. Savarkar and the Mahatma's Assassination', *South Asian History and Culture*, Vol. 11(3), August 2020, pp. 1–15.

as ethical. In a country that still venerates Gandhi, a national leader who developed non-violence as a weapon in politics, it will not be easy to whitewash violence. Savarkar did not gain historical significance because he supported violence. His analytical approach helped him see political developments in a larger context. This was the metaphysics that led to Hindutva itself. In other words, even as Savarkar weaponised politics, he fitted his politics into an ideological framework, thereby giving it an additional depth and dimension. By making Hindutva look like a legitimate ingredient of politics and public affairs, he made it possible for extremist viewpoints to gain ground and help platforms like RSS. Mahatma Gandhi's secretary Pyarelal wrote that, '...the RSS was a communalist, para-military, Fascist organisation. Their declared object was to set up Hindu Raj. They had adopted the slogan "Muslims clear out of India".' Gandhi and Pyarelal are dead and so is the India they envisaged. Government came into the hands of the BJP, the political wing of the RSS. Large sections of the population also became supporters of the nationalist agenda as conceived by the RSS and the BJP. Most of Savarkar's dreams came true within half a century of his death in 1966.

Perhaps his contemporaries knew that time was going to solidify his standing in history. Even those who were ideologically opposed to him were liberal in their praise. P.K. Atre, poet and educationist who enjoyed considerable influence among Marathi readers, wrote 14 articles in his paper assessing Savarkar's contributions to society. Communist leader Hiren Mukherjee demanded that Parliament pay homage to the departed leader. Indira Gandhi described Savarkar as a byword for daring and patriotism. The BJP government in Karnataka named a newly built flyover after Savarkar in 2020 in the face of stout opposition by non-BJP legislators. In Parliament a Shiv Sena member shouted: 'If you have courage, give Bharat Ratna to Savarkar.' That level of courage is yet to come.

6

C.N. ANNADURAI AND M. KARUNANIDHI

The Rise of Dravida

Conjeevaram Natarajan Annadurai was one of the shapers of India in the 20th century. Neither this nor its importance is adequately recognised because his theatre of activity was limited to the south of India and his cause was seen, largely by traditionalist chroniclers of a unitary subcontinent, as narrowly provincial. In fact, he represented the primal force of language in nation-building. India got it wrong on the language issue right from the start, hence the perception of language politics as a negative force in public life. A different approach at the right juncture could have made language a unifying force. Consider Indonesia at one end and Switzerland at the other. Home to 700 'living languages', Indonesia side-lined all of them when independence came and picked a composite called Bahasa Indonesia as its only official language. Thus Javanese, the language of the majority, did not get any advantage over others, a policy objective pursued by the country's first-generation leaders, many of whom were Javanese themselves. Compared to Indonesia with a population of 207 million, Switzerland has only 8.5 million citizens. As many as 65 per cent of this small population speak German but they put themselves on equal terms with French, Italian, and even the 1 per cent Romansh speakers. Both Indonesia and Switzerland devised policies that suited their separate sociopolitical circumstances and remained linguistically peaceful and reformist.

Very different has been the Indian narrative. Mahatma Gandhi stood firmly for Hindustani, a mixture of Hindi and Urdu, as the national language. Subhas Chandra Bose lobbied for Hindi in Roman script. But Hindi purists were opposed to adjustments of any kind. They not only ensured the enthronement of Hindi as the dominant language; their inflexibility alienated speakers of other languages. It was not merely a matter of sentiment. Language proficiency was a qualification for jobs. That gave Hindi speakers an advantage over others in the employment market. Even those who picked up Hindi well were at a disadvantage in comparison with those whose mother tongue it was.

The economic dimensions remained unchanged but the political scenario changed in 1952 with Potti Sriramulu fasting to death. The rattled Nehru government quickly announced the formation of Andhra Pradesh, India's first linguistic state. The reconstitution of the country into a conglomeration of linguistic jurisdictions, each patriotically sensitive about its uniqueness, paved the ground for permanent quarrels over river water among the southern states, over the ownership of Belgaum between Maharashtra and Karnataka, over territorial claims between Haryana and Punjab, over a who-is-who mess in Assam and neighbouring states. Then, in 2014, the very concept of linguistic states turned comical when one Telugu state was split into two Telugu states. The politician who led the agitation for the splitting, K. Chandrasekhar Rao, saw the new Telangana state as his private preserve, making his religious superstitions the basis of governance, appointing his son as minister and party leader, and ridiculing Potti Sriramulu himself. Language has been anything but a unifier in India. In fact, in a region that has been tormented by religious hatred, linguistic antagonisms proved even more lethal. This had been tragically dramatised by 'Mainland' Pakistan's treatment of East Pakistan, 1,800 miles away at the other end of the subcontinent. Language-based incompatibilities made religion-based unification impossible. Eventually, the military junta unleashed genocide in the east wing, where mass killings and mass rapes destroyed a generation. But they couldn't win. A civilisation based on Urdu-Punjabi just could not coexist with another based on Bengali. Religion did not have the strength to mediate in a clash of languages.

The pre-eminence of language in the affairs of the state acquired special significance in a multilingual polity such as India. It was an article of faith with Annadurai that language was the essence of a people's cultural heritage. He shared that conviction with iconoclast Periyar Ramaswamy and fellow film-writer M. Karunanidhi. The Trimurtis nurtured a previously unarticulated Dravida civilisational value system, thereby contributing a lasting component to India's socio-political ripening. Whether Indus Valley was populated by Dravidians and whether Aryans came from Central Asia are running controversies among academicians. Latter-day politicians have vulgarised it with partisan concepts of nationalism. The fact remains that Dravida civilisation's history goes into the ancient past and has sustained itself robustly into the present. It is a misfortune that this is sought to be denied by sections of people from non-Dravida areas, giving rise to a north–south confrontation. This polarity, manifested in the campaigns for and against the propagation of Hindi, continues as a vitiating influence in Indian public life.

Emotions against Hindi imposition are at their bitterest in Tamil Nadu. The irony—which deserves attention by Hindi partisans in the north—is that that Tamil people are not per se anti-Hindi. Most young people make an effort to learn it for various reasons. The Dakshin Bharat Hindi Prachar Sabha has been functioning with quiet efficiency out of Madras for a hundred years. Some 60 per cent of candidates appearing for its qualifying examinations are from Tamil Nadu. Clearly, public sentiment has not been against Hindi. It was the zealotry of Hindi's northern torchbearers that created the antagonism, a zealotry that generated matching zealotry in the south. When milestones along rural roads in the deep interior of Tamil country carry place names and numbers in Hindi, it is not just a provocation to local sentiment; it is plain stupid. When Hindi is made compulsory in CBSE and Kendriya Vidyalayas, Tamil aspirants feel they are at a disadvantage, however bright they may be. Resistance to Hindi was stronger in Tamil Nadu perhaps because Tamil is the oldest linguistic tradition in the south and Tamil speakers are more emotionally attached to their language than their counterparts in the other language territories. To see the importance of this aspect of Tamil tradition we only have to look at the way C. Rajagopalachari and K. Kamaraj were overtaken by time within one generation. Giants of the south and pillars of national politics once, they were warriors who got us freedom. But when language loomed as an issue of freedom, their 'national' status clashed with local aspirations. They were overtaken by protagonists of Tamil identity. C. Rajagopalachari as prime minister of Madras presidency in 1937 made Hindi compulsory in schools. He told people to look at Hindi as 'chutney on the leaf' which they could 'taste or leave it alone'. People did not want even to leave it alone. Massive protest kept the state on the edge of violence for three years. Police beatings led to two deaths. Ironically, when C.R.'s Congress government was succeeded by the British administration in 1940, Hindi was made optional in schools.

The strongest opposition to C.R.'s Hindi move came from Periyar E.V. Ramaswamy. As far back as in 1916, the Justice Party had raised the banner of revolt against Hindi. But the main fight of that party was against Brahmins. Seeing the Dravida cause as larger than anti-Brahminism, the Justice Party was dissolved in 1944 and its chief at the time, Periyar Ramaswamy, founded the Dravidar Kazhagam. That year, the Hindu Mahasabha made an effort to bring the Dravida leadership under its sphere of influence, somewhat unusual, given the Hindu Mahasabha's Brahmin orientation. Periyar's weekly publication, *Kudi Arasu*, published polite reports of his discussions with the Mahasabha's leader B.S. Moonje in Trichy. Annadurai, a follower of Periyar at the time, issued a press release on the discussions. Apparently, the newspapers of the day ignored him, for *Kudi Arasu* pointed to the press coverage as 'an example of how the Brahmin mind worked'. Annadurai's association with Periyar did not last. Concepts like 'self-respect marriage' conducted without priests as Brahmins had attracted him to the venerable Dravida pater familias. But even after the formation of the Dravidar Kazhagam, the patriarch continued his extremist position against Brahmins. Annadurai had no problem accepting Periyar's ideas on women's rights and superstitions, but he could not go along with the position that Aryans were responsible for all the ills of India. Periyar wanted 15 August 1947 to be observed as a day of mourning; Annadurai saw independence as a gain for all Indians, not just for Aryans. Periyar wanted elections to be boycotted; Annadurai saw elections as vital to democracy. While much of Periyar's revolutionary thrust came from his emotional commitment to causes he considered dear, Annadurai was driven by his intellectual bend of mind. With a clearer understanding of the way the political system worked, Annadurai found the Dravidar Kazhagam too romantic to be effective. There was no way the realist in him could carry on with the eccentric in Periyar. Five years after the Dravidar Kazhagam's formation, Annadurai left it to launch his own Dravida Munnetra Kazhagam (DMK) with M. Karunanidhi as his teammate. Both of them were influential literary figures. Their combined power had a transformational impact on Tamil sensibilities. They changed the history of Tamil Nadu and influenced that of India.

Annadurai was a small man, physically and socially. He was only five feet three inches, and he was born to a family of weavers. He went to college only because he got a Backward Class scholarship. He got a school-teacher's job that helped him make ends meet. But he was a dreamer. He dreamed big, about his people, his language, his country. These dreams took him to Periyar Ramaswamy and made him launch his own platform with its own action plans. The dreams made him perhaps the most educated among the early Dravida leaders. (He had a master's in economics and visited Yale

University as part of a fellowship programme. He studied and got attached to the theories and principles of three men who became his intellectual heroes—Lincoln, Garibaldi, and Mazzini.) The writer in Annadurai emerged early. So did the orator. His ability to grab the attention of readers with his articles was surpassed only by his power to sway the masses with his speeches. Using the medium of cinema as a political weapon was an Annadurai idea. It came naturally to him because he was a novelist, short story writer, playwright, and occasional actor. His films were loaded with social and political messages with no attempt to be subtle about it. *Nallathambi* (1948) exposed the zamindari system while *Velaikari* (1949) revealed the exploitative nature of landlords. Some of his movies and plays lacked even a plot, as poet-lyricist Kannadasan said, but they stirred the emotions. The combined power of Annadurai and Karunanidhi, with their heart-warming themes and bullet-like dialogues, filled cinegoers' hearts with Dravida pride, turning DMK into an unstoppable political force.

Annadurai had a down-to-earth approach that made ordinary people identify with him. His language was their language. His lifestyle was their lifestyle. He was famous for not wanting anything for himself, not even the governmental facilities to which he was entitled as chief minister. He championed the cause of the south as part of his identification with the people. He propagated the view that the difference between South India and North India should be openly accepted. In the early days, he considered these differences to be so deep-rooted as to justify the Dravida region seceding from the north to form a separate country called Dravida Nadu. His argument was that, 'India is a continent and should be divided into separate nations. There is no need for a single government.' He failed to see that this viewpoint ignored many historical and cultural realities that bound the subcontinental nation together. He was no doubt carried away by the divisiveness that had developed on the issue of language largely on account of the superiority complex displayed by the north. He abandoned his radical position in the wake of the

1962 Indo-China war and the Nehru government's anti-sedition law passed the following year. 'When the country is in danger, for us to advocate separatism would be to give way to the foreigner,' he said, recognising discretion as the better part of valour.

Giving up separatism, however, did not mean recognising the north and the south as one. What he perceived as the north's persistent efforts to impose Hindi on the south became a running irritant through much of his career. He put it once in disarmingly simple terms by asking: 'If Hindi is to be the common language because it is spoken by the majority in the country, then why do we claim the tiger as the national animal instead of the rat which is more numerous?' Matters came to a head in 1965 when a 15-year grace period given by the Constitution to use English alongside Hindi ended, effectively making Hindi the only language for the states to communicate with the centre. A letter from Annadurai to Prime Minister Lal Bahadur Shastri fetched no response. Violent protests spread across Tamil Nadu. Even Congress leaders in the south turned against the centre. Eventually, Delhi was forced to allow southern states 'to transact its own business in the language of its own choice'. That surrender gave DMK its finest hour. A massive wave of popularity swept the party to power in the 1967 elections, making Annadurai the people's chief minister. Neither he nor the people knew that fate had given him only two more years to live.

The state functioned with a fervour it had not known before. Its name was changed to Tamil Nadu. The legislature passed a resolution abolishing the three-language formula and replacing it with a two-language formula; that system has been in force ever since. He ordered the removal of pictures of Gods from public offices. He never flaunted atheism as Karunanidhi did nor did he attack other people's faith in God and spiritualism in general. He gave out the slogan 'Onre Kulam, Oruvane Thevan', one race, one God. He once described himself as a Hindu minus the sacred ash, a Christian minus the sacred cross, and a Muslim minus the prayer cap. His simplicity probably explained the economic populism he adopted as policy. He announced subsidised rice at one rupee a measure. The state did not have the resources to implement it immediately, but the concept of subsidy became a staple of government policy in Tamil Nadu.

Annadurai died suddenly, a victim of oesophageal cancer. The shocked populace reacted in a manner that became known as 'the tenth wonder in the world'. Every man, woman, and child dropped his/her work and went to say goodbye to their beloved leader. What was described as 'the largest gathering of human beings ever on earth' assembled to form the funeral procession—13 million. The turnout at Mahatma Gandhi's funeral was two million. Annadurai lives on in multiple ways in the everyday life of his Tamil Nadu. Chennai's arterial Mount Road gave way to Anna Salai. Anna Nagar overtook T. Nagar in popularity and spread. Anna University developed into a major centre of education with, for example, A.P.J. Abdul Kalam as professor of aerospace engineering. Anna Centenary Library is said to be South Asia's largest. Tamil Nadu has seen other cinematic, literary, and political titans rising to the top, but none reached Annadurai's height in creativity and in political acceptability.

Karunanidhi came close to him in writing and political perceptions but could not equal him in impact or popularity. One reason was that Annadurai was selfless while Karunanidhi gave his family undue importance. Annadurai and his wife Rani had no children. They adopted four sons, all of them Annadurai's sister's grandsons. The family fended for itself, deriving no advantage from Annadurai's political positions. Karunanidhi, on the other hand, brought up his family as a political dynasty, trying to ensure that his chosen son would inherit his power. Besides, Karunanidhi had to contend with rivalry from mega stars such as M.G. Ramachandran who subsumed the Dravida cause and later went his separate way with a separate party, the All India Anna DMK (AIADMK). Annadurai split from Periyar over ideology; M.G.R. split from Karunanidhi over power. Neither M.G.R. nor Jayalalithaa who claimed succession rights after him had anything of substance to contribute to the Dravida postulates.

Annadurai was all substance, all brain, all heart. If Dravida identity came alive in the 20th century to claim its place in history, it was primarily due to the way the scholar-activist in Annadurai developed it. He bought to the attention of the world as much as to his own brothers that Dravidian civilisational heritage was something that transcended the politics of his time and covered an extended era of creativity. In its classical days, Dravida genius had not only produced the wondrous temple architecture of southern India but also influenced the development of Khmer, Thai, and Javanese languages. Ridiculing 'Indo-Germanic scholars who held that everything valuable in the world originated from the Aryan', Sardar K.M. Panikkar wrote: 'Not only is Indian civilisation pre-Vedic, but the essential features of Hindu religion as we know it today were perhaps present in Mohenjo-Daro' (*A Survey of Indian History*, 1947). Political India was in thrall to Indo-Germanic attitudinising until this unassuming David stood up to the Aryan Goliath. Annadurai should not remain undiscovered by history.

Muthuvel Karunanidhi made his way across the path that Annadurai had traversed, through the Justice Party, Periyar's Dravidar Kazhagam, and then the Dravida Munnetra Kazhagam. He stayed in the bastions of power much longer than his mentor, but they represented two different eras: One recognised the supreme leader as supreme, the other saw a pride of lions all claiming to be king of the same forest patch. The result was that Karunanidhi was buffeted around, demonised, defeated, and jailed. But in the theatre of public life, he remained a dominant player, admiration for his literary contributions making up for the controversies that coloured his politics. In the title-loving Tamil political culture, he was Kalaignar, master of art, and one notch up on the admiration scale, Mutthamizh Arignar, master of the three forms of Tamil. In this play of titles, presumed to be bestowed by the people, Annadurai was Arignar, scholar, M.G. Ramachandran was Puratchi Thalaivar, revolutionary leader, and Jayalalithaa Puratchi Thalaivi.

Karunanidhi was only 25 when he joined Anna, 15 years his senior, to form the Dravida Munnetra Kazhagam. But his brilliance as a writer had impressed his seniors. He sparkled as a speaker as well. He and Anna became the DMK's most powerful public orators, stirring the masses with their magical words and their dramatic delivery. In 1956, the year they decided to fight the elections, the duo were the party's and the state's star campaigners. When Annadurai died after two years as chief minister, Karunanidhi successfully campaigned to be elected as his successor. He did not have the smooth sailing within the party that Anna had. The challenger was M.G. Ramachandran, who could well be called a protégé of Karunanidhi's. M.G.R. was a struggling stage actor looking for a chance in cinema. He got a supporting role or two in the 1930s, but his lucky break came in 1950 when he was picked for the lead role in *Manthiri Kumari*. It became a hit because it was a powerful film driven by a powerful script written by Karunanidhi. M.G.R.'s sense of gratitude stayed with him; even when political rivalry made them act against each other, M.G.R. continued to refer to Karunanidhi as Aandavar, meaning God. When M.G.R. died, Karunanidhi wrote a moving letter recalling their friendship and their shared values.

Although he became a megastar, M.G.R. was instinctively inclined to politics. Even in his struggling days, he was a worshipper of Gandhi, a wearer of khaddar, and a Congressman. When the Dravida concept gained ground, he joined the DMK. Then superstardom arrived and he did not find it easy to be second to someone, even if it was Aandavar. Irritations mounted over such mundane matters as party procedures about explanations for expenditure. The reality stared them in the face: the glamour of stardom had put M.G.R. on a pedestal that was unreachable by Karunanidhi who after all was a writer and therefore off-screen. The supremacy that glamour bestowed on M.G.R. made M.G.R. overconfident and Karunanidhi resentful. The rivalry led to M.G.R.'s expulsion from the DMK and the floating by him of the Anna DMK which later became the All-India ADMK. Chief Minister M.G.R. haunted Karunanidhi with cases and investigations and Chief Minister Karunanidhi returned the compliment with interest. The feud ended only with M.G.R.'s death. Although the magic of cinema helped them reign like emperors, M.G.R. and Jayalalithaa achieved next to nothing in the realm of ideas. They just enjoyed the power that glamour brought them. They became footnotes in the chapter written by leaders who could think and plan.

Winning all the 12 elections he fought and becoming chief minister five times, Karunanidhi became a legend in his own right. It was his sagacity that made a regional Tamil Nadu party a player in national politics. He teamed up with Atal Bihari Vajpayee's BJP first, but switched to the Congress in the 2004 general elections. The DMK alliance won 40 Lok Sabha seats that year, and seven ministerships in the union government. Dravida leaders wielding power in Delhi as well as in the state was something the early preceptors would not have imagined. Power also made Karunanidhi a law unto himself. His government was dismissed twice by the central government, in 1976 on charges of corruption and in 1991 for being too close to Sri Lanka's LTTE. Jayalalithaa's career-long enmity with him climaxed in a high-voltage drama past midnight on 30 June 2001. Police woke up Karunanidhi, roughed him up, no doubt on instructions from above, carried him downstairs in a scuffle, and dumped him in jail. It was such a highhanded revenge job by Jayalalithaa that it attracted all-round condemnation, leaders of various parties describing her action as atrocious, distressing, barbaric, and shameful. There was an element of crudeness in the way Jayalalithaa and Karunanidhi exhibited their hostility to each other. Karunanidhi had the weaknesses of all post-Emergency political leaders—the belief that the limits of power were ignorable, that the promotion of the self was equal to the promotion of the state, that the children of ministers were more equal than other people's children. He put these self-serving notions to good use as destiny gave him the time it denied Annadurai. He was a member of the legislative assembly for more than 60 years and chief minister for 19. These turned out to be years when the Karunanidhi clan became entrenched, powerful and self-seeking. It was not a small clan. Karunanidhi had three wives and six children in all. His original plan was to make M.K. Muthu, the only son from his first wife, his political successor. Muthu wasn't up to it. He went into films where he made no progress either. The second wife gave Karunanidhi three sons, Alagiri, Stalin, Tamilarasan, and daughter Selvi. The first two entered politics, the last two went their own way. Kanimozhi was the daughter of Karunanidhi's third wife. Keen to become a poet and writer, she found politics had claimed her in devious ways.

In practical terms Karunanidhi was left with Stalin and Alagiri to choose from as potential torchbearers. It was not much of a choice and the father was the first to realise it. He chose Stalin as his heir apparent and sent Alagiri away to Madurai where he was allowed to build an empire of his own. Not that the father had not given Alagiri a chance in politics. In fact, following the rise of DMK as a partner of power in Delhi, Alagiri had become Union Minister for Chemicals and Fertilizers. It proved a disaster. Alagiri neither understood nor was interested in understanding what was ministership or what were chemicals and fertilisers. He seldom attended meetings and turned out to be an embarrassment to all. For Alagiri had grown into a different kind of person. An insight was provided rather graphically in a *Times of India* report (3 September 2018). The correspondent who went to his house wrote: 'There he sat on a throne in the drawing room of his Madurai home, surrounded by nearly 20 men, some flanking him, some at his feet. One with a handlebar moustache held a mug of buttermilk or some such drink, offering it whenever the leader cleared his throat. Another stood with a hand towel, ostensibly to ensure that the drink didn't stick to Alagiri's moustache that looked as thin as his chance of survival in DMK.' Stalin was not exactly a born political heavy-weight, but there was no question of comparing the two. Karunanidhi was the first to admit this; he expelled Alagiri from the party. After the patriarch's death, Alagiri tried to make peace with Stalin and get back into the party. Stalin ignored him.

Karunanidhi died less than two years after Jayalalithaa. The departure of two towering personalities who had monopolised politics for so long created a vacuum that threw Tamil Nadu off balance. Jaya, who liked to see ministers prostrate before her, never allowed talent to come up in the party. When she vacated the chair, it was occupied by men who had no leadership qualities of any kind, reducing the administration of the state to a farce. So pathetic was the situation that the BJP, always considered a North Indian party and therefore shut out of the state's political landscape, found it easy to annex AIADMK leaders as its proxies. The DMK was slightly better off with Stalin as a formally anointed successor. But he had to wait till the 2019 election victories to find a measure of recognition in his own right. (The front led by Stalin won 37 of 38 Parliament seats and 13 of the 22 assembly seats.) Stalin's emergence from the shadow of his father coincided with the crowning of his son Udhayanidhi as the next party leader. Formally, the July 2019 ceremony was to appoint Udayanidhi as secretary of the party's youth wing, the post Stalin had held when he was the crown prince. Udayanidhi was a film actor with a better record than his uncles such as M.K. Muthu. But the dynasty bug had the last say and Udayanidhi began his apprentice period for the family job of chief minister.

But Karunanidhi's talent proved non-transferable. Neither his literary abilities nor his socio-economic ideas were inherited by his successors. For all his dynastic weaknesses and political compromises, Karunanidhi was able to hold on to his concept of liberalism and growth. His long stretch in power had a direct impact on Dravida empowerment. It gave voice to the marginalised millions, thereby changing the social fabric of the state. Administrative reform became the tool of entitlement—equal rights to girls in ancestral property, free flats to the poor provided all castes and religions were represented in a given building, ID cards to farmers so that they could avoid middlemen and sell produce directly in market places set up by the government. It is clear that Karunanidhi had an intellectual understanding of the issues that came before him. Only E.M.S. Namboodiripad in Kerala and to a limited extent, Devaraj Urs in Karnataka, tried to see issues in their larger socio-economic context as Karunanidhi did.

It is tempting to speculate whether the upper hand M.G.R. and Jayalalithaa gained over Karunanidhi was the aberration of a particular period. The absence of film-star influence in politics after the M.G.R.–Jaya period has been conspicuous. If the old standards had continued, Rajinikanth would have become an instant chief minister after Jayalalithaa instead of floating about like Pirandello's six characters in search of an author. Given his earnestness, Kamal Hassan would have become at least the leader of the opposition instead of pursuing *Viswaroopams* in serial order. In neighbouring Andhra, N.T. Rama Rao became the only film-star who broke into politics successfully. Wasn't that because of Rajiv Gandhi? Wearing dynastic arrogance as a crown, Rajiv thought it fit to refer to Anjaiah, former Andhra Pradesh chief minister, as a buffoon. It happened publicly at the Hyderabad airport in 1982 and all of Andhra felt insulted. They voted out the Congress the next year and enthroned N.T.R. whose solitary plank was Telugu aatmagauravam, meaning self-respect.

Karunanidhi's class was different. He was a crusader for social revolution with language as his weapon. He wrote all through his active life. He was chief minister when he wrote screenplays such as *Niyaya Tharasu* (1989). Writer, politician, rebel, iconoclast, Karunanidhi used his faculties to push his idealism. Even after the din and bustle of party politics quieten down, the thunder of his words will echo in Tamil hearts, because such words as Sivaji Ganesan delivered in *Parasakhti* (1952) in defence of 'crimes' are deathless:

I caused chaos in the temple, attacked the priest and I am charged with crimes. You expect me to deny them? No. I won't. I caused chaos in the temple not to protest against the temple but to stop the temple from becoming a centre of terror. I attacked the priest not because he is a devotee but to stop devotion from becoming a pretence. This priest, he asked my sister for her chastity as an offering. This priest pushed her into suicide, into killing her own baby. Luxury tempted my sister, she ran away in fear. Money wooed my sister, she ran again. Devotion frightened my sister, she ran and ran. What's wrong in me, her brother, running after the culprits? Whose crime is it that fake priests roam about, sinning in the name of God? Is it God's mistake? Or is it the mistake of morons who preach in the name of God?

That was Karunanidhi, the dialogue writer, at his biting best. We are left wondering whether those words were written in 1952. They sound so much like life in the 2020s.

7

M.G.R.

Politician, Magician

Maruthur Gopalan Ramachandran was a shudh Malayali, but M.G.R. was a powerful Tamil phenomenon. Maruthur Sathyabhama from Vadavannur village, 15 kilometres from Palakkad town, was living in Sri Lanka with her husband Melakkath Gopala Menon when Ramachandran was born. They were Nairs. Gopala Menon died when his son was not even three years old. Satyabhama returned to Kerala, but she was not welcomed by her family. She found employment as a housemaid in Madras and struggled to bring up her two sons. Young Ramachandra Menon developed as a devotee of Guruvayurappan, but turned rationalist after joining the Dravida Munnetra Kazhagam. The DMK took him to the higher realms of politics, C.N. Annadurai becoming his hero. M. Karunanidhi became a fellow wielder of power. In 1972, he broke ties with Karunanidhi and formed the All India Anna DMK. Winning the 1977 election, he reigned as chief minister for 10 years. He was the first film-star to become a chief minister. Tamizhagam embraced him so warmly that his Nair roots were as good as cut off. He was posthumously awarded the Bharat Ratna, again as a revered icon of Tamil culture.

M.G.R. died in 1987 when he was 70. His hold on the Tamil imagination surpassed that of all others. Jayalalithaa's name, supreme when she was alive, lost some of its effectiveness after her passing. M.G.R., who died almost three decades before Jayalalithaa, retained the magnetism of the name as a symbolic reminder of Tamil grandeur. One reason was that both Annadurai who laid the intellectual foundations of Dravida integrity and Karunanidhi who made it a mass emotion through cinema functioned unseen from behind the screen. M.G.R. was visible on the big screen dazzling the masses with his body and face and sparkling dialogue. He gave shape and voice to the new ideology.

A Tamil movie came out in 1952 that changed all notions about language and politics—and M.G.R. was nowhere in it. This was *Parasakti*, written by Karunanidhi and starring Sivaji Ganesan. The dialogue, rather Sivaji Ganesan's spirited monologues, demolished social evils such as the caste system and put Dravida politics on centre-stage. Sivaji entered politics but failed because he did not represent Dravida sentiments. He was, in fact, the Congress Party's last trump card in Tamil Nadu. He joined Congress because of his admiration for Kamaraj, the idol of the Congress in the south. He even formed the Thamizhaga Munnetra Munnani, but Tamil hearts had already moved away from the Congress and embraced the Dravida dream, shored up by anti-Brahminism and Tamil nationalism. The uncrowned king there was M.G.R.

From the time M.G.R. came in touch with Annadurai in the 1950s, he began taking an active interest in the DMK. He attended party meetings regularly. He became popular with special programmes organised to help the poor. He started orphanages and directly provided financial help to the poor he considered deserving. At one point Annadurai commented: 'When we show M.G.R.'s face, the DMK gets 40,000 votes. When he speaks a few words, we get four lakhs.' Ironically, DMK leaders who wanted the party to be above personalities had to watch Karunanidhi trying to make his son M.K. Muthu take M.G.R.'s place in the party. Serious behind-the-scenes moves were made to convert M.G.R. fan clubs into Muthu fan clubs. Poor Muthu! He sank without a trace.

M.G.R. would have been conscious of his pre-eminent position. When the politicians in the DMK saw him rising high on the wings of stardom, they wanted to bring him down to earth. M.G.R., by now an experienced politician, promptly formed his own platform. Karunanidhi was not impressed. He dismissed the new party as 'a successful movie's 100-day run'. He was pitiably wrong. In the next elections, held in 1977, M.G.R. won a landslide victory. He became chief minister and won the next three elections as well. Decades after his death, his magic continues undiminished. At election meetings in Tamil Nadu, the organisers only had to mention his name, and the crowds would go ecstatic with cheers.

As is the case with most political figures, there was a gap between M.G.R. the film star and M.G.R. the politician. M.S.S. Pandian's essay, 'The Image Trap', describes how M.G.R. always presented himself as 'a low-status underdog' who became a fighter for justice. R. Kanna's *M.G.R.: A Life* shows how the superstar remained an enigma even to his close aids. Analysing his subject with merciless objectivity, Kannan discusses the moral degradation of an icon who was too vain to admit he was ill and too self-consumed to name his successor; he was intolerant of dissent, trusted no one, and kept cabinet colleagues as well as opposition leaders under surveillance. 'No files moved when he was ill,' as Kannan put it. 'The mystique of M.G.R. rested on the fact that his film and political careers were intertwined in a remarkably symbiotic manner that gave him an unbeatable image... When people watched him on the screen, the party's message became M.G.R.'s message.' Was M.G.R. primarily a political man who used his filmic aura to promote his other interests? His political battle with Karunanidhi remains one of the uglier chapters of Tamil Nadu history. The M.G.R. camp accused Karunanidhi of corruption (which later led to an inquiry commission) while the DMK camp used its period of power to unleash the police on M.G.R. associates besides slapping defamation cases against them. When the merry-go-round put M.G.R.'s people in power, raids and arrests plagued Karunanidhi's people. The governing of Tamil Nadu assumed the aspect of a farce, or a slapstick. It was as though someone had written a lurid screenplay and chief ministers and political parties were acting out the roles allotted to them.

Debates are possible over the relative importance of the dialogues written by Karunanidhi and the characters enacted by M.G.R. The emotionally stirring declamations Karunanidhi wrote in firebrand Tamil ensured that the movies of the time were not only popular but also politically influential. It could even be argued that Sivaji Ganesan was a mighty character actor who gave the dialogue a power no one else could. Yet it was M.G.R. who got the louder applause from the public. Even when M.G.R. was hospitalised in New York, Karunanidhi could not get the voter support he wanted. Only after M.G.R.'s death could Karunanidhi get what he, as a more seasoned politician, could claim as his due.

Post the 1977 elections, Chief Minister M.G.R. ran into rough weather because of sudden and unexpected developments. The most important of these was the shooting of eight farmers during a protest against electricity charges levied on agriculturists. The chief minister made things worse by enacting a new rule that made anyone with an annual family income above ₹9,000 was not eligible to get benefits under the backward classes reservation quota. Electoral setbacks followed, despite all his filmic glamour. Five of Tamil Nadu's chief ministers were representatives of Dravidian politics, rather than caste politics.

Cinema's hold on politics in Tamil Nadu developed despite the power and influence wielded earlier by national leaders. C. Rajagopalachari, venerated as a leader for all of India, was surprisingly anti-cinema. Seeing it as a threat to morality, he held the view that cinema should be eliminated from life. K. Kamaraj, unquestioned king of the Congress in Tamil Nadu and beyond, once asked: 'How can there be government by actors?' Perhaps an answer was inherent in what Annadurai once said about his scripts. 'With a view to educating the people of Tamil Nadu, all my stories and screenplays have been on themes of social purpose.' Karunanidhi said the same thing when he explained that his intention as a film writer was 'to introduce the ideas and policies of social reform and justice'. Both Annadurai and Karunanidhi used popular Tamil devoid of all Sanskrit flavour, thereby having a special effect on the sensibilities of the masses. M.G.R. went a step further and brought active social work into his domain. He would finance orphanages, take part in disaster relief activities, and get involved in programmes meant to help the poor. He ensured that the social capital gained from such activities remained, without getting mixed up with the DMK.

M.G.R. lived a full life and became of course a rich man, a very rich man. His assets were such that he thought there could be problems after he had passed on. To make things smoother, he wrote a will. But problems cropped up. His adopted daughter, Geetha Madhu Mohan, and relative, Latha Rajendran, filed cases. Eventually the High Court ruled in favour of 'a court-appointed administrator [managing] the affairs of the estate and the Trust'.

The dictat that no file should move when the big man was ill had its own weird repercussions when he did fall ill. A severe paralytic stroke crippled M.G.R. in 1984 and official attempts to hide its seriousness from the public did not succeed. Foreign doctors who were rushed in for expert treatment said point-blank that there was 'not a chance' of his total recovery and that he would always have a tell-tale limp in the right leg and a permanent impairment in his speech. When it happened, it was worse than expected. Months later, an anonymous AIADMK leader said: 'Speech is still slurred as a result of the paralytic stroke, haemoglobin content of his blood necessitates occasional blood transfusions and he has suffered frequent bouts of epileptic fits.'

In a strange development, two paid advertisements appeared in local newspapers purportedly issued by the chief minister himself. One said M.G.R. did not like his wife's relative interfering in the state's administration and asked civil servants not to entertain any request from his wife V.N. Janaki. The other denied the existence of a 'personal and confidential cell' in the CM's secretariat and asked officials to be wary of such claims. That these points were made through advertisements in the papers showed that there were executives in the government plotting actions on their own. What the advertisements actually showed was that M.G.R. was no longer functional. Only the political brand value of those triple letters mattered to those who benefited from his legacy. The ancestral home in Vadavannur remained unattended with nothing to suggest that this was where he spent his childhood. A name board proclaims that it is an Anganwadi centre under the state's Social Welfare Department. Children play in the compound but the small-tiled house has windows coming off their hinges, walls with peeling plaster, and steps that are broken. But politicians have ensured that the walls of the house carry not only pictures of Annadurai and Jayalalithaa but also a calendar carrying messages from S.P. Velumani, representative of the Coimbatore area and a minister.

The Arcot Road house where M.G.R. lived is now the official M.G.R. Memorial. It was turned into a museum after his death, enriched with a wide range of memorabilia representing his life and work. On show even is his Ambassador car, with the registration number TMX 4777. He had modified the car to include a mini-television so he could watch cricket. The television in the house is a 1980s model. Even by Tamil Nadu's high-value traditions of film-star worship, the way M.G.R. was taken to heart was unique. The astonishing fact is that the mass worship of the star retains its unique intensity decades after his passing. No other film personality in Tamil Nadu commands the attention and adoration he commands. To the Tamil world, M.G.R. was more than Aayirathil Oruvan, one in a thousand. He was one in all of history.

8

JAYALALITHAA

Aayirathil Oruval

Jayalalithaa, with an extra 'a' added to the name as recommended by numerologists, was a windstorm that forced itself into the history of Tamil Nadu. For 15 years she reigned as the state's chief minister in a style that was unapologetically authoritarian. The thick layers of dogmatism that covered her public identity made the inner persona invisible. No one knew that she was a classic case of the could-have-beens of history. By virtue of ancestry and on the strength of proven ability, she could have risen high in academia. But events charted a course that pushed her into the pedestrian precincts of cinema and from there into the compromising culture of politics. The flair meant for trailblazing was expended on the give and take of streetwise one-upmanship.

In an age when pedigree mattered, Jayalalithaa, known as Ammu in family circles, was born to an erudite family of Iyengars. Her grandfather, Narasimhachar Rangachar, was a medical doctor in the service of the Mysore royal family. Her maternal grandfather, Rangaswamy Iyengar, was an officer in Hindustan Aeronautics in Bangalore. Her father, Jayaram Rangachar, qualified as a lawyer, but did not practise. According to published reports, he squandered the family's fortune and died under suspicious circumstances. Jayalalithaa was two years old at the time, but in reminiscences she wrote years later for Tamil magazines, she recalled in vivid detail the scene of her father lying dead. Jayaram's departure changed the course of his wife's life and with that, his daughter's as well. Vedavalli, widowed at the age of 26, took her son and daughter and moved to Bangalore where her parents lived. She managed to get a typist's job. But better prospects beckoned from Madras where her sister, Ambujavalli, was doing well as an air hostess with occasional appearances in drama and films. Persuaded by Ambujam, Vedavalli left her children in Bangalore and moved to Madras in 1953 to try her luck in films. Both adopted new names for the screen. Ambujam became Vidyavathi and Vedavalli turned into Sandhya.

Her mother's drift into show business did not affect Jayalalithaa's interest in books and studies. Sandhya had enrolled her in the best of schools, Bishops Cottons in Bangalore and Sacred Heart (Church Parks School) in Madras. Jaya stood first in all her school examinations. Picked for a government scholarship to pursue college education, she worked out plans to go to Stella Maris in Madras. That was when fate interfered for the second time. Sandhya, struggling to make ends meet with her work in films, wanted help. She did the obvious and pulled Jayalalithaa, now aglow with youthfulness, also into films. In the circumstances, it was a tribute to the scholar in Jayalithaa that she continued to educate herself through reading.

The actors she mixed with had no interest in the printed word, while she was never found on set without a book. She spent every spare moment reading. It turned out that she was a writer as well. In the 1970s, when her film career was in a slump, she flowered as a contributor to the leading Tamil magazines of the time. She wrote columns in *Tughlak* and *Bommai*. A series of personal reminiscence appeared in *Kumudam*. To the surprise of many, short stories by her appeared in *Kalki*. In the 1980s, she forayed into novels, too. She told the editor of *Kalki* that she had just finished writing a novel for an English magazine. The editor urged her to turn it into Tamil and the result was *Uravin Kaidigal* (Prisoners of a Relationship), believed to be inspired by her neighbour Rajinikanth's love for his wife Latha. Another novel followed some years later, *Nenjile Oru*

Kanal (A Fire in the Heart). This was about a drunken father dying suddenly and his wife taking up roles in films to bring up her two children. Any resemblance to her own family story was not exactly coincidental. The stories, essays, and novels written by Jayalalithaa became part of the periodical journalism of the time. There was no attempt by her or any publisher to bring them out as books and thus give them some kind of durability. That could be one reason the writer in Jayalalithaa did not make much of an impact. When politics finally consumed her, it consumed her in totality, so much so that it surprises most people today that Jayalalithaa was an author in the 1970s and early 1980s. (She became chief minister for the first time in 1991.)

It is idle to speculate what Jayalalithaa would have become if she had gone on with her higher education and taken to the profession of either her father or grandfather. In the event, she followed her mother into films. What made it a life-changing step was that it was Tamil cinema and it was the era of M.G.R., a historical juncture when cinema was politics and politics was cinema. Jayalalithaa, who paired with M.G.R. on the screen, paired with him on the political stage as well. She developed into a more consummate politician because, unlike M.G.R., she had to fight powerful opponents and crawl her way up, wounds and all.

The start was smooth when she was appointed propaganda secretary in M.G.R.-led AIADMK in 1983. The title was seen as a facade. The insider talk that she had access even to police intelligence reports was an indication of how others saw her status in the party. When a journalist asked her bluntly, 'What is your relationship with M.G.R.?', she spoke between the lines and said: 'He is one the finest human beings I have ever come across. There are just two people to whom I bow my head, my mother and M.G.R.... I do believe in what is called chemistry between two people. M.G.R. and I hit it off very well from the beginning... Tongues wag. I don't think we must pay attention to that.' (Bhagwan Singh, *The Week*, January 1984.) She had ups and downs with M.G.R. That did not matter as long as he was alive. The day he died in 1987, the ground shifted. Those who had looked upon her as a usurper now pounced upon her. She, too, realised that the moment had arrived for her to win all or lose all. Ugly scenes that marked M.G.R.'s funeral procession told their own tale. Jayalalithaa tried to climb the gun-carriage, only to be roughed up and pushed around. A relative of M.G.R.'s wife Janaki hit her on the head. More targeted aggression was witnessed when the state assembly convened in March 1989. She called Chief Minister Karunanidhi a criminal and he returned the compliment in unprintable terms. At one point, honourable MLAs assaulted her and the loose end of the sari got pulled, an incident that would duly be compared to Draupadi's disrobing by the Kauravas. That moment of humiliation was to change Jayalalithaa and Tamil Nadu politics. With sari in disorder, blouse askew and hair dishevelled, she stomped out of the Assembly swearing that she would return to it only as chief minister. When she returned two years later as chief minister, she was a changed person. Determined to make her authority felt by all, she emerged as a one-woman government, single-minded, autocratic, and totally unconcerned about what others thought of her. She ignored the checks and balances of the system and acted as an imperial ruler. She became intolerant of criticism. She demanded not just support but subservience from her followers. Elected by the people, she insisted that her cabinet colleagues, elected leaders themselves, prostrate before her as a matter of routine. She walked, talked, and took decisions as though it was her right to rule. She was Amma, queen, dictator, commander-in-chief, the monarch of all she surveyed. She assumed the title of 'Puratchi Thalaivi', revolutionary leader, parallel to M.G.R.'s 'Puratchi Thalaivar'. Additionally, she became 'Thanga Tharagai', golden star, and 'Kalai Selvi', literally meaning female artiste, but it is the Tamil term for Goddess Saraswathi. She became 'Aayirathil Oruval', one in a thousand women. (Her first movie with M.G.R. was the popular *Aayirathil Oruvan*, which means one in a thousand men.)

It is not uncommon in politics for women of grit to fight their way through and become icons as Indira Gandhi, Imelda Marcos of the Philippines, and Eva Peron of Argentina proved. As they vanquished their tormentors, each of them became autocratic and yet won popular applause. Threats and humiliations put iron into their soul. Jayalalithaa would recall with pride how she had a 'tempestuous life' and how she was always 'propelled by fate'. Like Indira, she would trust only her personal staff and, unlike Indira, she had no children to lean on. Fate turned her into a self-supporting mechanism, making her own rules and declaring, 'I don't take any nonsense from anyone.' She once confessed: 'I am surprised at the way I have changed.'

As chief minister, she introduced initiatives she considered progressive—programmes to give free education to girls, entrepreneurship training to women, free cradles where families who did not want girls could leave their babies. She launched all-women police stations. She started the Amma brand of products, from meals to medicines, salt to cement. The impression grew that she was a heroine of the masses. This was true to some extent, but it was also true that massive scandals eroded her image. Her nemesis was Vivekanandan Krishnaveni Sasikala who became Sasikala Natarajan after marriage but preferred to be known politically as V.K. Sasikala. A small-time video company operator, she contacted Jayalalithaa, then AIADMK's propaganda secretary, with proposals of video coverage. She rapidly firmed up her relations with Jayalalithaa who encouraged her because her services were helpful. Sasikala's husband and other relatives became activists in Jayalalithaa-related programmes, gaining considerable influence in the party and becoming known as the 'Mannargudi mafia'. Their thirst for power was so apparent that in 2011 Jayalalithaa expelled her and a dozen others from the party. But a year later, they crawled their way back into her good books with a letter of apology. Sasikala did not hide her intention to succeed Jayalalithaa as chief minister. When resistance developed within the AIADMK, she formed a separate party called Amma Makkal Munnetra Kazhagam (AMMK). Her plans ran into legal obstacles following court rulings against her in a string of cases. In 2017, the Supreme Court found her guilty in a disproportionate assets case and sentenced her to four years imprisonment. Sasikala kept her Mannargudi clan active so that when the court cases were over, there would be a political platform to make her chief minister. Things did not work out as she expected.

Court cases, trials, and sentences brought to light enormous assets acquired by Jayalalithaa in association with Sasikala. The quantities of gold (21.3 kg, silver 1250 kg), the saris (2140), the shoes (750 pairs), and the luxury watches (91) that she accumulated could perhaps be attributed to womanly ego. But the purchase of landed properties, sprawling mansions and massive spreads of land told a different tale. Gossip among the common people at the time was that Sasikala would drive around Chennai city and nearby areas and if a property caught her fancy, government agencies would immediately start acquisition procedures leaving the owners no say in the matter. It was left to the court to get her assets quantified to the extent possible. A judgment in 2014 listed 173 properties bought by Jayalalithaa, her disowned foster son Sudhakaran, Sasikala, and her sister-in-law J. Elavarasi. The investigating officer in the disproportionate assets case said there were properties running to more than 3,000 acres costing several thousand crore. Among them were farmland in Ranga Reddy district in Telangana, houses in Chennai city and suburbs, and a house in Secunderabad that had Sasikala's name on the gate. The biggest and most glamorous property that got involved in the scandal was the Kodanad Estate, the secluded resort where Jayalalithaa loved to spend time when she was in power and out of it.

Unrivalled picturesqueness combined with size to make Kodanad special. Spread over 942 acres (some accounts put it at 1,600 acres), it had a 10-acre lake, a 10-acre flower farm, a tea factory, and a plush-white mansion. It was valued at around ₹12,000 crore. The original owner Peter Jones, a planter from England, was not thinking of selling his estate. 'More than just a property, it was close to my heart,' he said. But Jayalalithaa and Sasikala wanted it and they saw to it that they got it. Jones was paid ₹7.6 crore by demand draft. 'They had agreed to pay ₹4 crore more in cash. We never got that. What we got were income tax raids and 150 goondas at our doorstep,' he told *The Week* (4 June 2017). The journal added: 'The Mannargudi family kept expanding and buying new estates till a few months before Jayalalithaa 's death, said C.Divakar who used to work at the estate. 'These included the Curzon estate spread over 200 acres, the Thai Cholai estate spread over 1,100 acres and a 750-acre estate near Edakkad. The land was bought and registered in the name of a firm called Kodanad Tea Estates in which Jayalalithaa, Sasikala and Elavarasi were partners.'

The Mannargudi brains had fitted things into a corporate empire which itself reflected elaborate planning. Sri Jaya Publications and Sasi Enterprises were used to acquire properties between 1991 and 1996. Sasikala and Elavarasi held important positions in companies like Riverway Agro Products, Lex Property Developments, Indo Doha Chemicals and Signora Business Enterprises. The shares they held in these, and several other companies were supposedly on behalf of Jayalalithaa, or acquired by using the name of Jayalalithaa. They were all money spinners. Jazz Cinemas, said to be owned by Elavarasi's son, was the largest multiplex in Chennai in the 2010s.

Peter Jones's beloved colonial bungalow in the Kodanad estate was demolished by Jayalalithaa because it was too small for her. The new mansion was not only big, it was nicely hidden by undulating tea gardens and dense pine forests surrounding it. The precise measurements of the house were never known, but estimates were made from the fact that the compound had ten gates, located so far apart that guards shouting from one gate would not be heard by guards at other gates. Such details lent poignancy to the horror stories that came out of the estate after its owner's passing. Within four months of her death, Kodanad had a break-in. A ten-member gang murdered the guard at Gate 10, tied up and assaulted the guard at Gate 8, and smashed their way into the rooms used exclusively by Jayalalithaa and Sasikala. Police made it look like a burglary, announcing that five watches and a crystal decoration piece had been stolen. They later said the break-in was plotted by Kanakaraj, a dismissed former driver of Jayalalithaa, and his friend from Kerala, Sayan. But suspicion mounted when Kanakaraj was killed in an apparent road accident in Salem and Sayan met with a car accident in which he barely escaped; his wife and daughter were killed. Three months later, the Kodanad estate employee in charge of the CCTV network there killed himself. Clearly there was some kind of pattern in the string of tragedies that rocked Kodanand. In January 2019, a video report surfaced claiming that the break-in and subsequent deaths were linked to Edappadi Palanisami who succeeded Jayalalithaa as chief minister. Based on conversations with men involved in the break-in, the *Tehelka* video charged that the purpose of the raid was to retrieve important documents from the estate. The chief minister not only denied the allegations but filed a complaint with the police. 'Ten people have been arrested in connection with the case,' he said.

The circumstances of her passing and the confusion, conspiracies, and crimes that followed were a reminder of the tragedy that was Jayalalithaa. She left no will. She did have immediate relatives: brother Jayakumar's daughter, Deepa, and son, Deepak, besides a clutch of cousins. All were strictly kept out of her reach. Well or ill, she would be cared for only by Sasikala and her approved relatives. This complicated the medical problems that plagued her in the final phase of her life. After she was admitted to Apollo Hospital in September 2016, dozens of doctors from AIIMS, Vellore, Tata Memorial in Bombay, and specialists from England and America examined her, but the information passed on to the public was minimal and misleading. She was the chief minister in office and had a mass following making her illness a matter of public interest. Large crowds that collected at Apollo every day made this clear to all. But the health bulletins issued by Apollo were 'always vetted by plastic surgeon K.S. Sivakumar, a relative of Sasikala,' as *Outlook* magazine reported, quoting 'a senior doctor in the Apollo team that treated Jayalalithaa' (G.C. Shekhar, 16 March 2017). The nature of this backroom control became evident when the state government released, three months after her death, a summary of reports from Apollo and AIIMS. According to the summary, Apollo said that she was admitted in a very critical condition. What the government told the public, as per the plastic surgeon's wisdom, was that she was admitted for fever and hydration. The summary said she was in the ICU, barely conscious on certain dates. On one of those dates, the plastic surgeon's government told the public that she held discussions with officials on the Cauvery dispute.

The public was aware that information was being manipulated. This strengthened the general feeling that the medical attention she received in the hospital was inadequate. Top officials in the state government were blamed by some for not taking her abroad for treatment. A former law minister charged that an expenditure of 1.7 crore shown on a hospital bill was, in fact, the food expenses the Sasikala family had incurred in the hospital. Every day, in every way, Jayalalithaa was being misused. It is difficult to believe that she was unaware of what was going on. Perhaps there were difficulties when she was in the hospital, but even when she was active she had let things drift. How easy it would have been to act with more imagination. A tiny portion of her wealth could have been used to set up a trust for promoting the women's causes she was interested in. The intelligent, worldly-wise Jayalalithaa threw it all away.

Was she unhappy? She tackled the world with chutzpah and said repeatedly that she was tough enough to face any challenge. However, for a person who peppered her speeches with quotations from Tennyson and lesser-known American authors, she must have regretted not having a university degree. For one who had a crush, as she once admitted, on cricketers Nari Contractor and Mansur Ali Khan Pataudi as well as on film-star Shammi Kapoor, she must have felt forlorn about her spinsterhood—or should we say the circumstances that forced her to put on the garb of spinsterhood.

(In her 2016 book *Amma: Jayalalithaa's Journey from Movie Star To Political Queen*, Vaasanthi says how she was told about Jayalalithaa's marriage to Telugu star Sobhan Babu. The narrator was Chandini, a school mate of Jayalalithaa. She said Jayalalithaa showed her 'a huge album with pictures of her marriage ceremony with Sobhan Babu'. Chandni was quoted as saying: 'It was a pukka Brahmin marriage with Pandithji and ceremony.')

That basic things like marriage and parenthood had to become subjects of gossip must have contributed to Jayalalithaa's sense of isolation. Adding another strand to it must have been the paradox of a Mysore Brahmin heading an anti-Brahmin Dravida movement in Tamil Nadu. As she withdrew into herself, the tyrannical use of power became a device to protect her turf. Critics were seen as personal enemies. She became paranoid about the media. An entire department was set up to scan all newspapers in all languages every day, measure the column inches devoted to her in every edition of every paper and prepare a table to be presented to her every day. She would check the table personally. The government's attitude to newspapers, not to mention patronage in the form of advertisements, depended on that chart. The only media person she was happy with was Cho Ramaswamy, editor and soul of *Thuglak*. But Cho was a lawyer, an actor, a director, a playwright, a satirist, and a speaker as well. She gave occasional interviews. The only one she enjoyed was her conversation with Simi Garewal in 1999. In fact, the 'rendezvous', as the TV programme was called, became famous for the way Jayalalithaa dropped her masks. She made an assessment of Garewal in the first two minutes, decided she was friendly, and then began talking freely and naturally. Two moments of that interview became permanently lodged in the popular memory. The first was her recollection of Bangalore when her mother had left her there and gone to Chennai to build a career in films. 'When I was about five,' she recalled, 'and she had come to Bangalore to see us, I always used to cry whenever she left, so she used to put me to sleep and I always used to sleep clutching her sari pallu in my hands. I used to wind it right around my hand. So my mother used to find it impossible to get up and leave. So leaving the edge of the sari in my hand, she used to gradually unwind the sari from herself, and she used to make my aunt drape the sari around herself and lie down beside me so that I wouldn't notice her leaving. And then, of course, when I got up and found that mother was gone, I would cry and cry and cry. Throughout those four years when I was in Bangalore, I was pining for my mother every minute, every second.' The other memorable snippet of the interview was Jayalalithaa melting into a song. They were talking about Hindi films and about Jaya's heartthrobs when Garewal brought up the subject of favourite songs. The next moment Jaya was reciting, alongside Grewal, lines from 'Aaja sanam madhur chandni mein hum', the Lata Mangeshkar–Manna Dey hit from *Chori Chori* (1956). At the end of the interview, Jayalalithaa went out of her way to say, 'It was a pleasure talking to you.'

There was another interview where the reverse happened. The anchor said formally, 'Chief Minister, a pleasure talking to you' and extended his hand. Jayalalithaa ignored the extended hand and said, 'I must say it was not a pleasure talking to you. Namaste.' She then walked out. That was in 2004 when Karan Thapar, in his usual overbearing style, shot 'tough questions' about her being 'undemocratic, unreliable, irrational, vengeful'. At one point, the interviewer himself felt the air was getting hot and said, 'You are a very tough person, Chief Minister.' The chief minister said, 'That is because of people like you.' As an interview, it was a flop, but Thapar listed it among his best.

Politics consumed Jayalalithaa so comprehensively that her gentleness was suppressed. She was all human, all woman, but she had to look and behave as though she was all steel. She yearned for friendships but could not find any that sustained her interest for a reasonable length of time. She yearned for a normal family life but became so disillusioned that she talked about the virtues of not having a family. She had everything at her disposal but could not find the enriching relationships she cherished. She was truly lonely. Her way of fighting loneliness was by demonstrating toughness. She became an imperialistic democrat. Sophisticated within, she chose to project a profile of boorishness. She stuck to the blacks and whites of politics, ignoring the grey in between. She could be gracious one moment, gross the next. She herself said once that no one could get anything out of her by threatening her which 'only makes me more stubborn, inflexible, unbending, determined'. She would cooperate only if someone were 'nice to me, pamper me, cajole me, talk to me kindly, softly'. Long after she is gone, those words sound like a lonely soul's call for help.

I should not fail to recall a personal experience that threw light on Jayalalithaa's ability to enjoy the simple things. I was a complete stranger to her, having never met her professionally or socially. But one day I got a letter from her. Bangalore had just got itself renamed to Bengaluru following U.R. Ananthamurthy's argument that the U sound had an enabling effect in Kannada. Arguing that what was enabling in Kannada need not be enabling in English, I published a poetic spoof in my newspaper column that went like:

> Do you visit Bengalooru
> Or perhaps Mangalooru?
> Do you live in Belagavi
> Or perhaps Kalaburagi?
> Do you live in Vijayapura
> As if it were Singapura?
> Do you go to Mysuru
> Though it is an eyesoru?

Several more lines followed, about our goondas giving our netas mysuru bondas, and how our liquor lobby and transport lobby saw financing our netas as their hobby. The column was evidently critical of political leaders, but the leader who sat in the chief minister's chair in Chennai saw the humour, not the criticism. The letter I received was not exactly what we understand as a letter. It came in an A-4 size envelope made of card-thick paper. Like the cover, the sheet inside proclaimed grandeur and authority, enhanced by the official insignia of the government of the state with its motto 'Truth Alone Triumphs'. But the four-line message typed on the sheet had no sign of putting on airs. It was just a reader being a reader. She said: 'Dear Shri George, I enjoyed reading your ditty on Bengalooru on 25th December 2005. It was truly hilarious. Congratulations—and thank you! I can't remember when I last laughed so much and so heartily.' Neither travails nor tribulations, nor the burdens of being a solitary autocrat dimmed Jayalalithaa's wit. The pity was that she got so few opportunities to laugh heartily.

Postscript

The U sound initiative that Ananthamurthy launched was to lead to unexpected denouements. At the 2005 Kannada Sahitya Sammelana, the writer–professor had said: 'In Kannada language U is a great enabler. Take any English word and you can make it a Kannada word by joining U. Chair chair-u, table table-u.' It was an overstretched thesis, but it appealed to popular sentiment and Bangalore, even in its English form, absorbed the U sound.

Seven years later, the unexpected happened. Out of nowhere, with no prior warning, appeared a daring iconoclast named Dhanush, guerrilla style, and hijacked the U sound. He was not even a Kannadiga. He was a Tamil film star. In a 2012 film called *3*, he wrote and sang a song that robbed Kannada of its specialty. The song 'Why this Kolaveri di?' (in Kodambakkam Tamil it meant 'Why this murderous rage, girl?') became a sensation, dominating channels, coffee shop discussions, and social media. What it did was to appropriate for Tamil the sound Kannada had already appropriated. He subjected the U sound to audacious subversion:

Whitu skinnu girlu girlu
Girlu heartu blacku
Eyesu eyesu meetu meetu
My future blacku
Why this kolaveri, kolaveri di?

Does it matter all that much if a girl's skin is whitu and heart blacku? What causes worry is that a shuddh Kannada enabler sound can be shanghaied by an alien language and turned into another kind of enabler. Perhaps it is not too late to recognise that narrow provincialism begets only narrow provincialism. It is never too late to return to the universally enabling sounds of Bangalore and Madras and Bombay.

9

A.B. VAJPAYEE

The Flexible Dharma

Machiavellianism suggests a conspiratorial approach of the contemptible kind. Atal Bihari Vajpayee was not quite that scheming. Expediency suggests a manipulative approach. Vajpayee was not quite that either. He was simply a politician ready to compromise for the sake of power. A harbinger of hope when he started out, he became a destroyer of dreams as he settled down. As a poet, he was a counterpoint to V.P. Singh, the other poet–Prime Minister. Vajpayee showed how the poet could be compromised by the politician. V.P. Singh showed how the politician could be rescued by the poet. Vajpayee was very conscious of the ephemerality of power. 'You may one day become an ex-Prime Minister,' he said, 'but you will never become an ex-poet.' He showed also that you may one day abandon what you considered 'Raj Dharma' and go after solutions of the adharmic kind.

Vajpayee was reared in the RSS school, attending a four-year officers' training course from 1940. He qualified as a full-time Pracharak the year India became independent. But rather than preaching the prescribed gospel, he showed more interest in reaching out to people in ways that went beyond his training. He is on record as saying, 'The Sangh is my soul.' That was in an India where it was possible to have the Sangh in the soul and yet appreciate what lay beyond and be appreciated for it. Vajpayee was a direct beneficiary of the liberalism of those days. He entered Parliament when he was 33. His speaking abilities made him an instant star. It is a part of contemporary legend that the young MP's oratory turned Jawaharlal Nehru into an admirer. The story goes that Nehru would rush to the House whenever Vajpayee rose to speak. Not trying to hide his appreciation of an opposition MP, Nehru is said to have told him: 'One day you will be Prime Minister.' As if to contribute his bit to that consummation, Nehru sent him to the UN General Assembly for international exposure and some training in diplomacy. That level of non-partisanship in the larger interests of the country is impossible in today's India, showing that the march of Indian democracy has not been forward. The very name of Nehru is taboo among 'patriotic' circles in Narendra Modi's India. One reason Vajpayee rose to greatness was that he lived in an age that valued political courtesies. What the poet in Vajpayee described as *darkness in the middle of the day* arrived during the watch of his own ideological brethren.

We cannot say that it arrived without warning. A signal had flashed across the horizon in the middle of Vajpayee's prime ministership. It had happened even as his stature was growing following his assumption of office in 1998. That turned out to be a year of significance for both India and Vajpayee, because in May, India exploded its second nuclear test and gained the status of a 'full-fledged nuclear state'. The weapon was ready a few years earlier and the then Prime Minister Narasimha Rao had ordered a test firing in 1995. At the last minute, however, he succumbed to international pressure and cancelled all plans. Vajpayee handled the situation differently. He ensured complete secrecy and the detonation was successfully conducted deep in the deserts of Pokhran. This was a bold initiative at a time when it was considered improper for non-superpowers to try for nuclear status. They had to go about it carefully. The control room was set up adjacent to the Prime Minister's residence with only four other cabinet ministers in attendance. All were tense and quiet. When news of the successful detonation finally arrived, 'the atmosphere was completely surreal,' as Shakti Sinha, present in the room, recollected. 'There was a visible sense of relief, almost as if the unreal had become real. There were a lot of tears in that room that day—all of us felt the rush of "we have done it" confidence.' (*Vajpayee: The Years That Changed India*, Shakti Sinha, 2020.) The heroic profile Vajpayee gained from the nuclear blast was lost, in political terms, when he made a dramatic peace overture to Pakistan: a bus ride to Lahore in February 1999. It looked like a bold initiative and an imaginative one because he took with him film-star Dev Anand, writer Javed Akhtar, and cricketer Kapil Dev. But it turned out to be mere showmanship. Pakistani incursions led to the Kargil war within three months of Vajpayee's visit to Lahore. As BJP's own hawks saw it, India disgraced itself by making a peace overture just as the enemy was secretly planning military strikes. A Viswa Hindu Parishad secretary described Vajpayee as a 'pseudo Hindu'.

The ultras got their opportunity to hit back when in March 2002 Gujarat exploded into communal frenzy. The burning of a train in Godhra had killed 58 Hindu karsevaks. For three days, armed marauders roamed the capital subjecting Muslims to gang rapes, mass murder, arson, and kidnapping. Officially, 790 Muslims and 254 Hindus were killed, though unofficial sources put the figure above 2,500. Scholarly studies later suggested it was a planned pogrom with even the train-burning a 'staged trigger'. Chief Minister Narendra Modi was accused of instigating the horror although a Special Investigating Team gave him a clean chit in a controversial report. Prime Minister Vajpayee was outraged that communal terror of such dimensions could rock a BJP-ruled stage. He visited Gujarat and it was there that he spoke of the state's failure to do the king's duty to uphold Raj Dharma. When Narendra Modi, sitting by his side, butted in to say that he, too, was trying not to discriminate between people of different faiths, Vajpayee dropped the topic. Evidently, he was apprehensive about an argument within the party leadership. He was a deeply worried man, aware of the bad image the country had acquired as a consequence of the Gujarat riots. But he did not stand up for his beliefs. At the BJP's national executive meeting in Goa a few days later, he showed that his position in the party was more important to him than his notions of dharma. Rattled by behind-the-scenes manoeuvres to make Modi look like a hero, he gave a stridently communal speech to safeguard his own standing in the party.

That flight to Goa was a turning point in history. Vajpayee had established himself as a strong-man Prime Minister by ensuring that the party chairmanship was held by men who could never challenge him and by keeping the RSS away. The crisis that developed over the killings in Gujarat was the first occasion that his opponents found it possible to challenge him. The issue that came up was whether Narendra Modi should be punished for the holocaust in Gujarat as Vajpayee wanted, or whether he should be applauded for holding up the Hindu cause as influential leaders such as Arun Jaitley wanted. On the flight from Delhi to Goa, Vajpayee had made up his mind. He hardly spoke to fellow passenger L.K. Advani, a known promoter of Modi. Prompted to talk, he 'muttered in his usual style about what had to be done... "Modi has to go." By the time they landed in Goa, the decision was taken: Modi would go.' (*The Untold Vajpayee: Politician and Paradox*, Ullekh N.P., 2017.) Advani was aghast. 'There will be chaos in the state,' he warned. At the national committee meeting, there was drama. According to a pre-arranged script, Modi moved up to the dais to announce his resignation. Even before he could actually do so, slogans in his favour rented the air. The atmospherics developed in such a way that 'a resolution was passed that Modi and his government had done their best while facing the challenge during the riots' as Kingshuk Nag put it in his *Atal Bihari Vajpayee: A Man for All Seasons* (2015). 'Thus Atal was stymied. Modi was a core RSS man who had become the chief minister of a state without being a legislator or an MP.'

It was the threatening attitude of the national executive that persuaded Vajpayee to depart from the moderation he had developed as a trademark and turn his Goa speech into a communal tirade. 'What happened in Gujarat?' he asked, in tones that echoed the Modi backers' thesis. 'If a conspiracy had not been hatched to burn alive innocent passengers, the subsequent tragedy in Gujarat could have been avoided. Who lit the fire?' He then went over the top: 'Wherever Muslims live, they don't like to live in co-existence with others, they don't like to mingle with others. And instead of propagation their ideas in a peaceful manner, they want to spread their faith by resorting to terror and threats.' The Prime Minister's Office later clarified that he was only referring to followers of militant Islam. He also told Parliament that he was as opposed to militant Hinduism as he was to militant Islam. Clearly, Vajpayee was swinging between conviction and realpolitik. After the Goa meeting, commentators were quick to point out that his true face now stood exposed, that he had identified himself fully with the 'Golwarkar–Savarkar thesis of India as a Hindu nation beset by Muslim trouble-makers' (Siddharth Varadarajan in *The Wire*). There were comments across the board expressing surprise at Vajpayee's anti-Muslim harangue. An editorial in the *Hindustan Times* said: 'This can't go on. India cannot afford a prime minister who shoots his mouth off on sensitive issues and then issues tedious clarifications two days later.' If Vajpayee's intention was to assert his supremacy in the party in the wake of Modi's challenge, he failed. The post-Goa Vajpayee was a politically enfeebled man. L.K. Advani now became deputy prime minister, a post he had long been canvassing for and Vajpayee had blocked. The RSS demanded a meeting with the prime minister and Vajpayee had to oblige. The meeting marked the restoration of the RSS's political influence which Vajpayee had kept at a near-zero level.

So why did he depart from his familiar line of moderation and adopt a position of extremism and intolerance? Was he scared by the challenge Modi represented? Was he unnerved by the noisy audience at the national committee meeting that shouted down moderate voices and gave Modi a halo? He could perhaps have swung things in his favour by standing firm. His popularity was high and his call for Raj Dharma had won applause. At the same time, the brutalities that were allowed to take place in Gujarat had caused widespread dismay in India and beyond.

Since the general impression was that Modi had given a free run to marauding gangs in the initial days, moderate Hindu opinion would have joined others in backing the central government action against the then chief minister. If Vajpayee had taken the position that India could not afford state-sponsored communal violence, he would have won considerable support. That, in turn, would have dislodged the challenge posed by Hindutva extremism with Modi as the flag-carrier. If Modi had been stopped then, he and his brand of divisive politics would not have marched on to Delhi. The ifs of history are haunting. Vajpayee let the moment slip, hurting himself as much as his country. The BJP-at-peace ended its run and the BJP-at-war began its Ashwamedha Yajna at the Goa conference of the party. In a sense Modi became king in 2012 itself; donning the crown two years later was but a formality. That eliminated from official India the kind of sentiment that the poet Vajpayee had expressed when he wrote:

> My Lord,
> Never let me climb so high
> That I'm unable to embrace
> a stranger.

Eventually politics embraced him in Dhritarashtra style. Vajpayee reached a stage where the very idea of embracing a stranger was anathema to him. He was now long past the ideas he had once aired. He had said that it was not right '...to adopt an attitude that what we have accepted as the final principle of our ideology is the ultimate truth. It is essential that our ideology stands the test of being beneficial for humankind as a whole. The thought process will not come to a halt at any time.' This was the man who now said: 'We are right. We alone are right. All others are anti-national and shall be treated as such.' His ideological successor turned that idea into the definition of patriotism.

10

ARUN JAITLEY

The Compulsive Contrarian

In India's political arena, Arun Maharaj Kishen Jaitley was the ultimate gladiator, ever-ready to pounce. He fought every battle as though he had already won. His vocabulary was as sharp a weapon as his conviction that he was always fair. He was felicitous in coining words (Maha-jhootbandhan to ridicule the opposition's Mahagathbandhan) and in devising phrases meant to knock down those who questioned him. In early 2019, as many as 108 economists from around the world had expressed concern over 'political interference' in influencing statistical data in India. The fact that the signatories included some of the world's best-known economists from India, Harvard, and MIT should have made the Finance Minister of India respond to the statement in a measured manner. But Jaitley dismissed them as 'compulsive contrarians' who routinely signed papers on 'manufactured political issues' against the government. In Jaitley's universe, dissent was immoral if it was directed against the establishment of which he was a part. When he was on the other side of the fence, dissent was the recourse of the righteous. The advantage Arun Jaitley enjoyed was the absolute conviction that the side he was on at any given moment was the only right side. He was the compulsive gladiator, forever fired by contrarianism.

That wasn't how young Arun started off. His father, Maharaj

Kishen, was a lawyer who could not afford to send his son to institutions of repute. Arun grew up in an atmosphere that was so ordinary it bordered on the pedestrian. His academic record was minimalist—BCom and LLB, both earned in Delhi rather than Oxford or Yale. Yet, in finance and law, he reached summits occupied by the best and the brightest. Some credit his Saraswat Brahmin heritage, some the dedication with which he applied his mind to a subject. He made his ideological choice fairly early in life. He joined the ABVP, the aggressive student wing of the BJP, and became President of the Delhi University Students Union in 1974 when he was 22. ('From childhood I have been a party member,' he once said.) Jaitley's original ambition was to become a chartered accountant, but circumstances pushed him into his father's career. He seemed comfortable with it because he was familiar with it, having watched his father at work. It also fitted into his extracurricular interest in ABVP politics. He once said: 'I did not contest elections because I thought I will settle down happily as a lawyer and work for the party.' The party seemed to appreciate it. His rise to power in the BJP was rapid. By 1991, he was a member of the national executive, becoming its principal spokesman in time for the 1999 elections and, post-election, a minister in the Vajpayee government. His ability to discuss and debate his way through thorny questions of policy made him more effective in the party than his titles indicated.

This had its impact on Gujarat. An unusually close relationship developed between Jaitley and Narendra Modi long before Modi was a factor in the politics of the state. He told journalist Saba Naqvi once: 'I have known Modi for years. We have worked together in Delhi much before he came to Gujarat and I see him as an exceptional talent.' This assessment of Modi by Jaitley was a key to the making of Modi because of Jaitley's influence in the BJP and beyond. It was he who proposed Modi for the chief ministership of Gujarat and, 18 eventful years later, for the prime minister's post. On both occasions, resistance was stiff. When Vajpayee himself wanted to remove Modi after the 2002 Gujarat killings, Jaitley led the argument in favour of Modi. Helped by L.K. Advani, he organised intra-party manoeuvres that turned the tables in favour of Modi. Jaitley was also the lawyer who defended Modi and his collaborator, Amit Shah, in vexatious cases they faced within the tumult of Gujarat politics. It is possible that Modi developed a feeling that he needed Jaitley for his advancement. This stemmed from his understanding of Jaitley's brain power and his insider status in Delhi society. The BJP is not exactly famous for leaders with grey matter. Most of their strength lies in rabble-rousing and the cadre support they build up. Jaitley was among the few who stood out. Modi understood the value of this. An outsider in Delhi, Modi was also aware of the importance of Lutyens' Delhi of which Jaitley was a veteran who knew everyone who was anyone. Such was his networking capabilities that despite being a BJP fighter, he was known to be close to Sonia Gandhi, Rahul Gandhi, and other Congress leaders such as P. Chidambaram. There was no one in any party to beat him in social skills.

For a man so pivotally placed, Jaitley was not exactly unassuming. His overweening manner of dismissing opponents became an identifying mark of his public life. As with most brilliant people, he tended to believe that those who had opinions other than his were dim-witted. References to Rahul Gandhi made no attempt even to sound polite. Rahul's hatred for Modi, said Jaitley, emanated from envy. 'A failed student always hates a class topper.' On another occasion, he referred to the Congress president and said, '...even a kindergarten student has better understanding than him.' When the BJP was humbled by setbacks in the 2018 state elections in Rajasthan, Madhya Pradesh, and Chhattisgarh, Jaitley's reaction was: 'Election is election, but people won't vote for Rahul Gandhi in 2019 against Narendra Modi. No country jumps in to commit suicide as a preferable option.' The 2019 Lok Sabha polls was described by him as a 'choice between Prime Minister Modi and chaos'. When *The Hindu* published government documents as proof of manipulation in the Raphael deal with France, Jaitley commented:

'The use of sliced document is unprecedented in history [and] is certainly not in consonance with the spirit of free speech.' There were occasions when Jaitley showed the facility with which he could shift from the courage of conviction to the courage of convenience. He supported the tactic of disrupting Parliament on a regular basis and later opposed it tooth and nail. With exactly the same elasticity of conscience, he attacked the misuse of CBI by those in power and, when he became a wielder of power, went for the wholesale politicisation of the CBI.

During the prime ministership of Manmohan Singh, it became routine for Sushma Swaraj, leader of the opposition in the Lok Sabha, and Arun Jaitley, leader of the opposition in the Rajya Sabha, to disrupt the proceedings of Parliament under one pretext or another. It went on and on, popular opinion expressing itself against it and media reports pointing out how many thousands of rupees were lost to the nation by each hour of a non-functioning Parliament. Sushma Swaraj's response to the criticism was: 'Not allowing Parliament to function is a form of democracy like any other form.' Jaitley also took the public for granted and said, 'There are occasions when obstruction in Parliament brings greater benefits to the country.' He then went pedantic: 'Disruption should not be described as preventing work from being done because what we are doing is very important work in itself.'

With neither regret nor abashment, he did a somersault when he moved from the opposition to the treasury benches. In February 2019, he said the disruption of Parliament by the Congress Party was tantamount to wrecking the country's institutions. He said: 'History will record that Jawaharlal Nehru's great grandson had singularly damaged India's Parliament as an institution more than anyone else. Attempts are made at 11 every morning by the Congress to disrupt both houses.' What was very important work when he did it, became singularly damaging when someone else did it. Jaitley in his avatar as leader of the opposition had one set of morals. Those very morals were dismissed as evil when he took his second avatar as minister. Perhaps this was natural for eminent lawyers. Jaitley could represent Coke against Pepsi in one case and Pepsi against Coke in another.

The same double standards marked his and his party's handling of the Central Bureau of Investigation, a supposedly independent agency which was used by all ruling parties for partisan purposes. From the opposition benches, the BJP was strident in accusing Congress of manipulating the CBI to target the Modi government in Gujarat in the Ishrat Jahan case, one of the murder cases with allegations of involvement by BJP leaders. The CBI had accused the Ahmedabad police of staging 'encounter killings' of four people including Jahan in June 2004. A BJP spokesperson charged that the CBI was 'acting like a private militia of the Congress Party'. Equations changed soon enough when the CBI began to be seen as the private militia of the BJP. In October 2018, heads rolled in the CBI as unprecedented infighting started at the top between the Director and the Special Director. With each accusing the other of corruption, unheard-of developments made a mockery of the CBI. At one point, the CBI raided its own headquarters, which were later sealed. The government sent the director on compulsory leave. The Supreme Court reinstated him. Within 48 hours a committee headed by the prime minister removed him from his post. Arun Jaitley pointed out, in his customary tone of righteousness, that in removing the Director the government had only acted upon the advice of the Central Vigilance Commissioner (CVC). 'That is all pretence,' said former BJP leader and cabinet minister Yashwant Sinha, one of the civil leaders who sought judicial intervention in the case. He expressed doubts about the bona fides of the CVC's appointment and said: 'The CBI has been thoroughly misused, manipulated by previous governments, but much more so by this government.'

In a Facebook post, Jaitley enlarged the scope of his accusations against his opponents. He said the Congress governments used to interfere not only with the CBI but also institutions like the RBI and the judiciary. This was of course true. In fact, it became a scandal during Indira Gandhi's brief experiment with Emergency. But it was nothing like the concerted programme of 'take-over' that the Modi government launched. In what looked like an ideologically driven campaign, the government attempted to make inroads into the Supreme Court, Election Commission, Right to Information Act, Central Information Commission, Reserve Bank, Central Vigilance Commission, Film and Television Institute of India, Indian Council of Historical Research, University Grants Commission, and a string of central universities beginning with JNU. In early 2019, the Human Resources Ministry asked vice chancellors to 'discourage research in irrelevant areas' and make PhD scholars work only on projects in line with 'national priorities'.

In the destruction of the Reserve Banks's statutory independence, Jaitley might have played a direct role. He insisted on absolute dominance in and around the Ministry of Finance. Even area specialists were expected to toe the line and not get into discussions, let alone arguments, with the minister. Internationally renowned economists were no exception. Aravind Subramaniam, associated with the Peterson Institute of International Economics and with Harvard's Kennedy School of Government, became India's Chief Economic Advisor the year Jaitley became finance minister. He quit four years later. Aravind Panagariya, Columbia University professor of economics, became the vice chairman of the NITI Aayog the year after Jaitley became Finance Minister. He quit in two years. Raghuram Rajan of the University of Chicago became the governor of the Reserve Bank of India one year before Jaitley became finance minister. He quit in three years. In 2016, following Rajan's departure, Jaitley handpicked Urjit Patel, a product of Yale University, as RBI governor. Patel functioned obediently when the country reeled under the impact of the hastily implemented demonetisation; he bore the brunt of public anger when ATMs failed to function and people couldn't withdraw their own money from their banks and the RBI guideline to restore order failed to work. Wags nicknamed the Reserve Bank as the Reverse Bank. Patel soon began asserting his authority. In an annual report, RBI said 99.3 per cent of banned currency had returned, thus putting an official stamp on the failure of demonetisation. He told banks to consider insolvency proceedings against defaulting borrowers, a move that could compromise government leaders whose friends were among the defaulters. In a speech, RBI's deputy governor, Viral Acharya, warned: 'Governments that do not respect central bank independence will sooner or later incur the wrath of financial markets and ignite economic fire.' Ignoring all warnings, the finance ministry took measures to limit RBI's independence on issues like liquidity management and disclosure norms for defaults. The Economic Affairs Secretary even suggested the setting up of an independent payment regulatory board. Urijit Patel resigned suddenly in December 2018 leaving the RBI headless. The government played safe this time and appointed a retired IAS officer Shaktikanta Das, as the new governor. That was a first in the history of the RBI.

Using banks' money to help businessmen friends has been a game all politicians play irrespective of party affiliations. In his 2017 book, Raghuram Rajan showed how large numbers of bad loans originated in 2006–08 when 'too many of them were made to well-connected promoters who have a history of defaulting on their loans'. Jaitley was eloquent when he spoke about Congress cronies running away with public money. When the Congress government allowed indiscriminate lending by banks, Jaitley said, the RBI had failed to check it. 'It was a regulator but it kept pushing the truth below the carpet.' As usual, truth changed its nature once Jaitley was in power. A parliamentary committee reported that non-performing assets went up by ₹6.2 lakh crore between March 2015 and March 2016, forcing the government to provide ₹5.1 lakh crore to public sector banks. Whoever governed, the plundering went on. Jaitley's approach won him right-wing supporters abroad. The *Wall Street Journal* profiled him as a pro-business politician who eased restrictions to allow foreign companies to fully own local ventures in key section like oil exploration, permitted overseas investors to own up to 70 per cent of local banks instead of 49 per cent as before, and opened the doors to foreign investors in some segments of the media. In Jaitley's own opinion, 'By being pro-business and pro-poor, I am not contradicting, but both have to exist at the same time.'

That statement was released to the world by Jaitley through Facebook. In late 2018 and early 2019, he had resorted to the internet to make himself heard because he had unofficially withdrawn from the cabinet for health reasons. A diabetic, he had been having problems since the 1960s. In 2014, he had a gastric bypass operation. Four years later, kidney-related problems forced him to be confined to a controlled environment at home. Actually, he had had a kidney transplant though it was not made public. In January 2019, he unexpectedly flew to the US for treatment. No official announcement came from any sources, but it was believed that he had undergone cancer-related surgery. According to a Gulf newspaper, he was diagnosed with soft tissue sarcoma, a rare type of cancer. Cutting across party lines, there was a rush of prayers for his recovery. Jaitley kept himself in the news with frequent commentary on current issues, spreading the impression that he was bravely coping with his problems. He was soon back in his ministry, appearing in public with customary attacks on critics and justification of everything the government did.

As with all diabetics, love of food was Jaitley's problem. He admitted it with no qualms. 'I am a Punjabi by birth and by culture,' he wrote in a 2010 article in *Outlook*. 'My all-time favourite is Amritsari Kulcha.' He was in charge of the kitchen when he was jailed during the Emergency and he recalled fellow prisoner K.R. Malkhani describing him as both a gourmet and a glutton. Eating was a problem while travelling. 'Foods of countries like Japan and Israel didn't suit my palate and I ended up having dal roti in my room ordered from Indian restaurants in those places.' Food at state banquets abroad were 'the world's most boring meals'. The title of 'the worst food in the world is reserved for what you get in trains and flights'. He was known for taking home-cooked food with him when he was traveling first class on reputed airlines. 'There is nothing quite like good, honest Indian food,' said the lover of stuffed parathas served with yoghurt.

The dinner parties Jaitley threw at his home in Delhi were famous—for the food, not the VIPs. Despite his diabetes and his surgeries, the Punjabi in him loved a good bite, and loved talking about it. It is ironic that a man who was so hospitable, educated, and socially active could turn into a one-sided combatant when he confronted political views opposed to his own. When the BJP's own senior leader, Yashwant Sinha, made critical remarks about the party, Jaitley dismissed him as 'a job applicant at 80'. He compared Indira Gandhi to Hitler. His reasoning was that she imprisoned opponents as Hitler did. But she didn't kill minorities as Hitler did—or indeed as the BJP's own ideologues have been attempting to do. There was no lynching during Indira Gandhi's days. Nor were there ministers like the BJP's Lal Singh who asked journalists in Kashmir to 'draw a line' because, if they didn't, they could meet the fate of Shujaat Bukhari, the Srinagar editor who was shot dead by unidentified gunmen in June 2018. Lal Singh remains un-reprimanded by his party.

Jaitley's refusal to see the suffering of the small businessmen and the working class as a consequence of demonetisation was typical. Millions had their businesses ruined, but the Finance Minister's position was that despite some 'initial inconveniences' the absence of social unrest and 'any significant economic disruption' showed that DeMo was a success. There was no social unrest even when Emergency denied citizens the right to life. But people kicked out Indira Gandhi. As for economic disruption, Surat and Tirupur, crown jewels of India's textile exports, were devastated overnight. It was a 400-crore-a-day business in Surat, a 50,000-crore-a-year backbone in Tirupur employing 10 lakh workers. Denied ready cash for spot business deals, both centres became graveyards. As the economist Kaushik Basu said, 'A bigger worry than demonetisation itself is the failure to recognise that it was a mistake.'

Authoritative voices often rose to point out the one-sided haughtiness in Jaitley's arguments. His response was to ignore them. Sometimes erudite people pointed out mistakes in his attempts to display his own erudition. He ignored them too. But what got into print stayed in print as proof of Jaitley's pretensions. Attacking his favourite quarry in Parliament in early 2019, he said: 'The Congress president must have watched James Bond films in which Bond says, if it happens for the first time it is happenstance, if it happens twice it is coincidence, and if it is thrice, it is conspiracy.' The House looked impressed and the Congress president had nothing to offer by way of a retort. But well-read and intellectually inclined MPs were not. Trinamool Congress MP Saugata Roy said, 'Jaitleyji, your memory is failing you.' Roy, a professor of physics, holder of a law degree and a National Science Talent Search Scholar explained: 'What Bond said was, if it happens for the first time it is happenstance, twice it is coincidence, and thrice, then it is enemy action.' For good measure, the learned professor also told the error-prone minister that he should learn to pronounce French President Francois Hollande's name correctly. Jaitley, true to character, pretended that he did not hear Saugata Roy. For Arun Jaitley, the one-man brains trust of the Narendra Modi junta, bon vivant and blogger–speaker who told the world what it needed to know, minor details like a literary episode or a foreign language nicety was of scant importance. What mattered was his conviction that the country needed him. He used the internet to heed that call even when he was away from Parliament and microphones on health grounds. He was a politician without a base. The people of Amritsar did not vote for him despite his love for Amritsari kulcha. He was never an elected member of any legislature. He had to be nominated to the Rajya Sabha from Gujarat. When the BJP did not have enough members in the Gujarat Assembly, he was nominated from UP. Despite being unelectable, he was a leader with a style of his own, known as Modi's 'special diamond'. He was also often described as 'every big man's friend'. The Modi government would have been seen as mere sounding brass and tinkling cymbals without the substance provided by the polished articulator in Jaitley. He was the behind-the-throne architect of the Modi superstructure. There were no greys in his universe, it was all dark black or stark white. This gave him the profile of a perpetual confrontationist, hiding the charming networker in him. He could argue with conviction that he was in the right even when he was in the wrong. He could be rude to opponents though gracefulness was his forte. When he attacked Rahul Gandhi as 'a clown prince,' a whiff of sympathy went to the victim. Covering himself with a tunic of immunity, Jaitley felt free to do what he criticised others for doing. Ultimately, he unified in his persona the three lucks that consummated Feng Shui Serenity—Heaven Luck, Earth Luck, and Man Luck. Destiny as determined by the Cosmic Trinity ensured that Jaitley won even when voters defeated him. He was blessed with the conviction that he was always right and others were always wrong. Beyond Heaven and Earth, he was blessed with Man Luck.

11

SANJAY GANDHI

Defiance as Play

Sanjay Gandhi was only a meteor that streaked through history and disappeared. But that momentary incandescence transformed not only the trajectory but also the political character of India. The progenitor of India's rebirth during the 1975–1977 Emergency was not Indira Gandhi who sat in the prime minister's chair but Sanjay Gandhi who ran the government. India's journey into dictatorial governance began with him.

Reckless and impetuous, Sanjay Gandhi grew up defiant. His Doon School days were noted for the 'fun' he had taking joyrides in other people's cars and abandoning them. He never went to college. His obsession with speed and automobiles made him join a British car factory, but his own attempt to make a car in India flopped amid a bundle of scandals. He didn't care; he lived by his own rules. When his mother's position seemed shaky following the Allahabad High Court's ruling against her election, Sanjay took a tough stand that encouraged Indira to declare an Emergency. With that he became the Aurangzeb of his own Indian Sultanate. The civil service became a toy in his hands, and VIPs and business tycoons his sycophants. Power at ground level was wielded by what became known as the Sanjay Brigade, a hotchpotch army of undisciplined youngsters whose Kurta-pyjamas became a licence for hooliganism.

India was governed by a set of proprietors. B.N. Tandon referred to them as the Palace Guard. Although he named no names, it was known that the inner core of the Palace Guard comprised Sanjay Gandhi, his wife Maneka, a 'family elder' called Chacha (Mohammed) Yunus, and two stenographer-turned-storm troopers: R.K. Dhawan and Yashpal Kapoor. Sanjay's parliamentary storm troopers included Jagdish Tytler, Kamal Nath, Ghulam Nabi Azad and Ambika Soni, great survivors who stayed on in power long after their patron was gone. Almost all references in Tandon's book to the way top appointments were decided in Delhi mentioned Sanjay Gandhi's and Dhawan's names together. Kapoor was no less of a terror at the time. Perhaps the best description of him was provided by Indira Gandhi's friend-turned-critic, Raj Thapar. In *All These Years*, one of the first insider accounts of Delhi's political class, she summed up Yashpal Kapoor in a few words: 'One glance at [him] and you felt the grease all over you. He was smooth and unintelligent, outwardly vacuous and inwardly scheming.' And totally devoid of grace, she might have added. For this was the man who took charge of the *National Herald* and hounded out and humiliated one of the great editors of India, Chalapathi Rao, who had built up the paper and was a friend and partner of Jawaharlal Nehru.

Why did the few 'intrinsically good men' around Indira Gandhi hang on to their posts and ignore Sanjay's insults? According to B.G. Verghese, 'Dhar did think of resigning but abandoned the thought and decided to soldier on...Indira Gandhi too would not let Dhar go. The presence of men like him lent respectability to the PMO in howsoever small measure.' Sharada Prasad, though crestfallen, was held back by his sense of loyalty. Even in retirement, he never spoke about the subject and declined to write his memoirs. But there was no doubt he was an unhappy man. B.N. Tandon's diary entry dated 21 June, nine days after the Allahabad High Court set aside Indira Gandhi's election and thereby triggered the actions that led to the Emergency, said: 'Sharada told me that in the last eight days, the Prime Minster has given no demonstration of the greatness of her character. Day by day her personality is shrinking.'

The Emergency made possible what Indians had considered impossible. The Constitution, debated and devised by some of the finest legal and political minds of the 20th century, was summarily suspended. The Supreme Court became a tool of politics. Parliament succumbed to street culture; shouting down opponents and blocking proceedings became standard patriotism. The press crawled when asked to bend. Subservience became an art, flattery a way of life. Cronies were kings. It was no longer necessary to maintain the façade of propriety in public life. Indians were divided into two groups—a minority that chose to fight and the majority that devised ways to profit from the situation. The fighters were permanently scalded. The opportunists established a culture of obeisance that rapidly turned into an Indian way of life. Two years is not a long period of time, but the Emergency altered the timbre of democracy and the thinking habits of a large number of Indians. In the process, the ruling elite lost its legitimising moral fibre. Democracy returned after two years, but morality did not. The negative traits of political India had by then re-emerged and taken root. The Emergency took the guilt out of selfishness in politics. That power could be misused with an easy conscience transformed the vocabulary of governance. Sanjay Gandhi's influence seemed to go deeper than himself had expected. His experiment transformed Nehru's liberal India to the Gandhi family's authoritarian India. It did not merely turn the Constitution upside down; citizens were specifically deprived of their right to life by a trumped-up Supreme Court. Arrests, tortures, and killings went on unbeknown to the families of the victims because the press was censored. Journalists crawled, industrialists cringed, politicians in the Sanjay camp strutted. Under the direct influence of Sanjay Gandhi's Youth Congress, thuggery became an accepted political norm. Up until the Emergency, some decorum was considered appropriate in public life. After the Emergency, blocking proceedings in Parliament became routine.

The idea of dynastic succession would have outraged Mahatma Gandhi and Sardar Patel who left their children to fend for themselves. Even Nehru had to use roundabout ways, and that too apologetically, to get Indira into the party's higher echelons. After the Emergency, a chief minister's unlettered wife considered it her right to assume office when her husband was jailed. Across the country and across parties, sons and daughters of leaders projected themselves as such, and were accepted as leaders because of their parentage. Sanjay Gandhi and his mother established a pernicious practice that grew into India's bone marrow. When the Congress won a landslide victory in 1980 after the farcical rule of the Janata Party, it was clear that Sanjay had reached the very summit. There was talk that he might not even wait for his mother to complete her term and retire, that he might take over while she was overcome with motherly love. That was when an exciting new aerobatic aircraft, the Pitts S-2A, came into the possession of the Delhi Flying Club at Safdarjung Airport. Electrified by the new machine, Sanjay flew into the sky, showing off with a swoop near his Willingdon Crescent residence, rose majestically higher, and then, in a split second, nosedived into a cluster of trees. His face was split down the centre. His co-pilot's body was even more gruesomely mangled. It was an end one would not have wished on one's enemies. The crash also marked the end of any prospect of India being ruled by the Sanjay Brigade. India after Sanjay Gandhi was very different from the India he had tried to build. Political players were forced to accept the reality that the man who had been about to put his stamp on India was gone. It was to his brother Rajiv that the spotlight now shifted.

Two brothers could not have been more different in character than Rajiv and Sanjay Gandhi. Suave and soft-spoken, Rajiv would have been happy as a pilot leading a quiet life with Sonia, the girl he fell in love with while in England. Sanjay was a completely different personality, 'a wild, wayward youth... rebellious, destructive,' as chronicled by Pupul Jayakar, family friend and biographer of Indira Gandhi. Aunt Vijaya Lakshmi Pandit marked him out as 'rude and crude'. The writer Khushwant Singh, who showed singular interest in promoting Sanjay's wife Maneka, called him the 'loveable goonda'. The 21-month Emergency that came into force in June 1975 was Sanjay's idea. He persuaded his mother with the argument that if she lost political power, her enemies would go after her, and her own as well as her family's lives would be in danger. At the height of the Emergency as many as 1,50,000 people were in jail. Sanjay's pet project of sterilisation injected an unprecedented dose of suffering into the populace. Targets were fixed for government officials and school-teachers and those who failed to reach them were denied salaries, or suspended. In the rush to meet targets, old men and unmarried men and one-child fathers were sterilised. In one year, the sterilised population rose from 26.24 lakh to 81.23 lakh. A controversial Sanjay associate, Rukhsana Sultana, took Sanjay's message to the Muslim areas of old Delhi. Rasheed Kidwai's book, *24 Akbar Road: A Short History of the People Behind the Fall and Rise of the Congress* (2011), describes Rukhsana as 'an exotic character, an unabashed exhibitionist' who never missed an opportunity to say that she and Sanjay were 'ice-cream buddies'. As the book puts it: 'In the Jama Masjid area, the sight of Rukhsana, perfumed, painted and bejewelled to within an inch of her life, wearing pink spectacles, a silk saree and a low-cut choli was a complete put-off for both men and women.'

Sanjay had a constructive streak in him. He promoted self-employment, industrial parks, and the grand Maruti car although it materialised only after his death. But the good in him was obliterated by the dictatorial methods he used to impose his will. Internal feuds made things worse. His death was followed by a spectacular exhibition of enmity among family members. A denouement occurred when, in full view of television cameras, Maneka Gandhi was thrown out of the house along with her utensils and personal belongings. Maneka bided her time, and, two decades later, in August 2002, damned Indira with an account of their estranged relationship. She said that after Sanjay's death, Indira '...was never normal again. She was not Indira Gandhi. She lost everything in that plane crash.' As Maneka saw it, 'The country's most formidable politician suddenly turned into a puppet at the hands of her elder son Rajiv Gandhi and his Italian-born wife Sonia.' It is a bit difficult to imagine Rajiv Gandhi reducing anyone to a puppet. He was completely uninterested in politics and only got into it because, as he put it, 'Mummy wants me.' Maneka never tried to hide her disdain for her brother-in-law. 'Rajiv and Sonia are very Western. Sanjay was completely Indian... It's odd that in one family two brothers and their wives could be so different.' A philosophical proclamation followed: 'You don't become a relative just by being related.'

Indira Gandhi, powerful as she was, presided over a warring kitchen. B.K. Nehru's book *Nice Guys Finish Second* (1997) put it nicely by saying that there was a 'servants' problem' at Wellington Crescent. 'Sonia was the cook, Maneka merely ate. Indira's two sons and their wives were certainly not on the best terms with each other.'

The extent to which family discordance vitiated the atmosphere in Indira's household became public after Sanjay's death. This was deftly conveyed by Janardan Thakur, the gifted journalist who wrote *Prime Ministers, Nehru to Vajpayee* (2002). In gentle terms, he conveyed a grim message as he described Indira's concerns after Sanjay's death. She went to the hospital where she could be alone with her son's mangled body. 'From the hospital she rushed to the crash site a second time. The whole area had already been cordoned off. Mrs Gandhi walked around the rubble, her eyes searching. She told the guards that she was looking for a bunch of keys and a wristwatch. Both were found... Why did the shattered mother have to go looking for a bunch of keys and a watch? When and how did she know that the two things were not on the body?... Two days later Maneka asked her mother-in-law for the keys. Mrs Gandhi refused.'

Realising that the Gandhi part of her name had lost its relevance, Maneka tried to carve out a role for herself. But she was not enough of a politician to make a mark singlehandedly. She ended up joining the BJP. It was a public relations gain for the BJP, but not of any consequence because Maneka was a light-weight in the political sphere. The headlines disappeared in no time and Maneka was forgotten. Sanjay and his tribe inflicted what injuries they could on the concept of India. Thomas Carlyle got it right when he said that history was not a distillation of rumour but a play of personalities.

12

A.P.J. ABDUL KALAM

From Missiles to the Stars

The position does not make the man; Neelam Sanjiva Reddy became the President of the Republic of India but only the record books remember him. But a man can rise above his position; A.P.J. Abdul Kalam's retirement from the presidentship of India did not merit even a comma in his saga. His public engagements, mass appeal, and the number of organisations that requested an appearance saw no dip after he left Rashtrapati Bhavan. He designed inspirational maxims such as: 'Every pain gives a lesson and every lesson changes a person.' The common man loved them. The guiding spirit within Kalam contributed more to his pre-eminence than the offices he held. The enlightenment of India's first-generation leadership also helped. Without Jawaharlal Nehru giving wide powers and generous funding to Homi Bhabha, would Indian science have progressed so far, so fast? Without Bhabha encouraging Vikram Sarabhai, and Sarabhai's collaboration with Raja Ramanna, and Ramanna providing inspiration to Kalam, would we have become leaders in innovation? They were masters of the arts, not just men of science. Bhabha was a widely admired portrait artist, Sarabhai a patron of the arts, Ramanna a pianist of distinction, and Kalam a veena player. A Mysore brahmin who excelled in Chopin and Beethoven, a Rameswaram Muslim who celebrated Thyagaraja and vegetarianism—this was India at its finest.

Irony played a role in the development of Avul Pakir Jainulabdeen Abdul Kalam. His ancestors were wealthy but 'progress' reduced his father's generational status to lower middle class. Natives of the Hindu pilgrimage town of Rameswaram on Pamban Island in the southern tip of India, the family had attained prosperity by trading groceries between Pamban and Ceylon, 40 kilometres away, and by running a ferry service between the island and the Indian mainland. The ferry was a lifeline for pilgrims who came from all corners of India to worship at the Ramanathaswamy Temple, considered one of the holiest in the country. The ferry was always busy. The family acquired land in nearby areas. Then came progress in the shape of the Pamban sea bridge. It was a narrow-gauge rail line laid by the British in 1914. But it was enough to kill the ferry service run by Kalam's ancestors. It also affected the grocery business with the Lankan coast. Kalam's father had a ferry boat but passengers were few and far between. He was also the imam of the local mosque, a position that added to his status as a man to be respected. In his writings, Kalam has acknowledged the influence his father's liberal views exerted on his own ideas.

Evidently, there were other unseen influences at work that sent Kalam in directions no one in his family had considered. No one knows why, but he was a vegetarian when he joined St Joseph's College in Trichy where he studied physics. Because a Muslim vegetarian was something of a novelty and because Kalam was so devoted to his vegetarianism, he became known as Kalam Iyer. His fellow students enthusiastically elected this unusual Iyer as secretary of the college's vegetarian mess.

His habits were special too. He shared a room with Sampath who was doing maths and Alexander who was into biology. He would get up at 5 a.m. so that he would have undisturbed time for study before his roommates got up. Similarly, he would stay awake till 11 p.m., well after his mates had gone to sleep. A sense of purpose guided Kalam from an early age. Transferring from physics to engineering was a short step. Hoping to become a fighter pilot, he completed an aeronautics course at the Madras Institute of Technology. He qualified in the preliminary tests and got into a nine-man list for final selection. He was ninth on the list and it turned out there were only eight vacancies at the time. Chance pushed him into the Directorate of Technical Development and Production as senior scientific assistant. From there it was a short step to the committee for space research, the early version of ISRO, the Indian Space Research Organization. The stage was set for the emergence of India's Missile Man.

He flowered when he joined the satellite launch division of ISRO at Thumba, the equatorial site near Thiruvananthapuram. That was a crucial turn in the development of both Kalam the man and Kalam the rocket scientist. Thumba was the arena of the men who turned out to be Kalam's heroes. 'I learned leadership,' he once said, 'from three great teachers—Dr Vikram Sarabhai, Professor Satish Dhawan and Dr Brahm Prakash.' Those were the pioneers of India's journey into space. Sarabhai and his fellow visionary, Homi Bhabha, headed departments a newly independent third-world country was not supposed to possess. Power centres in the West knew that these young scientists had nuclear ambitions for their country and the wherewithal to pursue them. Homi Bhabha had quietly started a nuclear programme as early as 1944 under the Tata Institute of Fundamental Research. Jawaharlal Nehru's perceptive approach to scientific advancement strengthened Bhabha's hands and made him aim for an atomic bomb. Sarabhai was more circumspect, but those who worked with him said later that his goal was the development of nuclear missiles. The West, led by the US, considered it a sin on the part of India to nurture atomic ambitions. They were happy when the sinners were stopped in their tracks. Bhabha died in an air crash in 1966. Five years later, Sarabhai went to sleep hale and hearty—and was found dead in the morning. The cause of death was never discovered because no postmortem was conducted. Bhabha was 57, Sarabhai 52. Who killed them? Why? Speculate as much as you like, but not a clue would be found anywhere. Such were international relations when the US ruled the roost.

Kalam was closely associated with Sarabhai's plans. Actually, he was working on advanced concepts of missile attack technologies when others of his rank were into more conventional research. A programme he devised for the development of ballistic missiles appeared so close to a military operation that the government officially denied him permission to proceed. Indira Gandhi came to his rescue and provided secret discretionary funding. In due course, he succeeded in making it an approved military programme, though in civilian clothing. The sutradhars of Pokhran-II—India's first nuclear bomb test—were Raja Ramanna, Homi Sethna and P.K. Iyengar, the designer of the bomb. Kalam was present at the site as a representative of the Defence Research and Development Organisation. Pokhran-II, in 1998, saw Kalam as the chief coordinator alongside R. Chidambaram of the Department of Atomic Energy (who had participated in Pokhran-I as the metallurgist). Kalam was described as the brain behind the multiple nuclear tests that constituted Pokhran-II. He led the weaponisation of strategic missile systems and played his part in the elaborate arrangements made by the government and the army to keep the test hidden from America's spy satellites. (Like other scientists at the site, he wore military uniform and assumed the nom de guerre Major-General Prithviraj.) He called the Thar desert explosions a 'defining moment' in Indian history, second in importance to economic liberalisation in 1991.

Kalam is regarded as the 'Father of India's Missile System'. The title of 'Father of the Indian Atomic Bomb' is Homi Bhabha's. Neither is known to have expressed any contrition over their achievements, as J. Robert Oppenheimer, the 'Father of the Atom Bomb', did. Their inventions were not used to wreak havoc of the kind the atomic and hydrogen bombs did over Japan at the end of World War II. Such was the horror of American overkill that Oppenheimer famously said he was reminded of the Bhagavad Gita: 'Now I have become Death, the destroyer of Worlds.' Einstein regretted urging US President Roosevelt to go atomic as a way of stopping Nazi Germany from becoming the first nation to develop a nuclear bomb. Bhabha and Kalam represented an era that judged nations by the fire power they possessed. Their contributions gave India a place in an exclusive club.

Ironically, the Missile Man's flowering reached its fullness after he had passed the missile stage. It was teaching, in which he immersed himself by the end of 2001, that found him at his passionate best. The passage in *Turning Points* (2012) where he describes his work at the Anna University in Chennai is aglow with his ardour for teaching. 'The authorised strength of my class was sixty students, but during every lecture the classroom had more than 350 students,' he wrote. A course of ten lectures for postgraduate students was specially designed for him at the university. It was when he was immersed in this work that he got a phone call from Prime Minister A.B. Vajpayee. 'Kalam, how is your academic life?' asked the Prime Minister. 'It is fantastic,' said the teacher. That was when Vajpayee told him of his coalition's decision to make him President. Kalam took a couple of hours consulting friends and colleagues before he agreed. But he made the point that there should be 'a consensus among all political parties on my nomination'. In the event, 'all political parties' did not agree; the left came up with their own candidate. The Congress Party agreed to go along with Vajpayee but only after it realised it had no choice. As Kalam himself put it: 'Vajpayee consulted with Mrs Sonia Gandhi, the opposition leader. When Mrs Gandhi asked whether the NDA's choice was final, the Prime Minister responded in the affirmative. After due consultation with her party members and coalition partners, she announced the agreement of the Congress's concurrence.'

Various accounts proved that Kalam was essentially the BJP's choice for the post of president. The party's principal strategist, Pramod Mahajan, acted as his election agent. There was not much discussion then or thereafter why the BJP picked Kalam or why Kalam agreed to be the BJP's nominee. A rare comment on this subject came from Muchkund Dubey, former ambassador who had taken to academia after retirement. He said that the BJP zeroed in on Kalam '...to establish its non-existent secular credentials and to refurbish its image tarnished by the Gujarat carnage. The Congress and other so called secular parties are supporting him in the belief that this would enable them to retain, if not augment, their Muslim vote-bank. Thus, we have here the case of the right candidate being nominated for the wrong reasons.' However wrong the reasons, the candidate became the most interactive president India had seen. In his decisions and actions, there was no suggestion whatever that Kalam felt indebted to the BJP. He set his own style without displaying any kind of political partisanship. His only partiality was in favour of children and young people. Rashtrapati Bhavan became an open house for students and youth. Many were engaged by the president in question-and-answer sessions. These sessions were interspersed with lectures, now at an academic gathering, now before legislators. The official duties of the president attracted attention only on occasions where a decision proved controversial—like ignoring 20 out of 21 pending mercy petitions and acting only in the case of the rapist Dhananjay Chatterjee to let him be hanged. But there was one issue on which he firmly, if somewhat unconventionally, asserted presidential authority, leading to unexpected consequences.

In 2006, the penultimate year of his presidency, when the Congress was in power with Manmohan Singh as prime minister, Kalam found on his desk the Office of Profit Bill (OPB). It had been passed by Parliament and needed only the president's signature to become law. But the president was in no hurry to sign. He noticed that the bill provided exemptions to certain individuals and institutions. Suspecting that this could be to show undue favours to a chosen few, he consulted some judges and then took the unusual step of sending the bill back, not to the prime minister, but to the speaker of the Lok Sabha and the chairman of the Rajya Sabha. This led to moves within ruling Congress circles to convert the OPB into an ordinance to circumvent the presidential assent. The opposition led by the BJP mounted a vociferous campaign against the move. It went so far as to petition the president for disqualification of Congress President Sonia Gandhi on the ground that she held an office of profit as chairperson of the National Advisory Council (NAC). The Chief Election Commission added its bit to a mounting sense of crisis by saying that the law was the same for everybody. Sonia Gandhi was miffed that only she and her party had been brought into the line of fire. She reacted in a way that surprised friend and foe alike. She announced her resignation as chairperson of the NAC and also as Member of Parliament. Subsequently, Parliament set up a joint committee to work out a comprehensive definition of the office-of-profit concept on the lines suggested by the president's office. President Kalam formally approved this, providing relief to as many as 45 MPs, including speaker Somnath Chatterjee, who had held offices of profit.

The episode added to the grudge Sonia Gandhi was believed to have held against Kalam. Two years before her resignation from Parliament, in 2004, she had what was generally interpreted as a confrontation with Kalam although no first-hand account of it appeared anywhere. The 2004 general election had put the Congress Party in the driver's seat and Sonia Gandhi had gone to Rashtrapati Bhavan to stake her party's claim to form the government. What happened between her and the president remains a matter of speculation despite Kalam's account of it in his autobiography written eight years later in 2012. According to unofficial reports that circulated at the time, Sonia wanted to lead the government as prime minister and Kalam advised her against it considering the discontent it could generate because of her Italian origins. According to official accounts, however, Kalam was ready with an appointment letter with Sonia's name on it, but was surprised when Sonia proposed Manmohan Singh for the post. The president had to get the appointment letter re-typed, he noted in *Turning Points*. However, he wrote: 'There were many political leaders who [requested] me not to succumb to any pressure and appoint Mrs Gandhi as the prime minister, a request that would not have been constitutionally tenable.' Sonia, for her part, told party faithfuls that she had listened to her inner voice and decided against taking up the prime minister's post.

Who was leaving what out of the narrative? If it was all about Kalam being surprised by the Manmohan Singh nomination and Sonia being guided by her inner voice, where did the bad blood between Kalam and Sonia come from? Even the US embassy in Delhi called Washington at the time about the 'longstanding animosity between President Kalam and Sonia Gandhi'. Kalam would have signed on for a second term as president, but withdrew when the Congress Party along with the Left made it clear that it would not support him. The Congress instead supported Sonia's nominee Pratibha Patil who, it turned out, was eminently unfit for Rashtrapati Bhavan. She became the only president who continued asking for cars and petrol allowances long after she left office. As president she took a dozen family members on her foreign tours, and a special post-retirement mansion was built in Pune for her pleasure, ignoring convention. This petty president was Sonia's revenge against those who stood in the way of her ambition.

Out of office, Kalam remained busier than ever. Apart from accepting the posts of chancellor of the Indian Institute of Space Science and Technology in Thiruvananthapuram and professor of aerospace engineering at Anna University in Chennai, he became a visiting professor at the IITs in Ahmedabad, Indore, and Shillong, and an honorary fellow at the Indian Institute of Science in Bangalore. He also taught information technology in Hyderabad and Banaras. He became a familiar sight across India, lecturing with his laptop in front of him. He kept writing books, taking collaborative assistance from fellow researchers and friends. A hit title of 1999, *Wings of Fire*, was co-written with Arun Tiwari, a professor of biomedical engineering. *India 2020*, written a year earlier, was a joint effort with Y.S. Rajan while *A Manifesto for Change: A Sequel to India 2020* (2014) had V. Ponraj as collaborator. *Ignited Minds* which appeared in 2002 was also a kind of sequel. Inspired by a

Gujarati school girl who, when asked, 'Who is our enemy?' replied, 'Our enemy is poverty.' This book found Kalam at his motivational best. *Re-ignited* and *Advantage India*, both published in 2015, were written with Srijan Pal as collaborator. A somewhat different kind of book was *Transcendence: My Spiritual Experience with Pramukh Swamiji* (2015) which was written with Arun Tiwari as co-author. In the course of these writings, phrases and sentences emerged with the clear stamp of Kalamism. 'A leader should know how to manage failure.' 'Dreams are not those that we see in our sleep. They should be the ones that never let us sleep.' 'You have to dream before your dreams can come true.' Kalam become a quotable speaker/writer.

Behind all the didacticism that propelled him and the faith he had in his fellow beings, there lurked a very personal Kalam with very personal ideas about himself. No one knows why he never married, although he was very much a family man as son and brother. He had no possessions of his own except his rudra veena; the highlight of the pictorial show put up at his memorial in Rameswaram is a painting of him in traditional Carnatic music dress, silk dhoti, full-sleeved shirt with a white shawl around the neck, sitting cross-legged in Bhagavathar style. He did not start veena lessons in his childhood as is the practice in Tamil Nadu. He learned to play the veena when he was already at DRDO working on missile technology. For reasons of his own, he chose the rudra veena which is essentially a part of the Dhrupad tradition of north India.

Of all his various traits, the one that stood out as a registered trademark was the Kalam hairstyle. It turns out that he was hair-conscious from early on. As a young scientist, he would always look out for mirrors and, when he saw one, take out a pocket comb and do a quick, spruce-up. He had noticed that his hair had a tendency to grow fast. 'It grows and grows,' he once said. From boyhood he was in the habit of keeping his hair long. There were some references to his being born with a malformed ear and the hair coming in handy to cover it. After he became a Delhi resident, he used to go to a salon in Lodhi Road where Habib Ahmed had made a name for himself. (His father Nazir Ahmed had attended to Jawaharlal Nehru and Rajendra Prasad.) Habib gave Kalam a serum that softened his hair and gave it a shine. His client liked it. But it was Habib's son Amjad who created the Kalam we know. Tired of the familiar old look, Kalam once asked for something new. Amjad Habib rose to the challenge and, with the deftness of an artist, worked out a new cut. As he himself described it, 'The style I gave him is called "reverse gradation". It had been very famous among rock-stars. 'I gave him the haircut with limited steps to keep it convenient for him.' Some days later, Kalam phoned him and said, 'If I ask you to change my haircut again, never do it.' Kalam had found his bliss. The silver shine now acquired a glow, fanning out at the back of the neck to provide a touch of prosperous sufficiency. The locks hesitate momentarily at the forehead only to turn into twin half-moons, a decorative framework. Add a touch of grey in the eyebrows and a work of art comes into view leaving you confounded and envious in turns. When Kalam became president, protocol demanded that only government barbers have access to his hair. The president told the tonsorial bureaucracy not to make an iota of change in the style that had turned his hair into a crown. To drive the point home, Amjad, his wife, children and grandchildren were invited to the Rashtrapati Bhavan more than once, the president himself showing his guests rare sights such as the Mughal Gardens. If Kalam had any vanity in him, it was about his hair. The 'Kalam cut' became a civilisational marker in the aesthetics of coiffure.

With two or three exceptions, the presidents of India were great souls who brought honour to the country. S. Radhakrishnan and Zakir Hussain were internationally respected scholars. Two who became extraordinary because of their ordinariness were K.R. Narayanan and Kalam. Interestingly, those two were also presidents that the political system got rid of after one term each. But no one could rob them of their popular appeal. Narayanan became the first president who exercised his vote as a citizen. Kalam wrote more than a dozen inspirational books, 22 poems and four songs, and was twice nominated for the honorific of 'MTV Youth Icon'.

Perhaps Kalam's most significant achievement was that nobody thought of him as a Muslim. He bore a 24-carat Muslim name, did his namaz, and observed his Ramzan duties without fail. But he was also a vegetarian who read the Bhagavad Gita and listened to Carnatic devotional songs every day. It must be the atmabala, the strength of the soul, he thus gained that enabled him to sit in the political jungle of Delhi and still remain apolitical. The gods blessed him by allowing him to die quietly and quickly in the midst of what he loved most—teaching. In death as well as in life, he remained true to the message he conveyed to his young listeners: 'Look at the sky. We are not alone. The whole universe is friendly to us.' This was a man who belonged to the stars.

13

P. LAL

The Word, the World

Indians spend more time reading than any other national group in the world—10 hours 42 minutes a week. Thais come next with 9 hours and 24 minutes, followed by the Chinese with 8 hours a week. Americans are way below with only 5 hours and 42 minutes. The figures, put out by Culture Score Index,* may help us understand phenomena such as Donald Trump. But they also point to some anomalies. For a non-celebrity writer, something like 10,000 copies makes for a bestseller in India. In America, it takes at least five times that number to be anywhere near bestseller status. That means moderate sales are enough to hit the jackpot in the country with the most readers while massive numbers are needed to reach comparable success in a country with fewer readers. What explains the conundrum?

Bestseller is a word authors, publishers, and the media love, yet there is no agreement on the methodology of identifying them. The trade sees Nielsen-Bookscan as the only quantitative dataset on the Indian book industry. But Bookscan cannot be comprehensive as it covers only 60–70 per cent of the book market. The *New York Times* bestseller list, arguably the world's most famous, is said to be

* Sangeeta Bose, 'Indians spend more time reading than anyone else in the world', www.moneycontrol.com, 1 November 2017.

based on confidential reports from booksellers, but they keep the details secret. (William Blatty, author of *The Exorcist* (1971), filed a $9 million suit against the paper claiming it damaged the sales of his new book *Legion* (1983) by not including it in the bestseller list in the 1980s. He lost the case.)

While the term bestseller remains largely a matter of perception, the pull of the written word has been something of a phenomenon in India. An important contributory factor was the banning of titles for one reason or another. *Rama Retold*, a 1955 spoof on the Ramayana by Aubrey Menen, and *Nine Hours to Rama* (1962), Stanley Wolpert's sympathetic account of Mahatma Gandhi's assassin, were officially banned, which increased the popular demand for these titles, a demand that was met one way or another. Exaggerated nationalism led to the banning of V.S. Naipaul's *An Area of Darkness* (1964). Those who wanted copies got them. The most famous example of a ban helping sales was Salman Rushdie's *The Satanic Verses* (1988). India was the first to ban the book in a bid to please the Muslim lobby. In 1983, four years after he retired as prime minister, Morarji Desai tried to get Seymour Hersh's *The Price of Power* banned because it had portrayed him as a CIA spy. He filed a case in the US claiming damages worth $5 million. The court rejected his arguments. *The Polyester Prince* (1998), Australian writer Hamish McDonald's biography of Dhirubhai Ambani, did not get an Indian edition because the publishers feared legal action. 'Unauthorised' copies became available.

The rise of communal politics in India led to a new wave of intolerance in the literary field as activists of ascendant Hindutva objected to liberal views. Ironically, Hindutva activism helped increase the sales of the books they wanted to suppress. The most famous example was Perumal Murugan's Tamil novel *Madhorubagan* (2015). Scared by criticism and threats from Hindutva activists, he not only withdrew all his books from the market but announced that he was giving up writing. All he had done was to base his story on an old village tradition of a childless woman, urged by her husband

and family, having consensual union with a man participating in a local festival. Warnings and ultimatums from communal groups made him famous. The English translation of the book, *One Part Woman* (2010), became a bestseller. Encouraged by the unexpected success, he returned to writing and grew into a star speaker as well. Kerala, seen as the country's most literary state, witnessed comparable drama when the serialisation of a novel was abruptly stopped by a magazine. A reference to women decking themselves up to go to temples with lust on their minds offended the Hindutva lobby. The magazine that unilaterally decided to discontinue publication made it appear as though it was forced to do so. It made the novelist say that it was his decision to stop the serialisation when it was actually the magazine's decision. The game was exposed when DC Books stepped in and quickly published the novel *Meesa* (2018) by S. Hareesh without deleting any of the passages the religious right had objected to. A plea to ban the book was rejected by the Supreme Court which said the culture of banning books impacted the free flow of ideas.

All these were pointers to the robust health of the book trade. The Nielsen Book report of 2015 valued the Indian book market at $3.9 billion, growing at 20 per cent a year. Some estimates listed India as the sixth largest book publisher in the world and the second largest in English language publishing. Towards the end of the 1980s, established publishing houses from the West started opening offices in India attracted by the size of the market. Penguin set up shop in Delhi in 1987 and later developed into Penguin Random House. HarperCollins started its India operations in 1992 and Hachette in 2009. They joined the ranks of art-books publisher Roli started in 1978, Westland in 1996, Pan Macmillan in 2010 and Aleph in 2011. The dates are important. After Rupa & Co. started by D. Mehra in Calcutta in 1936 and Jaico established by Jaman Shah in Bombay in 1946, English book publishing in India saw a barren stretch that lasted four decades until Penguin appeared and others followed. For the generation that belonged to that protracted period, book publishing was some kind of an alien dream. Aspiring authors, including those who would become famous in due course, had no place to take their manuscripts. England, the dream destination, remained just that because even Mulk Raj Anand, who lived half the time in England, needed E.M. Forster's help to get a break, just as R.K. Narayan needed Graham Greene's. Young hopefuls in India with no such connections found themselves marooned. Then something happened. P. Lal came up as publisher extraordinaire, T.N. Shanbhag as bookseller extraordinaire and K.S. Padmanabhan as book trade campaigner extraordinaire. They were simple men, driven by nothing but an addiction to books. None of them became famous. None was guided by the profit motive. For all three, it was love's labour not lost.

P. Lal's place in the literary history of India is, and will remain, unique. He achieved what others did not even attempt. Three addictions governed his life—the Mahabharata, publishing books by newcomers, and campaigning to make English accepted as an Indian language. All were perilous pursuits but he persisted in his quiet an unobtrusive way. For a man born in Kapurthala and transplanted to Bengal in his childhood, it was unusual to be self-effacing and quiet. Perhaps it was his vocation as a teacher that made him. For forty years he taught English at St Xavier's College in Calcutta continuing in an honorary capacity after formal retirement. His position as professor led people to call him Profsky, reminiscent of D.G. Tendulkar (biographer of the Mahatma) calling Dom Moraes, Domsky. Neither Lal nor Dom were radicals in the tradition of Trotsky or even Laski. Perhaps his admirers thought that a touch of Russification would add to the gravitas of their favourite professor. Lal was visiting professor at various universities in the US. His oeuvre included poetry, literary criticism, stories for children, translation, and anthologies.

His translation of the Mahabharata was unusual because it was in fact trans-creation, a word he invented. He took it up as a 20-year project and ended up with 100 cassettes of 60 minutes each with the creator reading his creation. He took Vyasa in his entirety, all 1,00,000 slokas. In quality, too, it was unusual. The poet in him was unafraid to have different renderings of the same passages, a result, he explained, 'of changes in my understanding and appreciation of Vyasa'. His aim was 'to re-tell the story... in Vyasa's own words, without simplifying, interpreting or elaborating'. And how did he understand Vyasa? 'The Ramayana rouses compassion, the Mahabharata an almost cosmic awe... Vyasa posits an intricate dharma, where right and wrong are bewilderingly mixed... No epic, no work of art, is sacred by itself; if it does not have meaning for me now, it is nothing, it is dead.' There was a pleasing emphasis on the oral/musical tradition of the epic. He took a characteristic step towards bringing this to public attention when he began spending an hour every Sunday morning at the Sanskriti Sagar Library hall in Calcutta reading aloud his transcreated slokas. He continued this practice until about a week before his death on 3 November 2010.

A limited hardbacked edition in 18 volumes comprising 18 parvas of the maha-kavya came out and quickly went out of print. It had a typical Lal-designed, Lal-executed cover with characteristic Lal typography. Recommending this for lockdown reading in 2021, Shashi Tharoor wrote: 'A wonderfully racy, contemporary translation of the timeless epic, melding poetry and prose and full of contemporary idiom, Prof. Lal's is unarguably the best and most readable one-volume version of Mahabharata.'

The Mahabharata might have been a magnum opus for P. Lal, but the world paid scant attention. His magnum opus in the eyes of others was the publishing house that accidentally became his baby. Facing a situation where serious book publishing had not yet developed in India, half a dozen idealists in Calcutta got together in 1958 and setup an organisation to bring out original writings by Indian authors. They called it Writers Workshop (WW) which seemed to suggest the tentativeness of a work in progress. It was an idea ahead of its time. Either for that reason or because of the pre-finished feel of the title, the sponsors lost interest. One by one, they dropped out until only P. Lal remained, in solitary splendour. He decided to stay put.

What followed was a one-man operation, herculean in its efforts and historic in its consequences. P. Lal made Writers Workshop a one-of-a-kind phenomenon in the annals of publishing, using facilities that were primitive by today's standards. But his approach was imaginative and it produced results. Lal was never a rich man and finding the resources to bring out his books was a burden. He earned a little from his lecture tours and visiting professorships. These 'shekels', as he called them, went into the production of WW's books. Whenever travels were stopped on health grounds, the shekels also stopped. That made him devise the system of asking his authors to buy 100 copies in advance. If an author was too impecunious to afford this, Lal went ahead anyway. Each WW book was a curious work of art. The types were handset by P. Lal. The titles and chapter heading were handcrafted by P. Lal, a recognised calligraphist. The cover design was executed in handloom silk and the book hand-stitched by P. Lal. Editing, proofreading, and page layout were all handled by P. Lal who was also in-charge of all correspondence with all authors; he never had a secretary or an assistant or even an office. He did have a treadle press but no place to keep it until a neighbour, P.K. Aditya, emptied his garage and gave it to Lal. These were the circumstances under which P. Lal brought out about 3,500 titles. Many were the critics who dismissed him as a vanity publisher. His reply was: 'My mission was to provide opportunities to writers when opportunities were not there and aspiring writers could not find a publisher.' That mission became a milestone in the development of English literature in India. Among those whose early efforts appeared under the Writers Workshop imprint were writers who evolved into celebrities—Vikram Seth, A.K. Ramanujan, Nissim Ezekiel, Kamala Das, Anita Desai, Agha Shahid Ali, Ruskin Bond, and G.V. Desani. Kamala Das (Madhavi Kutty, Kamala Suraiya) spoke for them all when she wrote: 'If not for P. Lal encouraging me, I would possibly never have become a serious writer in English.'

Writers Workshop did not merely give a chance to unknown writers. P. Lal had an ability to spot talent and, once spotted, to provide motivation and guidance to his discoveries. The importance of the service he provided began to win appreciation towards the end of his career. Started during the 'barren stretch' of English publishing in India, WW began losing its relevance with the rise of mainstream publishing companies from 1987. But appreciation for the role played by WW during the difficult decades began growing at the same time. P. Lal was a widely admired man when he died, aged 81. The spartan English professor who never smoked or drank would have been surprised by the various epithets people used to sum up his personality—Father of the Indo-Anglian Revolution, Dream Catcher, PPPP (Prince of Poets, Professors and Publishers), The Man Who Saw Everything, Faith Giver to Indo-Anglia, the Calligrapher of Calcutta, Eternal and Evergreen Parrot. Among those who published obituaries were *The Guardian* and *The Economist*. Finally, the P in his name stood out like a title his country had bestowed upon him—Purushottam, jewel among men.

If innovative publishing in the eastern metropolis of Calcutta turned P. Lal into an institution, innovating book selling in the Western metropolis of Bombay made T.N. Shanbhag something of a curiosity. For Shanbhag's bookshop was not really a bookshop; it was just a wall. Shanbhag was a small boy when he lost his father. It was a double catastrophe for him because life without a father meant life without money to go to school. Shanbhag wanted badly to go to school because he was precociously inquisitive by nature. It was luck that brought him a scholarship. He grew up as an eager young man, always interested in the books he came across. He left his village near Mangalore and went to Bombay where it was easier to find jobs. He wanted work because he wanted more education and the only way to acquire that was to finance himself. With the money earned from part-time work, he graduated from St Xavier's College. Once he got his basic degree, he did not go looking for a regular job like other college graduates did. There was an urge that kept him wedded to books. Fresh out of college, he started carrying selected titles around with him and talking select people into buying them. In an interview years later, he recalled that the first book he sold was in 1946. It was a copy of Winston Churchill's war memoirs and the buyer was Richard Burton, not the heart-throb of Elizabeth Taylor, but the chief of the Standard Vacuum Oil Company (predecessor of Esso) in Bombay. The felicity with which this young Indian described Churchill's exploits left Burton with no option but to buy. The Shanbhag trademark was already in evidence: knowing the contents of a book and making that knowledge the main tool of his selling method.

Shanbhag always knew that all that he wanted to do in life was to sell books. After the initial successes with individuals, he realised that he needed a bookshop to do justice to his chosen vocation. But a bookshop meant space in a city like Bombay. It had to be space where footfalls would be high. For a man who knew nothing more than a hand-to-mouth existence, it seemed no more than a fantasy in the bustling space-short metropolis. But this was Shanbhag. He considered the possibilities, discussed the matter with anyone who would listen, separated the practical from the ideal, and finally reached the original conclusion, keeping his lack of capital firmly in mind, that the foyer of a cinema hall would serve his purpose. High footfalls were guaranteed and if it was an English cinema, the quality of patrons would also be advantageous from a bookseller's point of view. Shanbhag got someone to introduce him to Keki Modi, owner of Strand Cinema in Colaba. All he wanted was Modi's permission to display some books along a wall in the lobby of the cinema house. Shanbhag's eyes had a way of burning bright when he put his heart into his words. Which happened every time the words were about books. Impressed by the young man's enthusiasm and assured that books would not damage his wall, Keki Modi gave his permission. That's how Strand Bookstall was born. It was 1948.

The 1940s and 1950s were a period when Hollywood's leading production companies like 20th Century Fox and MGM had resident business managers in Bombay, usually Kamaths and Kulkarnis from the same coastal Karnataka that was Shanbhag's native ground. Strand was the cinema where most Hollywood movies had their pre-release press previews. That meant that the Kamaths and the Kulkarnis knew Strand's owners and managers fairly well. Because of the previews, Strand was a regular meeting place of film journalists—and other journalists who pretended to be film journalists so that they could see the latest Hollywood hits for free. I belonged to the latter group, for a good decade. I am inclined to think that South Canara camaraderie must have helped Shanbhag to think of Strand Cinema as a possibility and perhaps to get access to its owner Keki Modi. What is certain is that Shanbhag became a friend to all the journalists who attended film previews at the Strand. He evidently cherished those friendships as much as we loved to see and hear about books we had not known of before.

Strand Cinema turned out to be a perfect location for Shanbhag's idea of a bookshop. It was in the heart of the upmarket Colaba area. It was a house that showed English movies, thus making it a regular haunt of the English-oriented public. A wall in the spacious foyer displayed books on each of which the ever-present stall owner could wax eloquent. Apart from the location, two other factors made Strand Bookstall an instant hit: the freedom with which a passer-by could browse for as long as she liked, and the expertise with which Shanbhag would describe the contents of each book. His enthusiasm alone was enough to make customers buy.

Additionally, he introduced the system of discounts, breaking the Net Book Agreement booksellers generally followed. Among the many legends about Strand Bookstall is the one about Jawaharlal Nehru buying 21 books at one go attracted by the 20 per cent discount offered. The location and the word-of-mouth publicity about Shanbhag's knowledge of every title on his shelves made Strand Bookstall a favourite of the rich and the famous. Oft-quoted names on his visitor's list included Manmohan Singh and A.P.J. Abdul Kalam, Vikram Sarabhai, N.A. Palkhivala and Sham

Lal, Narayana Murthy, and Azim Premji. There was no comparable space in Bombay where the literati felt at home. They would even get excited when Shanbhag announced a daring decision, such as importing 1,000 copies of the Boris Pasternak opus *Doctor Zhivago* (1957). Such was the acceptance Strand Bookstall attracted that Shanbhag found it necessary to have an occasional 'sale' to satisfy his clientele. Thus was born the Strand Book Festival, held annually at the Sunderbai Hall in Churchgate. It became something of a mass movement. One would feel lucky if one could squeeze oneself through the crowd and get inside the spacious hall on any of the twenty days the festival lasted. It became an amazing spectacle year after year, best described by poet-critic Ranjit Hoskote as 'the secular version of the Kumbh Mela'.

It was clear that Strand Bookstall had become too big for Strand Cinema. In 1993, just five years after its birth as a hole-in-the-wall adventure, Strand Bookstall moved to spacious premises in the Pherozeshah Mehta Road business district, retaining its iconic name. It kept the flag flying there for half a century. But dark clouds were appearing in the skies. The book trade had been affected by the internet and online sales. Shanbhag had health problems. The excitement that kept his spirits up in the 50s and 60s had gone. New trends were high-tech and convenient but lacked the warmth of personal interaction. Shanbhag withdrew from active involvement and passed away in 2009. His daughter, Vidya Virkar, threw herself into keeping the legacy running, opening branches in other cities. In the end, she was forced to admit: 'People's reading habits have changed. It is not viable to run a bookstore.' The five branches she had opened closed down. Nine years after Shanbhag passed away and 70 years after the Strand Cinema's foyer sported a book wall, the historic Strand Bookstall shut down.

Does bibliophilia, love of books, put one alongside writers, publishers and booksellers? K.S. Padmanabhan had nothing in common with P. Lal or T.N. Shanbhag. He did not have the writer's itch and he was not a zealous bookseller. All he had was a certain ability to put an organisation together and the instinct to direct whatever abilities he had in the direction of spreading the culture of books. Promoting book appreciation was as important to him as publishing new titles. Holding book reading sessions for small groups of interested persons was his idea of time profitably spent. He became a social influence among the cognoscenti without anyone noticing it. He himself never projected his role or claimed anything. He was, as the poet said, in his simplicity sublime.

Padmanabhan began his career with a job at the International Book Shop in Bombay. He moved to Calcutta to look after his ailing father and took up a job in an automobile company. In the 1960s, he moved to Delhi, where he began his active book career. On behalf of the New York-headquartered Van Nostrand Reinhold company, he looked after the reprinting of American academic titles under the US government's PL 480 programme. The contacts he made there gave impetus to his dream of launching a venture of his own. Thus was born the Affiliated East West Books, the affiliation being to the international textbook publisher with whom he was already associated. Those initiatives made him feel that he must leave Delhi for the south where he thought he could make closer personal contacts helpful to his publishing dreams. His instincts were right, for his move to Chennai saw him flower into an ideas man with a firm footing in literary pursuits. Mahesh Dattani's award winning *Final Solutions and Other Plays* (1993) was among the earliest titles that came out under the East West banner.

Padmanabhan's innovative urges were too wide-ranging to be contained by the single activity of publishing. He spread himself out into organising reading sessions and eventually launching two flagship projects that spread excitement all around, a journal called the *Indian Review of Books* (IRB) and the Madras Book Club (MBC), a social platform. The IRB fondly recalled the *London Review of Books* and the *New York Review of Books*. The editor's chair went to S. Muthiah, the antiquarian who became an institution as the chronicler of Madras. The journal became a lively forum with reviews and discussions. For the MBC, Padmanabhan would rope in N. Parthasarathy of Oxford Publishers and Abdullah of Longman as co-founders. When the US Information Service and the British Council also joined, the club became confident enough to hold its sessions in the prestigious Connemara Hotel. The management of the hotel provided a sumptuous tea-time spread for the club's meetings for a nominal charge; that was their way of fulfilling their corporate responsibility. Set up as a trust and with membership that shot up from a dozen to 300, the club became a sought-after platform for the release of new titles. Muthiah recalled in one of his columns of reminiscence: 'Although almost every meeting and speaker was the result of Padmanabhan's effort, he would never take a front seat, standing somewhere at the back in almost every meeting with that ever-present gentle smile on his face, enjoying the interest shown by the audiences.'

The fact remained that the burden of running the projects rested squarely with Padmanabhan. He had neither the corporate strength nor the cooperation of the literati that gave publications like the *New York Review of Books* its halo of success. Padmanabhan kept it going hoping for reader support and advertising backing that never came. He struggled for a full decade and then found it impossible to carry on. When the last issue of the IRB came out in 2001, writer Shashi Tharoor spoke for all book lovers: 'India's best literary journal has finally been defeated by the hard mathematics of the market.' The Madras Book Club faced the same hard mathematics. The Indian economy had gone into a crisis in the 1990s, the rupee was devalued and the country's gold reserves airlifted to the International Monetary Fund in exchange for a survival loan. Liberalisation followed and released new forces in the economy. But Indian traditions remained unchanged. Enlightened leaders of the corporate world could have given the lift initiatives like the IRB and the MBC needed. But that did not happen. The MBC tried valiantly to carry on even after Padmanabhan had passed on. But there was not enough patronage to make it viable.

Old timers were reminded of how similar ventures did well in the past because of the positive role played by one corporate leader. When Mulk Raj Anand returned to Bombay in the mid 1960s, after a prolonged sojourn in England, he was fired by the ambition to start a magazine that would be a 'loose encyclopaedia of the arts of India and related civilisations'. It was a romantic ideal, but it became a reality when J.R.D. Tata agreed to give Mulk a start-up fund along with 'seven advertisements per issue and two rooms' in the historic Army & Navy Building. *Marg* was born as a quarterly and Mulk Raj Anand remained its editor from 1946 to 1981.

The magazine continues online with books and documentaries as additional activities. Marg Foundation is still supported by the Tata trusts. Seven advertisements and two rooms would have kept the *Indian Review of Books* flourishing. And the Tatas had a responsibility to consider such possibilities because the entrepreneur in Padmanabhan had expanded his company with mergers and tie-ups, until East West books, Westland, and the Landmark Book Store in Chennai had all become part of the Tata group in 2006. But J.R.D. was gone by then and the Tatas were no longer the Tatas of his time.

Indians may spend more time reading than any other people in the world, but they somehow lack the wherewithal to sustain literary magazines. As far back as the 1900s, Ramanand Chatterjee's *Modern Review* had become an important forum for the intelligentsia of the country. When Raj and Romesh Thapar started *Seminar* in 1959, the early issues had Nirad Chaudhuri, Amartya Sen and K.N. Raj as contributors. In the 1950s and 1960s, magazines such as *Quest*, *Encounter*, and *Imprint* made an impact before they were found to be CIA-backed. Their demise caused no heartburn, but why did *Modern Review* die and *Seminar* lose its lustre? Why could the reading public not sustain the titles that came up in the closing years of the 20th century. The *Times of India* which claims to be the 'largest selling English-language newspaper in the world' started the *Times Review of Books* in 1995. It was a concession to the then editor Dilip Padgaonkar. Soon, the *Times* establishment recovered, got rid of Padgaonkar and his fancy initiatives, and returned to its philosophy that marketing executives, not editors, were the decision makers in newspapers. Padgaonkar and friends launched *Biblio.* It carried on, liked by the few and unknown to the many. The story of literary magazines is yet another reminder that India is a developing country, not a developed one.

It is one of the tragedies of literary India that K.S. Padmanabhan never tried his hand at writing. His personal reminiscences would have been a chronicle of modern India's romance with books, of expectations that were met and those that were not, of failures that were worth the try, of the private joy of having books as one's living companions. Padmanabhan, did the next best thing—persuade his wife to become a writer. Chandra, who graduated from Calcutta University and completed post-graduation studies at Delhi University, was happy to stay in her husband's shadow, assisting him in his publishing activities. The husband noticed that his wife had unusual abilities in cooking. It took some persuasion from his end to make her agree to write a cookery column in S. Muthiah's *Madras Musings.* From there it was a short step to books. Chandra emerged as a prize-winner producing instant bestsellers—*Dakshin* (1992), *Southern Spice* (2006), *Simply South* (2008). When she published *Dosai* in 2014, she referred to the importance of combining proteins with complex carbohydrates and said, 'A simple dosai made with parboiled rice, husked blackgram and fenugreek seeds fulfils this need.' By the time *Dosai* hit the stands, however, the man who had pushed its author into writing, was not around to savour its success.

When some of his cherished dreams like the *Indian Review of Books* and the Madras Book Club did not succeed the way he thought they would, Padmanabhan appeared to take it in his stride, but it must have caused some disappointment. He seemed to withdraw more into reading. Literary critic and author Nilanjana Roy noted: 'When I met Padmanabhan, I expected to meet a man who took himself very seriously... He didn't see himself as a legend. Instead, he saw himself as a reader and talked of books and authors and what they had meant to him, of the old bookshops of Chennai and people in the trade.' A touch of resignation crept into the smile. After East West and allied units merged into the sprawling world of the Tatas, he found himself with less and less responsibilities to handle. Although that gave him more time to read in his suburban home at Old Mahabalipuram Road, it was not the same as running a beloved project. In his 70s, Padmanabhan looked like he had regrets about some of the things that had happened in his life. That the *Indian Review of Books* had wound up was a big disappointment. He seemed to wonder, too, if he had done the right thing by walking into the Tata group in the name of consolidation. He had done it in good faith, but the outcome was less satisfying than it ought to have been.

The businessman in Padmanabhan was not in tune with the literary connoisseur and he seemed to realise it at a stage when he could do nothing to reverse the steps he had taken. As a publisher, Padmanabhan had found his fulfilment. As the face of changing commercial brands, he saw in himself a stranger. Not feeling all that good about the way things turned out slowed him down. It was too late when they discovered that cancer had invaded his colon. Emergency operations followed but without effect. After several weeks in and out of ICUs, Padmanabhan succumbed to his malignant tumours in 2013. A shinning chapter in Indian publishing closed with him.

14

USTAD VILAYAT KHAN

The Unawarded Bharat Ratna

I feel no need to apologise for repeating an oft-repeated story about Ustad Vilayat Khan's adventures as a prodigy. It happened when he was 11 years old. By then quite a few other things had already marked him out. He had given a public performance when he was six. His first recording was in 1936 when he was eight. A performance that year organised by the All Bengal Music Conference had Rabindranath Tagore in the audience. Then Vilayat lost his father, Ustad Inayat Khan, and a period of penury began. The unwritten tradition in the culture of Hindustani classical music was that, when a great ustad died, his prosperous disciples would take care of the family. Inayat Khan's prominent disciples proved an exception. They abandoned their guru's family and denied Vilayat continued training. What wounded young Vilayat more than the poverty into which the family was suddenly plunged, was the humiliation his father's disciples heaped upon him. It steeled his resolve. He left Calcutta swearing never to return until he had become the best sitarist in India. He proceeded to Punjab and Bombay where he had family. On the way he landed in Delhi.

Those were the days when All India Radio was the platform that could make or unmake a musician. To be an AIR artiste was the ultimate recognition a singer or instrumentalist could receive. The 11-year-old from Calcutta went to the headquarters of AIR and, security guards and commandos being unknown in those days, managed to get into the chambers of Z.A. Bukhari, the legendary arts patron and director-general of AIR. The boy told the big man, emotion choking his voice, 'I am Vilayat Khan, son of late Inayat Khan Saheb. If you try to send me back, I'll run away again.' Bukhari sensed something. Trying to sound casual and friendly, he asked, 'Can you play that sitar you are carrying about?' Instantly as it were, vibrant notes of Raag Bhairavi filled the air. AIR staffers drifted in to listen. One of them couldn't contain himself and said 'Arrey Inayat Khan is alive!' Bukhari arranged for the boy with the sitar to live in a garage. He also enlisted him as an AIR artiste. That was recognition, and it made the monthly salary of ₹10 nothing short of princely.

George VI was emperor of India and Linlithgow was ruling the country as Viceroy when Vilayat got his first job as an AIR artiste in 1939. That was the year World War II broke out. India would be consumed by the all-out British effort to win the war which included appropriation of Indian resources even if it caused famine among the masses. The national movement for independence would march ahead. In the midst of the turmoil, art found a way to keep the flame burning. For Vilayat Khan there was no let-up in his saadhana. The impact of his father's death was so severe that he would spend days doing nothing but practice, stopping briefly to eat and sleep. It took time to pull himself out of poverty. The 10-rupee job in AIR was great to begin with, but he found it prudent to move to Bombay, the business capital of India and home of the Hindi film industry, where young men from all over the country gathered in search of opportunities. Acquaintances who knew him in those years said he often survived on tea and biscuits in a single-room tenement with just enough space for a bed. If luck brought him an invitation to give a concert, he would get a fee of ₹500, provided there was no middle man taking a cut. In the midst of deprivation and suffering, his humanity never left him. For instance, he collected ₹5,000, a massive sum in those days, to help a friend whose wife was going in for surgery.

The move to Bombay proved beneficial. At 16, he got the chance to participate in a programme organised by the Vikramaditya Sangeet Parishad, at which Bade Ghulam Ali Khan was the main performer. It would not be incorrect to say that this was the show that made Vilayat Khan a star. Audience enthusiasm was such that he was obliged to give five encores. There was no looking back. It was 1944 and war was raging. The end of the war and India's hard-won independence were followed by a decade of optimism and pride, with artists and musicians and writers and filmmakers turning out their best work. AIR continued as an arbiter of culture, aided by the recording industry. Vilayat Khan emerged as one of the shakers and movers of the classical oeuvre. The thoroughness of his training aided by his unusual memory led to an inventiveness that was to turn him into a virtuoso. He could combine orthodoxy with innovation. The interpretative freedom the Hindustani tradition allowed was used to re-imagine the sitar itself. He changed the instrument, changed the way it was held, changed the style of plucking the strings, changed even the way the player sat on the stage. No one before or after him was such an all-rounder, and paid attention to such minutiae.

Central to Vilayat Khan's achievements was his saadhana, his riyaz, or training. The way the great gurus imparted training could, in modern parlance, only be described as punishment meted out in a bit of a mess. Vilayat himself gave us an idea of it when he said that in his time, 'Masters say "Sit, learn this tan and this raga, memorise it, and if you cannot remember we will do it again, now go home." In my house music infused every moment of life, riyaz was continuous. You would learn a technique and you would keep practising it. When my father or grandfather sits to teach, you would repeat and eventually you would understand.'

Repetition and tireless practice were the foundations of the gharanas that sustained Hindustani music for generations. Inayat Khan would light a candle and practise until it burned out. Men like him belonged to a tradition where nothing mattered except their muse. Pedigree and a sense of duty were basic to the value system that guided them. Vilayat Khan's pedigree had a modern six-generation phase and a remembered past that went all the way back to Tansen, the legend of Emperor Akbar's court. Sahabed Khan's son Imdad Khan's son Inayat Khan's son Vilayat Khan's two sons Shujaat Husain Khan and Hidayat Husain Khan represented a distinct gharana, the social system that bound musicians by lineage and apprenticeship to a singular style. The power and reach of the family/gharana tradition was reflected in the list of gurus who shaped the musician in Vilayat Khan—his father, paternal uncle Wahid Khan, maternal uncle Zindo Hussain Khan, maternal grandfather Bande Hussain Khan, and the strictestest disciplinarian among them all, his mother Bashiran Begum. But gharana loyalty was more a sense of responsibility to the muse than an enforcement of style, more inspirational than constraining. It provided a foundation that left the artist free to construct the superstructure according to his imagination. At a 2015 seminar on sitar gharanas of India organised by the National Centre for Performing Arts, composer–sitarist Shubhendra Rao (who was a student of Ravi Shankar and had thus become, since Ravi Shankar had trained under Allauddin Khan, part of the Maihar gharana) said: 'What is my style? Annapurna Devi's? Pandit Ravi Shankar's? Pandit Nikhil Banerji's? Or Ustad Ali Akbar Khan's? How did they all groom their musical talents under the same guru and yet became so distinct from one another?' Vilayat Khan himself developed under the Imdadkhnai-Etawah gharana. But as his stature and impact grew, it came to be known as Vilayat Khani gharana. It always remained one of the half dozen top-rated ghranas of Hindustani music.

A notable feature of the gharana system was the irrelevance of religion. Although Ravi Shankar, a devotee of Sri Anandamayi Ma and a Hanuman Bhakt, got Allauddin Khan's daughter converted to Hinduism before marrying her, she already had a Hindu name, Annapurna Devi, given to her by her father's royal patrons. In any case, Ravi Shankar was an exception. Vilayat Khan's family had no problem living with its Rajput roots. His great grandfather Sahabad

Khan was originally known as Saheb Singh. Inayat Khan was also called Nath Singh. Vilayat Khan sometimes composed pieces under the name Nath Piya. Theirs was a tolerant India and they would not have imagined that it would change. (The severity of the change became obvious, as coincidence would have it, the year Vilayat passed away. The Culture Minister of Madhya Pradesh, Anup Mishra, said the name of the Allauddin Khan Sangeet Academy in Bhopal should be changed since the Ustad was a Bangladeshi. What he meant, but did not have the courage to admit, was that the Ustad was a Muslim and therefore unworthy of recognition in a state committed to 'cultural nationalism'. He exposed his ignorance more than his haughtiness. Firstly, there was no Bangladesh when Allauddin was born, which makes him as Indian as those born in Karachi in the 1920s, such as L.K. Advani. Secondly, Allauddin was a lifelong devotee of Goddess Saraswati. He was known to insist that his pupils begin their day with the Saraswati Vandana. In his cultural essence, Ustad Allauddin was a better Hindu than many a Hindutva warrior.)

Vilayat Khan was 'Bangladeshi' too, born in Gouripur almost half a century before Bangladesh was created. He grew up as a Calcutta Bengali though biographical notes list him as a resident of Dehradun, Bombay, and Princeton, USA. When he died, in what had by then become Mumbai, it was to what had by then become Kolkata that he wanted his body to be taken—to be buried beside his father. That was a pointer to his gharana fidelity. If his decisions were wholly personal, he would have ended up a singer instead of a sitarist. He had a natural talent for singing, but his mother who was a singer herself insisted that his family duty was to continue the sitar tradition. Vilayat did, but he also kept singing, eventually inventing ways and means that would enable the sitar to mimic the human voice. This is where his ability to re-imagine his instrument and his music reached the summit of creativity. When a sitar string is plucked, it produces a note of limited duration. Prolonging that note was one of Vilayat Khan's aims. He achieved it through a new technique that gave the note a fluidity. With it, he could make patters in the vocal idiom. To suit this new architecture of sound, he would sit down with leading sitar manufacturers and help re-design the instrument and try out new kinds of strings. He also figured out that if the instrument was held at an angle of exactly 45 degrees, the movement of the left hand would be easier. He discovered that if the player folded his legs in a particular way, the instrument's positioning would become significantly more convenient, helping to change its acoustics. All these ideas came to him, as he once said, intuitively. The net result was that the Vilayat Khani Sitar revolutionised instrumental music. His name became synonymous with the technique of gayaki ang (singing strings). As the sitar began singing, many followed his ideas as far as they could. Admirers often reached a point where they did not want to listen to other sitarists. They appreciated his adherence to artistically nuanced music in preference to music adjusted to win mass appeal. Some called this an elitist approach. It was elitist in so far as he did not aim at audience applause. He always included popular ragas in his repertoire but he also expected his listeners to rise to higher levels of understanding.

He did become elitist, if that is the word, when it came to the nitty gritty of stage presence. He believed that an artist should look authentic, graceful and elegant when he appeared on stage. It was more than the innate aristocracy born of generations of ustadhood. It was his way of respecting music. He maintained, and wanted others to maintain, a certain reverence. There were instances of his chastising ministers when they left halfway through a concert. The importance he attached to grace and elegance led to his becoming perhaps the best dressed maestro of his time. He had spent time and effort to zero in on an exceptional kind of silk for his kurtas. I had occasion to learn about this directly from him. A relative of his, a struggling music director in Bombay's filmdom in the 1950s, invited me to his flat one evening, saying excitedly that the Ustad would be performing. There were just about 10 of us sitting around the maestro in the tiny hall as living-cum-dining rooms were called in Bombay's flatlets. I was too ignorant to appreciate the nuances of the music that filled the room through the night, but even I could feel the soothing impact of his lilting twangs. During one interval, I expressed admiration for the fabric of the kurta he was wearing, its comforting sophistication and the elegance of its creamy texture. With a tinge of a smile, Vilayat explained the uniqueness of Do Ghoda Boski, the variety of silk he was wearing. It was the most classic-looking silk, he said. I discovered later that it was premium Chinese silk of the spun variety as distinct from reeled silk. I hunted for it in the shops but could not find it. Apparently, its marketing was also along exclusive lines. (These days it is advertised by online companies.) Beyond the best of silk, Vilayat was an expert on perfumes. He enjoyed riding horses and was good at billiards and snooker. He loved partying. He had a teacher who used to offer him one bidi if he practised for one hour. He, of course, practised for several hours for several bidis. This smoking habit plagued him all his life.

In the final analysis, the master of the strings described as 'one of the all-time greats of Hindustani music' was an unhappy man. For all the adulation that came his way, he remained discontented and grudging. He resented the limelight that seemed to go past him towards the other maestro of the time, Pandit Ravi Shankar. The accident of the two men being born in the same generation led to a perceived competition between Vilayat Khan and Ravi Shankar which affected Vilayat Khan more than Ravi Shankar. The international glamour that surrounded Ravi Shankar made Vilayat Khan feel that his own position was not properly appreciated by the world. It was Ravi Shankar who became the darling of the Western press. It was Ravi Shankar who was befriended by the Beatles and by Yehudi Menuhin. It was Ravi Shankar who got Grammy awards. All of it struck Vilayat Khan as unfair. In many ways, it was.

Ravi Shankar gained a great deal from his natural talent for public relations. Vilayat Khan knew nothing about public relations. If he had understood the difference between publicity-based glamour and talent-based reverence, Vilayat would have had no reason to feel embittered. In peer recognition and acceptance by the cognoscenti, he was second to none in his field. He was not and never wanted to be a showman as Ravi Shankar often tended to be. He would have considered it infra dig to be market-savvy as Ravi Shankar was. The feeling that he did not get state recognition that was his due could also have been avoided if he had looked dispassionately at what had happened. The government did approach him with offers of its high awards, Padma Shri in 1964 and Padma Vibhushan four years later, but he was unwilling to receive them. He took the view that government officials were not competent to judge artistic quality. He was only 36 and 40 when the Padma honours went seeking him. Ravi Shankar, though eight years older, was awarded Padma Vibhushan only in 1981 when he was 61. Eighteen years passed before Ravi Shankar received the Bharat Ratna in 1999. Perhaps the government was too scared to ask Vilayat Khan whether he would accept the Ratna.

In her masterful biography, *The Sixth String of Vilayat Khan* (2018), Namita Devidayal describes a drama that was enacted during a music concert in Delhi's Constitution Club in 1952. It was a special performance before an elite audience. Ravi Shankar and Ali Akbar Khan were to play a duet. While the two were tuning their instruments on stage, Vilayat Khan, unannounced and uninvited, went up and said he was going to join the concert. The audience was taken aback, but the artistes on the stage took it in a sporting spirit. Soon the two sitarists got going, side-lining the sarod artiste. As Namita Devidayal puts it: 'At some point it became evident to the audience that a subtle musical duet was taking place... The notes had become sharp arrows shot with the intention to annihilate. Twenty-four-year-old Vilayat Khan was declared the winner in the battle of sitars.' It is a pity that Vilayat let the battle carry on despite his winning it. He carried it through the years of his glory. He carried it to his grave. He died in 2004 aged 76 when Bismillah

Khan was 88, M.S. Subbulakshmi 86 and Ravi Shankar 84, all of them alive. What looked like an early departure added to the sense of loss felt by music lovers across the world. The tributes that followed made it clear that to generations of connoisseurs, Vilayat Khan would always remain Bharat Ratna, Pahela Varg.

There is a large (896 pages) reference compendium called *The Penguin Companion to Classical Music.* Note that title again. It does not say Western classical music. Therefore, one would assume that the book, in convenient dictionary format, is about classical music from all over the world. But it isn't. In all those hundreds of pages the word Hindustani does not appear, or Carnatic. There is no mention of Tyagaraja or Bismillah Khan. The word 'India' is mentioned, to inform us that Indian music had the same sources as music in modern Europe. That would mean that the 18th century Shaivite saint, Thirujnana Sambandar, who devised the gamaka, learned his ropes from European sources. What would Indian civilisation have done without Europe!

While peddling Eurocentric misinformation, the Penguin Companion was gracious enough to include one, just one, Indian musician in its listing: Shankar, Ravi. He gets a five-and-a-half line mention of which three-and-a-half lines are about Ravi Shankar's tour of Europe and contacts with Yehudi Menuhin and George Harrison. But that is five-and-a-half lines more than Muthuswamy Dikshitar, although he re-invented the violin to bring it from the West's shoulders to South India's lap. There is a lesson to learn from the Penguin Companion's version of classical music. It is that recognition of talent assumes meaning only when it is recognition by the West, that what the West does not accept does not exist. This is one reason for the ignorance that abounds in the West about things that are not Western.

That Ravi Shankar is the sole Indian talent recognised by

Penguin's compilers is of course no reflection on Ravi Shankar. His mastery of classical sitar was acquired through dedication and saadhana. But he appeared more equal than others because he was seen as someone the Beatles and therefore the West approved. Actually, that bought his stature down by a notch or two by giving the impression that his greatness was derived from the West's affirmation of it. This is not a problem confined to music. An Indian author achieves greatness only when he is published in the West. An Indian movie becomes great when it is applauded in Cannes. An Indian scholar grows in stature when he is appointed a Visiting Professor in Berkeley or Yale. Perhaps this is a reflection of the poor standards of intellectual institutions in India. Perhaps it is a hangover of the colonial inferiority complex.

Long before the likes of George Harrison appeared on the horizon, however, the westernisation of Rabindra Shankar Chowdhury alias Pandit Ravi Shankar had begun. He was born in opulence. His father was a Middle Temple barrister who served as Dewan in Jhalawar state in Rajasthan for a while, then went off to London where he married an Englishwoman and practised as a lawyer. The eldest of Chowdhury's five children, Uday Shankar was the one who brought art into the family. He spent two years at the J.J. School of Art in Bombay and then, at 20, joined the Royal College of Art in London. The chance event that changed his life—and brother Ravi Shankar's—occurred in 1923. Anna Pavlova, the world's most celebrated ballerina at the time, had come across Indian dance during one of her tours and wanted to know more about it. She called Uday Shankar simply because he happened to be in London studying art. The meeting led to Uday Shankar giving up art studies and joining Anna Pavlova's troupe. He devised some India-themed ballet pieces and performed in them although he never had any formal training in dance. The months he spent with the prima donna of ballet led Uday Shankar to decide that dance was his life's mission. By 1930, he had his own troupe with his own adaptations of Indian themes. Ravi Shankar joined him in Paris, aged 10.

It was possible that the younger Shankar would have stuck with his brother and developed into a star dancer in due course. But another coincidence occurred. Uday Shankar had managed to persuade the Rajah of the princely state of Maihar to let the principal court musician join his troupe in Paris as a soloist. The court musician was Allauddin Khan, and when he was with the Uday Shankar team, Ravi Shankar got a chance to listen to the sitar. Allaudin Khan liked the way the boy showed interest and told him a thing or two about music and the rigours of training. Ravi Shankar found himself watching and listening to the sitarist with growing interest. Allauddin Khan finally offered to become his teacher on condition that he travelled to Maihar and lived with Khan Sahib's family as a gurukul student. That is what Ravi Shankar did in 1938. He completed his saadhana in 1944 along with two fellow students, Khan Sahib's son Ali Akbar Khan and daughter Annapurna Devi, nee Roshanara Khan. Training over, he took a career path that was his own. He seemed determined to play key roles in music that would put him on top of the heap. For a decade he focussed on India, writing music for the ballets produced by the left-leaning Indian People's Theatre Association of Bombay, becoming music director of All India Radio from 1949 to 1956, writing the musical score of Satyajit Ray's *Apu Trilogy* and other Hindi movies, and founding the Kinnara School of Music in Bombay. But it was the glamour of the West that seemed to entice him most. His early years in Europe with brother Uday had led him to pick up French, enjoy Western music, and develop Western social customs. The familiarity thus earned, began to influence his music as well. Just as Uday Shankar developed a dance style that mixed European theatrical techniques with Indian classical tradition, Ravi Shankar welded Indian systems with Western orchestral features. He evolved into a universal symbol of Indian classical music, touring Europe and the US on a regular basis, making Western connoisseurs marvel at the intricacies of the Indian traditions. The sitar itself was an object of fascination for them, used as they were to the handy violin. By contrast, here was an Indian classicist sitting comfortably on the floor and holding the instrument as if he was hugging it and tickling it with love. Conductor Zubin Mehta made a point when he said: 'When India was an unknown quantity in the world, Ravi opened up our country to everyone. Everybody got to know India through Ravi.' The West embraced him and honoured him with a clutch of prestigious positions in institutions such as the California Institute of Arts, University of California San Diego, City College of New York and guest lectureships in other citadels of learning. He won the Magsaysay Award in 1992, and the French Legion of Honour in 2000. In the rush of such international acclaim, the interlude with the Beatles seemed a minor detail.

The flood of honours, however, did not hide a streak of contrarianism in Ravi Shankar's makeup. He liked the spotlight so much that he didn't want anyone to share it with him. There are many versions about the collapse of his marriage with Allauddin Khan's daughter, Annapurna Devi. Other than his own version set out in his autobiography, others suggest that Annapurna Devi was more sinned against than sinning. The breakup of his marriage, the freewheeling love life he seemed to prefer, and the circumstances of the untimely death of his first-born, all add up to indicate a narcissistic element in his constitution. He exemplified the difference between popularity and respect. Think of Bade Gulam Ali Khan or Bismillah Khan, of Hariprasad Chaurasia or M.S. Subbulakshmi, and a sense of respect rises within. Think of Ravi Shankar and the anomaly of Westernisation and the tragedy of Annapurna Devi come to mind. She was on her way to becoming India's greatest sitarist of the 20th century. But she became instead a recluse, invisible and unheard. Her only son had shown the promise of becoming as accomplished as she in the discipline of the sitar, but he lost his way and died young.

Ravi Shankar and Annapurna Devi were music's most ill-matched couple. He was a man of the world, she an ascetic. Perhaps she was also too stubborn a daughter to become a successful wife. Her world began and ended with her father and guru, Allauddin Khan. She was 13 years old when Ravi Shankar, 18, joined the household gurukul. She would tell a biographer: 'I was brought up in an ashram-like atmosphere. There was no question of my getting attracted to Panditji. Ours was an arranged marriage.' Ravi Shankar, far from being an ashramite, had found her 'very bright and quite attractive'. With his talent, good looks, and exalted family background, he succeeded in marrying her, but only after getting her converted to Hinduism. Their only son was born when Annapurna was 14. Trouble began as soon as Ravi Shankar returned from the gurukul to the glitzy world he loved.

There were conflicts at the professional level and nastier conflicts at the personal level. Professional problem surfaced as soon as they started giving performances in public. Annapurna was a better player and the audiences made their preference clear. This was bluntly pointed out by a music critic, Madanlal Vyas, who was earlier a student of Ravi Shankar. He wrote: 'After concerts people would surround Annapurna which Panditji could not tolerate. He was no match to her. She was a genius. Even Baba, the unforgiving and uncompromising guru, called her the embodiment of Saraswati.' Her brother, Ali Akbar Khan, expressed the same idea famously when he said: 'Put Ravi Shankar, Pannalal Ghosh and me on one side and put Annapurna on the other side, and her side of the scale will be heavier.' The image-conscious Ravi Shankar couldn't take it. Arguments at home became increasingly bitter until the wife took an oath never to perform in public again. Some accounts say the husband's prodding led her to it. Ravi Shankar himself made light of it. 'Maybe she does not like to face the public or she is nervous or whatever,' he said.

Problems arose in their personal relations because of Ravi Shankar's roving eye. For the Paris-bred city boy it seemed natural that appreciating comely ladies was an aspect of his aesthetics. Peripatetic as he was, several ladies were recipients of his attention at the same time. He was uninhibited about admitting it. His second autobiography, *Raga Mala: An Autobiography* (1999), bristles with statements such as: 'I felt I could be in love with different women in different places. It was like having a girl in every port—and sometimes there was more than one.' Marriage to Annapurna Devi did not stop him from continuing an affair he had begun with Kamala Shastri, once a member of Uday Shankar's troupe, until Kamala left him and married another man. Ravi Shankar began a new relationship with a New York concert promoter named Sue Jones and had a daughter Norah from that union. But he did not have the time to meet his daughter for many years. He took up with a Tamil girl, Sukanya, who had trained in Carnatic music and had played the tanpura for a Ravi Shankar concert in 1972. She was 18 then and Ravi Shankar 52. In a few years, they became lovers and their daughter Anoushka was born in 1981. Again the maestro had no time to meet his new daughter. Just as Norah Jones was brought up by her mother, Anoushka was brought up by Sukanya who divorced her first husband and moved to England. Ravi Shankar had reservations about continuing his relationship with Sukanya. There is no record of what finally made him overcome his objections, but they were married in Hyderabad in 1989 when Anoushka was 11 years old. That was perhaps the most sensible decision he ever made, for Sukanya turned out to be a homemaker. She was the opposite of Annapurna Devi, ready to accept her husband's former lovers even when some of them came to spend weekends with the now freshly married beau. She seemed determined to make a success of her opportunity. She took control of managing the affairs of the household after they moved to Ravi Shankar's hilltop mansion in Encinitas, California. Eventually, the master of extracurricular relations began to understand what family life meant. He became attached to his daughter and trained her into an accomplished sitarist, sharing the stage with her in concerts in many countries. California became the home of children, brothers, cousins, and grandchildren of sitar–sarod families with Ali Akbar Khan's third wife, Mary, also settled there. Sukanya Rajan Shankar presided over the brood with pride.

The success of Ravi Shankar's career leading up to the luxurious family life on the Pacific Coast added poignancy to the failure of his first wife's career leading to her self-imposed isolation. There was something frightening about the finality with which Annapurna Devi vowed never to perform in public. In *An Unheard Melody* (2005), described as an authorised biography, Swapan Kumar Bondyopadhyay refers to the many versions of the vow-taking story and says that she '...told me that something worse had happened than Ravi attempting to make her take the oath. But she added that she would divulge it to none. "That will go with me when I go."'

What happened must have been soul-shattering, for Annapurna disappeared from the stage and never again gave a performance, never made a recording, never spoke to anyone about the inner secrets of her wrecked marriage. In the privacy of her abode, in the dead of night, she kept her practice going. She took some disciples, too, for tuitions after midnight. Among them were Hariprasad Chaurasia and Nikhil Banerjee. She was Guruma to them. She lived in a flat in Warden Road in Bombay, but nobody in the high-rise building ever saw her. There was no maid. She did all the cooking and cleaning herself. A man called Rooshikumar Pandya had been sent from America by her brother, Ali Akbar Khan, for training in 1980. He was allowed to stay with her and later became her companion until he died in 2013. A notice on the front door of her flat asked potential visitors to ring the bell only thrice and informed them that doors would not open on Mondays and Thursdays. Her resignation from life reached an extreme severity following the loss of her only son. She had taken Shubhendra with her when she ran away from her two-timing husband. In Maihar, she had trained him rigorously in sitar. By chance, Ravi Shankar heard a piece of Shubho's melody in a recording studio and was shocked to know that the performer was his son. Again, there are conflicting versions of what happened thereafter. Ravi Shankar said that he took Shubho with him to the US, trained him, and presented joint concerts in various Western cities. Annapurna noted that 'there were rumours that Shubho was going to be a better player than Panditji'. Torn between the glamorous life offered by his father and the loving training given by mother, Shubho developed a rebellious dislike for music itself. He turned to American junk food culture, married an American girl who knew nothing about India or sitar, took up dead-end jobs, including that of a liquor-shop clerk, and died of pneumonia at the age of 50. Annapurna lived for 26 more years, a desolate life of solitude with no one to turn to, and nothing to look forward to. Her own death came in 2018 when she was 91. With less than a dozen public performances, she had been celebrated as miraculously gifted. How rich would have been the legacy if a private hurt had not snapped the strings of her genius?

Such questions and the numerous ways they are answered or ignored are best seen as the eternal conundrums of the creative arts. Talent is inextricably mixed with human frailty. Juxtapositions are made for no particular reason. For all his spectacular success, Ravi Shankar could not get out of comparisons with Vilayat Khan, or the view among connoisseurs that Vilayat was his better. The Ustad's acerbic personality might have contributed to his being less celebrated than Ravi Shankar. Vilayat Khan focussed on classism, Ravi Shankar on populism. The contrast is reminiscent of the ideological clash that turned into a personal clash between abhinaya queen Balasaraswati and Kalakshetra supremo Rukmini Devi. The debate still rages as to who served Bharatanatyam better—Rukmini Devi who cleansed it by eliminating sringara, or Balasaraswati who said that it was a dirty mind that saw a dirty intent in classical art. Who wins in the end: ego or art, contrived orthodoxy or traditional classicism? Fundamentally, were Vilayat Khan and Ravi Shankar comparable at all? One answer is a counter question: How comparable are California and Maihar?

15

M.F. HUSAIN

The Artist in his Labyrinth

In 1947, in the first flush of Independence, leading artists of the day got together to set up the Bombay Progressive Artists Group. It proclaimed both their self-confidence and the honourableness art enjoyed in India. Within three years, however, founding members F.N. Souza and S.H. Raza announced that they were moving to Europe because 'you can't grow as an artist in India'. M.F. Husain, declining to share that view, stayed on in his country. Irony colours the rest of the story. Souza and Raza rose to great heights as artists but were always seen as Indians; they, as well as Indians, took pride in it. Husain, in some ways, grew taller than them, but was driven out of his country in the final phase of his career; he died in London as a Qatari citizen. Those who left their country won. The man who stuck to his country lost. Who in the end was the real loser?

It was a Joe McCarthy style of witch hunt that drove India's most celebrated artist out of the country in 2006 at the age of 91. McCarthyism represented a shameful period in American history when trumped-up accusations were used to destroy reputations. That nightmare of the 1950s gave the word McCarthyism its current meaning : 'Demagogic, reckless and unsubstantiated accusations as well as public attacks on the character and patriotism of political opponents.' Eventually, McCarthy was exposed and he died a drunken wreck. McCarthyism in India cannot be contained that easily because it is fuelled by religion. Husain was hunted by Hindutva zealots who ransacked his exhibits and swore to murder him. For a while Husain fought back. 'There are more than 900 cases filed against me,' he told reporters in 2005. 'For 12 years now I have been paying my lawyer 60,000–70,000 rupees a month. I have not fled from the Indian legal system.'* But ground realities changed within a year.

The timeline of Husain's travails is a reminder that Hindutva intolerance started raising its head even before the Narendra Modi–Amit Shah leadership got its hold on power. Husain's 'expulsion' from his country happened when Manmohan Singh was the prime minister. That supposedly 'secular' government made no effort to provide him protection. When Qatar offered citizenship to Husain—a smart move that enhanced Qatar's profile as a modernistic state—India looked petty-minded. Home Minister P. Chidambaram said, as though he was doing the world a favour: 'We would be very happy if M.F. Husain returns to India. There is no danger to him.' Those were empty words, uttered too late, and supported by no action. And Chidambaram's casual, lofty style of declamation made it sound even more irrelevant than it was. The Delhi High Court quashed criminal proceedings against the artist in 2009 saying that his paintings were expressions of creativity. Even then no climate of safety was created by the Congress government to facilitate Husain's return. Governmental indifference to communal issues amounted to encouraging the BJP's hate campaigns.

To see the absurdity of India's handling of the Husain issue, we only have to look at Britain's handling of the Salman Rushdie issue following Ayatollah Khomeini's fatwa against him in 1989. That Rushdie, although born an Indian, had become a British citizen was enough for the UK government to extend 24/7 protection to him. Margaret Thatcher was the prime minister at the time, and she had

* 'I have not fled India, said M.F. Husain in his last interview', *Times of India*, 9 June 2011.

reasons to adopt an Indian-style policy of platitude without action. In his writings, Rushdie had referred to Thatcher as 'Mrs Torture' and as 'Maggie the Bitch'. He had also described the British police as 'neofascist'. Yet when the call of duty came, Mrs Torture and the Neofascists heeded it for the honour of Britain. The protection provided to Rushdie was so efficient that he could continue to write and travel. In one defiant challenge to his detractors, he appeared onstage with U2 at London's Wembley Stadium during a packed music concert. Diplomatic relations broke between UK and Iran, but the UK establishment kept its citizen safe for nine years until the fatwa eased. India uttered banalities and left its citizen to the wolves.

It is bad luck that controversies overwhelmed Husain's career. Some of them were of his own creation, but most of it occurred because of the circumstances of his life. Born in Pandharpur town in Maharashtra in 1915, Maqbool Fida Husain grew up in Indore. When he was about 20, he moved to Bombay where, after some training at the J.J. School of Art, he found work in the cinema hoardings business. The hoardings were enormous and Husain would get ₹10 for each one he painted. The experience left him with a lifelong addiction to large canvases and three-feet-long brushes. In Bombay he became one of the founding members of the Progressive Artists Group (PAG). He also got involved in printmaking and cinema. His *Through the Eyes of a Painter* (1967) won the Golden Bear at the Berlin Festival. As his career soared, government recognition came to him in a steady flow—the Padma Shri in 1966, Padma Bhushan in 1973, and Padma Vibhushan in 1991. In 1986 he was nominated to the Rajya Sabha. He never spoke, preferring to spend his time working.

Even as accolades came, the tendency to say and do eccentric things grew. In appearance and behaviour he developed his own style. To understand the female form in a country where nude models were virtually unthinkable, he watched a Madhuri Dixit movie 67 times. He never explained how much of the female form could be understood by watching Hindi movies. His habit of arriving at a friend's house unannounced, staying there for a day or more, and departing without informing anyone was tolerated only because he was Husain. He once covered his car with paintings of nude gopis playing with Krishna. He turned shoelessness into a private religion, finding explanations that sounded contrived. On one occasion he said: 'Wherever you go, the first thing they see is your footwear. Then they will decide your status. I said, okay, you recognise me as I am.' On another occasion, he explained: 'Not wearing shoes is good for the knees. I can sit on the floor.' According to Bombay gossip, he neglected his family to the point of being cruel to them. (He had married Fazila Bibi in 1941 and had Shafaat, Shamshad, Mustafa, and Owais as sons, Raza and Aqueela as daughters. His wife died in 1998. In old age, however, family portraits showed him as a patriarch surrounded by sons and grandsons and their spouses. Two sons became artists in their own right.) He was a wandering free spirit who never had a permanent home. Often, hotel rooms were turned into studios. When inspiration struck he would do on-the-spot drawings no matter where he happened to be. Many Irani restaurants in Bombay had Husain drawings done on hastily acquired canvas or paper or a wall surface, proudly preserved. The childhood habit of spending time on the street stayed with him. He considered loitering as important. Till the end he remained unusual, arbitrary, and unpredictable, all of it adding to his aura. Restless, Husain liked to be in the news. It was not enough for him to be known as a noteworthy artist. That might have been all right for Souza, Tyeb Mehta, Ara, Hebbar, Manjit Bawa, Anjoli Ela Menon, B. Prabha. But Husain had to be in the headlines more actively. There was turbulence when he depicted Indira Gandhi as Durga riding a tiger, ignoring the fact that she had suppressed freedom of expression in the name of Emergency. He tried to get out of the unfavourable publicity by saying that the government '...exploited the paintings to get favourable publicity. I am not interested in politics.' How could he expect a bland statement of that kind to settle the matter? He should have been political enough to know how to be apolitical and be accepted as such.

Publicity and controversy spread the impression that Husain was India's most successful artist. If success was measured by the prices paintings fetched, he was nowhere near the top. A list of 'the most expensive Indian paintings ever sold' put out by an organisation called The Arts Trust placed V.S. Gaitonde's 1995 *Untitled* on top of the heap. It sold for ₹29.3 crore in 2015. The same year F.N. Souza's *Birth* (1955) ranked second, fetching a prize of ₹23.7 crore. In the list that mentioned 73 paintings, there were only three Husains as against 23 Tyeb Mehtas. That was reflected in the prices Husain attracted. *Untitled* (1956) got the 29th rank with a sale price of ₹10.01 crore, *Sixth Seal* (1964) the 43rd rank at ₹7.17 crore and *Ganga Jamuna* (1972) the 54th rank with a price tag of ₹6.5 crore. Gaitonde was among the least publicised of Indian artists, 'a quiet man and a painter of the quiet reaches of the imagination', as one votary described him. Yet he was way above the most publicised artist of his time.

It was clear that in Husain's case market valuation was a poor guide to public assessment. To art lovers he was exceptional. In his command of multiple disciplines, the originality of his interpretations, his celebratory approach to colour, and in sheer productivity, Husain was a class apart. His ability to give ancient symbols a contemporary edge was remarkable. Few artists splashed colour with Husain's controlled abandon. His vivid yellows, blues, and reds, not to mention the power of his blacks, gave his canvases an ethos of rejoicing. His horse became an articulate emblem of muscularity reminiscent of the howling critter at the centre of *Guernica*. Sometimes galloping in rage, sometimes roaring in agony, always projecting an ethereal vitality, the horse had a tendency to dominate his canvases. It became a recurrent motif in his work, suggesting a spiritual link with its creator. It symbolised the exuberance and vitality Husain himself projected in his life. Seldom influenced by his surroundings, Husain probably believed that his surroundings would be influenced by *him*. In the early effervescent days of Independence, the country was alive with political ideals, reformist movements, and leftist influences. Ideological affinities did not influence art as they did theatre. The Indian People's Theatre Association (IPTA) was openly leftist, with Communist Party General Secretary P.C. Joshi playing a leadership role in it. Nevertheless, the term 'Progressive' carried connotations of left leanings and the Progressive Artists' Group was assumed to be left of centre. Husain was either unaware of this or unconcerned. His indifference in fact diluted whatever leftism the PAG might have had. As far as he was concerned, PAG was a window to Western modernism as opposed to Eastern traditionalism. He was 'eastern' enough to understand the historical importance of movements like the Bengal School. What Abanindranath Tagore did was to reclaim nationalist art as distinct from Raja Ravi Varma's imitative art with its dependence on European realism. Nandalal Bose as an art teacher at Santiniketan, and his student K.G. Subramanyan as teacher at Sayajirao University in Baroda went on to influence a generation of artists.

Husain developed a modified cubist methodology while his thematic focus stayed on the classicism of Indian traditions. Modern art incorporated Hindu images and symbolism in significant ways. This was natural because religion was an inspiration to art from the Gandharva and Amaravati periods of the first century BCE. Initially, the theme was Buddhism. From the Gupta period, known as the Golden Age (4th to 6th century CE), Hindu temple art began advancing in conspicuous ways. Temple architecture and temple sculpture embraced regional styles as they matured. Outstanding monuments took shape, from the shore temple in Mamallapuram with its monolithic rock relief and sculptures of Hindu deities, to Khajuraho and Konarak, where temple walls displayed eroticism without inhibition, proclaiming that Kama was as important as Dharma, Artha, and Moksha in the human journey. Although PAG was formed to redefine the postulates of Indian art in the post-colonial era, there was no way artists could detach themselves from the symbolism and vocabulary of traditionalist Hindu art. The plurality of Hindu deities and belief systems was a stimulus to the artistic imagination. The conceptual originality of a god with a human body and elephant's head made Ganesha an all-time favourite with artists. Ganesha and other Hindu motifs figured prominently in Husain's art. He even saw a personal factor behind it. His mother had died when he was less than two years old. He told *The Guardian*'s Tim Adams: 'Without a mother, there was no real care for me. From seven or eight years old, I was on the street all day, just going back to my father's house to sleep... In Hindu culture, it is the mother, Shakti the Goddess, who takes care of us. My paintings have always been a kind of searching for that.'* With his range, his command of form and colour, his sheer inventiveness, Husain could have been to India what Picasso was to Europe—an undisputed genius, living life as he pleased, admired by all and bothering none.

But Husain was not Picasso. His own mannerisms were an obstacle. The more serious obstacle was his name. When India slipped into a phase where religion coloured judgments in all walks of life, Husain stood out as a Muslim. Indifferent though he was to religion, Husain had grown up in a Muslim household. His father was informal about religion. He sent his son to a Muslim boarding school as a matter of duty, but never bothered to keep track of the boy's progress. Husain spent his time drawing human forms on whatever surface came handy despite his teachers' warning that his habit was forbidden by Islam. In his adult life, Husain did his namaz routines without fail. But there was no indication at any time that his Islamic practices were anything more than a gesture. His sadhana as an artist took him to the realm of temples and Hindu divinity because that was where Indian classic art had found its identity. The

* Tim Adams, 'MF Husain: The barefoot "Picasso" of Indian art', *The Guardian*, 1 June 2014.

Ramayana and Mahabharata were familiar ground to him from his boyhood days when he appeared as Hanuman in a stage play. His themes and characters, in so far as they were rooted in historical lore, had the Hindu cultural connection because Hindu and Indian were interchangeable words in art. Hence the proliferation of gods and goddesses in Husain's work. And they were often in the nude because that was the Hindu-Indian inheritance. Not only Khajuraho and Konark but also the Sun temples in Gujarat and Orissa and the Virupaksha Temple in Karnataka are magnificent jewels in Indian art. The carvings depict sexual union in the most explicit permutations and combinations imaginable. All the temples were built and all the carvings made under the command of Hindu kings who proceeded to worship there. Not a whisper arose about vulgarity casting its shadows on religion. On the contrary, the carvings and sculptures were seen as evidence of the wholesomeness of Hindu–Indian aesthetics. Husain took the much-travelled path and was recognised as a savant of Hindu–Indian art. Norms changed as Hindutva forces gained ground with the dawn of the 21st century, overtaking the universalism of Hinduism.

Overnight, as it were, Husain ceased to be an Indian artist and turned into a Muslim artist. His work, which until then was seen in terms of art, now began to be seen in terms of religion. His depiction of nudes took on a religious dimension it did not have for decades. The question now arose: Husain paints Hindu goddesses in the nude but why are there no Muslim nudes? It was a non-issue with aesthetes because Indian goddesses appearing in the nude was part of a timeless, universally recognised iconography whereas Muslim art had no such tradition. But the logic of history was no longer the issue. The issue now was not the traditions of iconography and the practices of centuries, but religious sentiment. Hindutva dogmatism was now calling a Muslim artist to order. There was no way Husain could escape, let alone win. Bajrang Dal activists attacked his house in Bombay in 1998 protesting against a painting of a nude Sita sitting on Hanuman's tail. In 2006, London's Asia House Gallery closed a major Husain exhibition after three men sprayed black paint on some of the paintings. Hindu Human Rights and the Hindu Forum of Britain had objected to the exhibition on the ground that it contained obscene images of Hindu goddesses. The next year, Shiv Sena activists sneaked into India International Centre in Delhi and attacked an ongoing Husain exhibition despite a heavy police presence. Pamphlets distributed by the attackers threatened to disrupt any Husain exhibition anywhere in the country. In 2008 activists shouting 'Jai Shri Ram' damaged paintings, prints, and furniture at a 'symbolic protest exhibition' of Husain's work at the Constitution Club in Delhi. The symbolic protest was against the non-inclusion of Husain's paintings at the India Art Summit which had just concluded in Delhi. In 2013, Vishwa Hindu Parishad activists destroyed paintings by Pakistani and Indian artists displayed at an Ahmedabad gallery that had been established by Husain and architect B.V. Doshi.

It can be argued that this was part of a worldwide trend. Freemuse, an international organisation working for freedom of artistic expression, noted that there were 553 cases of freedom violation in 78 countries in 2017 and called it 'the tip of a big iceberg'. Ten countries were identified for exhibiting 'alarming developments in how they treat artists and their freedom of expression'. Third in the list after China and Cuba was India. According to this study, India accounted for one-third of prosecutions and threats against film makers, actors, and artists in 2017. In Turkey, artist Zehra Dogan was jailed for two years and nine months for exhibiting paintings which the state considered propaganda. There were prominent film industry leaders in India who, upon receiving warnings from extremists, went silent if not apologetic. The seminal role played by Hindutva extremism made India a special case. Threats to his life finally convinced Husain that it was wiser to shift base. He had been a recognisable face in most countries and had in many ways become a world citizen. He had sons settled comfortably in Dubai. He joined them, fitting into the high society of the rich and famous there. He acquired apartments in high-end towers and went to parties in his new black Cadillac. He also spent hours loitering in the Dubai Creek beehive, sipping Suleimani tea at the Moplah eateries there. Invitations came from the royal family of Qatar and steel magnate Lakshmi Mittal of London. He accepted both. As a Qatari citizen, he began a 99-paintings sequence symbolising the '99 Beautiful names of Allah'. He completed 35. In London he started on a set of 30 large triptychs covering Indian civilisation. The eight he finished reflected his freewheeling imagination linking Gandhi with Ganesha and Mother Teresa with the Mahabharata.

But his heart was in India. Art critic Kishore Singh, who met Husain in London wrote: 'Husain missing familiar places and faces in India, was known to have painted extempore at the homes and offices of a large number of Indian families, demanding nothing more than affection and a home-cooked meal in exchange for a hastily improvised drawing or painting.'* Husain's son Owais said: 'He had this idea that he could take a flight, just slip in, perhaps sit for a while at a teashop, and slip out.' But of course he could not do that in an India that could be extraordinarily efficient in implementing the wrong kind of law. Besides, time was against Husain. By the end of 2010, age-related problems started bothering the 95-year-old. He was forced to spend several months in a sick bed. On 9 June 2011 he died at the Royal Brompton Hospital in London and was buried the next day in Brookwood Cemetery, south of London. The Indian government offered to fly his body home for the last rites. Husain's children considered the offer, but decided to honour their father's wish to be buried wherever he died. India sent its high commissioner to place a wreath on behalf of his country.

Even as he stayed with the religion he was born into, Husain was too large to be confined to a single ideology, political or religious. Art was his religion. When pettiness scored, Indians proud of their Indianness moaned. Qatar's offer of citizenship to Husain made Sharmila Tagore lament: 'We recognise our national treasures only when they are gone.'

---

* Kishore Singh, 'MF Husain's "last" works', *Forbes*, 13 May 2014.

16

VEERAPPAN

Dreaded not Hated

For a man who made a living by robbing, killing, and taking captives for ransom, Veerappan, shockingly, developed the profile of a folk hero. He was dreaded but not hated. The combined forces of the Tamil Nadu and Karnataka governments tried for years to project him as a bandit, murderer of enemies as well as of his own people, an elephant poacher, and sandalwood smuggler. He was all that. According to figures released by official sources, he killed 184 people, half of them police and forest officials, poached 200 elephants (one account put it at an incredible 2,000 elephants, which may not necessarily be the work of a printer's devil), and felled 10,000 sandalwood trees. Despite all that, he was recognised as a celebrity of sorts. He had political ideas, but preferred not to go into politics as an occupation. There were people who exploited him just as there were people who hunted him. When he fell to police bullets at the age of 52, a wave of sympathy swept across and beyond the territory he had made his own. Movies about him were made in Hindi, Kannada, and Tamil. A 125- episode television serial ran in Tamil. Books were written, including one by the police officer who finally tracked him down and caught him. To the surprise of many, *The Economist* of London found him important enough to be featured in its famous obituary page. It described him as vain and vicious but also acknowledged that a romantic aura surrounded him.

In the criminal annals of India, there never was a figure comparable to the brigand of Sathyamangalam forest.

Koose Muniswamy Veerappan Gounder, born in 1952 in Gopinatham, Mysore state, and shot in 2004 in Papparapatti village, Tamil Nadu, was a child of history. The forested trijunction of Tamil Nadu, Karnataka, and Kerala is rich with three natural resources that are rare and in high demand—sandalwood, elephant tusks, and special-grade granite. This made the region attractive to generations of traders. But they had to be traders with a penchant for adventure because the precious items in demand could not be harvested easily. If the topography was challenging, the forces that controlled the area were powerful. There were three layers: the trader, the politician, and the mafia. The trader needed the politician to get around the laws and most politicians, seeing the lucrative margins, were ready to become partners. The trader–politician combine in turn needed local gangs to procure the sandalwood, to kill the elephants, and to protect quarry operations. Gang leaders were only too happy to team up with VIPs. In this union of interdependent lawbreakers, two retained their social respectability while one became criminalised. Traders and politicians teamed up with Veerappan in order to achieve the ends they could not openly pursue. They profited from their association with him. They no doubt gave him the price he demanded, but it was not enough to save him.

Veerappan, Mathaiyan, and Arjunan were the sons of Muniswamy, a farmer in Salem district who was forced to abandon his village Thampalli when it was submerged along with numerous other villages by the Mettur Dam. The family moved to Gopinatham. For residents in this forested area, it was routine to hunt for animals for meat. Muniswamy would go out regularly hunting deer and wild fowl. Veerappan accompanied his father always. The boy developed not only great interest in hunting expeditions but also became an unusually good sharpshooter. At 12, he killed an elephant singlehandedly, cut off its tusks, and sold it to the leading-poacher trader Sevi Gounder. Impressed by the boy's skill, Gounder presented him with an English-made gun. Veerappan was well on his way. It was a time when many gangs were operating in the forests. Elephant tusks commanded good prices. So did sandalwood and granite. Business was brisk because profits were shared by important people as well as by poachers and smugglers. In 1972, when Veerappan was arrested in Tamil Nadu, it was a ruling party MLA who helped him secure bail. In the 1980s, he openly took part in the election campaigns of politician friends. In 1986, when he was detained in Bangalore, it was a senior police officer who helped him escape. Walter Devaram, acclaimed Director-General of Police in Tamil Nadu, said in 1993: 'Veerappan is not just a bandit. He is able to analyse the psyche of his opponents thoroughly before launching an operation.' He had extraordinary jungle skills, too. He could identify animals by the crunching sound they made while eating leaves.

Does a society get the criminals it deserves, as Voltaire said? While his father and other elders in the family began poaching as a vocation, Veerappan developed it into a profession with his own rules. He outdid his elders by bringing in new ideas, new techniques, and a new devilry into the business. He had a brain the locals had not come across before. He also had an uncompromising style with dimensions of unthinkable cruelty. Close associates would be beheaded if he suspected them of being informers. Some of his killings became infamous because the victims were brave policemen doing their duty. A landmine attack he arranged in Palar in 1993 killed 22 uniformed personnel in one go. Many civilians were also summarily disposed of because he received complaints against them. He went wild when his sister committed suicide. Convinced that she had been raped by forest guards and policemen, he went on a killing spree that sent shock waves across the region.

His cruelty is often attributed to his formative years. People in and around his Sathyamangalam base lived in miserable conditions. Successive governments in Tamil Nadu and Karnataka paid no attention to the sufferings of the people although political leaders were interested in exploiting the natural resources of the region.

Those who eked out a living in the area were subjected to exploitation as well. Villagers were routinely persecuted by government officials seeking information about Veerappan's whereabouts. Many died in the course of ' interrogation'. No woman was safe when officials arrived in their search missions. Harassed forest dwellers saw Veerappan as a protector. This was one reason the government's prolonged efforts to project him as a terror did not cut much ice with the locals.

Veerappan grew to enjoy his power. By the 1990s, he found that kidnapping for ransom was relatively easy, less messy, and potentially more paying. His early targets were police personnel and forest officials. These were agents of government and when they were taken away by the Veerappan gang, the government found it advisable to pay ransoms unofficially. Veerappan developed the habit of making big demands. Once he asked for ₹1,000 crore to release his captive. Other ransom demands included the grant of a 100-year lease for quarrying in the MM Hills, and the filming of his life story in all Indian languages. He was persuaded that these were demands even the government could not meet. However, huge caches of cash came into his possession and he developed a style of his own when putting them in safe custody. He procured iron trunks, filled them with the note-bundles, and buried them in carefully selected spots in the forest. The trick was that only he could identify the spots. But it was a trick full of holes, for he was a hunted man and there was no guarantee that he would be around to unearth each trunk as needed. After his death, there were reports of young trekkers, setting up tents for a night's stay, digging and finding steel trunks. At one time, secret service cells of the government saw 500-rupee notes circulating freely in some villages around Sathyamangalam. At least in one instance Veerappan caught a thief red-handed. Selva Mary was a small-time 'operator' in the forest along with some of her family members. She and her brother-in-law managed to steal some of Veerapan's hidden money, She was caught and forced to marry Velayan, a senior member of the Veerappan gang. She was a teenager at the time, and quite adventurous. She took part in some of Veerappan's most murderous operations such as the attack on the Palar police camp. An arrest warrant was out, but she went underground. For 27 years she remained untraced. Velayan had died, she had married again, and settled down in the border district of Chamarajanagar as a labourer. When an elephant invaded a sugarcane field they were tending, she used a gun to scare it away. The gun was used with such expertise that the police enquired about its owner and found it to be Selva Mary. They took her in. We do not know if others have gone in search of the trunks hidden in the forest by Veerappan. Possibly, whatever interest remained in the fabled fortune would have vanished after demonetisation.

The kidnap that rocked the country and threatened the Karnataka government took place in July 2000. The Kannada actor, Rajkumar, accompanied by his wife and relatives, had gone to Gajanir for a house-warming ceremony. The house was located at the edge of a forest area via Erode district, four kilometres from the Tamil Nadu–Karnataka border. The weather was ugly with non-stop torrents threatening to drown everything. Around 9 o'clock at night, those in the house retired into various rooms to rest after a meal. Quietly, a gang of about a dozen men stormed the house. They were armed with self-loading guns. They surrounded the people in their rooms. In a jiffy the man with the unmistakable moustache appeared. Rajkumar and those with him instantly recognised Veerappan who firmly but politely escorted Rajkumar out of the room. On the way out, he gave an audio cassette to Rajkumar's wife, Parvathamma, and asked her to give it to the chief minister in Bangalore. The moment Veerappan and gang left the house with their prize catch, Parvathamma started the long drive to Bangalore, reaching chief minister S.M. Krishna's house at about three that morning. At that hour began the most agonising days of Krishna's life. When news of the hero's arrest was out the next morning, rioting broke out in the city. Tamil newspaper offices in Bangalore were attacked. The government was forced to declare a two-day public holiday.

The cassette Krishna received from Veerappan did not demand any ransom. It only asked the chief minister to depute an emissary with whom Veerappan could discuss terms. Given Rajkumar's eminence in public estimation and the state government's existential need to get him released, the kidnap became a landmark in Karnataka's history. Veerappan treated his captive with respect during the 108 days of the star's vanavas. But the Karnataka government was in a continuous panic, reminded by sporadic violence of what could happen if something went wrong. Setting the ransom amount became a vexatious problem with frequent toing and froing by emissaries who remained necessarily unseen and unidentified. More nerve-racking was the means of delivery in Chennai as was decided by the unknown emissaries. Informed speculation was that a ransom of ₹20 crore was fixed; it could well have been more. How could so many bundles of currency notes be transported from any point in Karnataka to Chennai even if it was a government that wanted to do so?

During those high-strung days, Chief Minister Krishna lost weight and visibly aged. A year later, I had occasion to imagine what he must have gone through. I came across confidential police reports describing how vehicles were readied, plans drawn up to handle possible checking by Tamil Nadu police at border points, and how delivery addresses in Chennai kept changing. The task was of course entrusted to handpicked police personnel. The confidential papers showed the expertise with which the officer in charge of the transportation planned every step, with attention to every detail. Reading the file filled me with respect for the professional capabilities of our police force. All the care they took seemed worthwhile when, in the end, Veerappan got what he demanded and Rajkumar landed in Bangalore in a specially arranged helicopter. The applause of the masses echoed across the state. It could as well have been for Veerappan for becoming one of the wealthiest men in the state overnight.

It was strange—then again, perhaps not—that the Rajkumar

kidnapping added to the larger-than-life profile of Veerappan. There were rumours that the granite lobby had had a hand in it. The demand for black granite from the area was high because of its superior quality and the high prices it fetched. Quarry operators routinely exploited more than the area that had officially been allotted to them. They saw the backing of Veerappan as essential for their operations. Influential people linked to Rajkumar had got into the granite business and upset the applecart of the established mafia. Rajkumar was unaware of all this, but the mafia found their own ways to keep outsiders from their racket. Also involved in the politics of the kidnapping, according to reports in circulation at the time, were Tamil nationalists with ideological links to organisations like the Sri Lankan Liberation Tigers of Tamil Eelam. Veerappan was said to be sympathetic to the Tamil cause. The political ambitions he nurtured at one stage in his life were linked to his belonging to the Gounder Vanniyar caste. In Tamil politics, the party of the Vanniyars, Pattali Makkal Katchi, was an influential entity. It had looked upon Veerappan as one of their own. For that matter, even the DMK and its leader, M. Karunanidhi, had a soft corner for Veerappan on the basis of Tamil camaraderie. There were, however, no concrete plans at any stage for Veerappan to become an active player in politics.

One reason for Veerappan's place in the popular imagination was the soft side he displayed in married life. The initiative for marriage was taken not by him but by a plucky girl named Muthulakshmi. She was impressed by the audacity with which he chased and eliminated his enemies. She managed to meet him and was further dazzled by the manliness of his moustache. She was quite an attractive girl herself and Veerappan in turn was impressed by her firebrand nature. Muthulakshmi's people objected to her marrying an outlaw. But the strong-willed couple paid no heed. Veerappan simply took Muthulakshmi with him and disappeared into the deeper recesses of the forest, to live there happily ever after. Two daughters were born of the union. The parents' decision that the girls should get a proper education made Muthulakshmi return to her village in due course. This brought the police into the picture and Muthulakshmi spent time in and out of jails, facing interrogations and experiencing police-style third degree treatment.

But her plans worked. Vidyarani, born 1990, and Prabha, born 1993, were enrolled in schools. As a widow, Muthulakshmi turned into something of a cult figure. She addressed the media and issued statements. At one press conference, she warned filmmaker Ram Gopal Verma against portraying 'en kanavan', my husband, in a bad light in his movie. She threatened the police sometimes, and warned politicians that she would reveal who among them were in collaboration with Veerappan. By 2002, the gritty lady said she had completed a book on police atrocities and 'sent it to Delhi for copyright', as one report cryptically put it. Even the number of pages was mentioned—654. Nothing more was heard about that sizeable volume. She kept giving interviews for a while. She claimed that policemen in Karnataka and Tamil Nadu used to take money from Veerappan. She reminded people that when Veerappan kidnapped Kannada matinee idol Rajkumar, his principal demand was that policemen who tortured villagers should be punished. Muthulakshmi saw her kanavan as a Robin Hood figure. In time, she withdrew from the limelight (or should we say that the authorities ensured she withdrew?), giving Veerappan's daughters the chance to grow up as ordinary citizens. Fortunately for her, Veerappan had proved a caring husband. Two houses in Mettur had been acquired for her. Two earth movers had also been bought to ensure a steady income for the family.

In due course, the daughters would add their own contributions to the family saga. Prabha had never had occasion to meet her father. After she went to Mettur to attend Veerappan's last rites, the convent school at Cuddalore where she was studying wanted her to leave. It suited her, for she was keen to move to Chennai for studies. Her ambition at the time was to specialise in computer sciences. Her older sister, Vidyarani, tried to live up to Veerappan's desire to see her become a doctor. But she later switched her interest to the civil services and joined an IAS training institute. 'One needs authority to carry out good deeds,' she said. In 2020, at age 30, she took another route to achieve authority. She joined the BJP along with 1,000 others from different political parties. By way of explanation, she had a script ready: 'I want to work for the poor and the underprivileged. Prime Minister Modi's schemes are for the people and I want to take them to the people.'* Evidently, it was an operation that had been well orchestrated by the BJP's strategists. At least in the Krishnagiri area of Tamil Nadu, the party acquired a measure of recognition through the surprise acquisition of a well-remembered bandit's lineage.

Alongside his murderous instincts, Veerappan possessed some surprising character traits. He was a religious man. He did the Surya Namaskar and walked a minimum of ten miles a day. He loved to dance, his own rustic formulation of measured steps. He would cut bamboo into flutes and enjoy the sound he made from them. He was proud about his moustache and would tend to it with great care using special oils and herbs. He derived pleasure from rolling the mouche with his fingers, shaping it carefully, fondling it. In 2015, Lush, a foreign cosmetic company marketed what it called Veerappan Moustache Wax at the impressive price of $15.95 for an 8-gram jar. When some noise arose about 'glorifying a bandit', the company stopped producing the wax. For all the glamour that surrounded him, a man as shrewd as Veerappan must have known that the life of a fugitive could end abruptly. Muthulakshmi could not have been unaware of it either. The daughters themselves must have felt the unusualness of the circumstances that surrounded them.

After his murder of police officers, Tamil Nadu and Karnataka governments set up a joint force in 1991 to track him down. It became known as the costliest operation of its kind in Indian

* 'Sandalwood smuggler Veerappan's daughter joins BJP', *Hindustan Times*, 23 February 2020.

history, eating up one billion rupees in 12 years. At one stage, experienced and capable officers such as K. Vijaya Kumar and N.K. Senthamarai Kannan were put in charge of the hunt. Vijaya Kumar would eventually put details of the hunt in print with his book *Veerappan: Chasing the Brigand.* The all-out operation to capture Veerappan turned out to be not only expensive but also time-consuming. In the end, they trapped him with a complicated plot, as the official version went. Police agents apparently infiltrated Veerappan's inner group and bided their time. When their quarry developed an eye problem, they suggested a visit to the hospital. An ambulance was organised which, unbeknown to Veerappan, happened to be a police vehicle. The driver was an undercover policeman. The old suspicious Veerappan turned into a new trusting Veerappan and boarded the vehicle. He and his closest associates who accompanied him were all armed. When they reached a village in Dharmapuri, the ambulance was suddenly challenged. Instantly, the area exploded with an exchange of gunfire. The ambulance driver ran to safety while Veerappan was killed in the vehicle along with his companions in crime.

It all sounded very neat. A bit too neat, perhaps. Quickly, unofficial versions began to circulate. According to one, the gang was killed by a double agent who poisoned their buttermilk. Another said the men were sedated (the buttermilk?), taken into custody, tortured for two days, then shot. A credible doubt that arose could not be easily brushed aside. This centred round the police claim that Veerappan was already trapped in a police vehicle driven by a police driver. If that were true, it must have been easy to capture him alive. So why was he killed on the spot? Those who raised the question also supplied the answer—that arrest, imprisonment, and a possible trial could have led to disclosures inconvenient to many leaders. A dead Veerappan was safer. Chief ministers and home ministers who took policy decisions and top police officers who conducted ground operations were all aware of Veerappan being in a class of his own. The operation chief who finally nabbed him,

K. Vijay Kumar, was insightful when he wrote: 'I never saw him only as an adversary. If he had taken competent STFs on a ride for over a decade, there must have been something going for him. What was that? Tactics? Intel? Good PR? or all of it.... He had audacity and cunning. He was a beast with a human brain. Give the devil its due. Minus some negative energy from his persona, and he could have been a terrific commander of any fighting force.'* That was high tribute from the commander of a fighting force.

An assorted mix of people gave their own tributes in their own way. The number of men and women from the villages who collected to attend his obsequies was a pointer to his hold on the popular imagination. Dignity marked the conduct of people who assembled to bid him goodbye. Two days after his death, the body, wrapped in a white shroud, was buried near Mettur. A youth brigade dressed in white trousers stood in silence at the site, like an honour guard. Thousands attended the 15-minute ceremony, thousands more stood some distance away, cordoned off by the police. For days, hundreds of common folk queued up to pay homage to the man who was called a brigand. Crowds still collect there on special days.

Does Veerappan, the idea, have a life of its own? His formidable moustache has become something of a fashion accessory across Tamil Nadu. And the consequences of continuing misery in the forgotten hamlets of the forest keep raising questions. There were unconfirmed reports about a 'Junior Veerappan' appearing in the hills. Given the wretchedness of the villagers and the all-round exploitation that is still goes on, a senior Veerappan might well emerge. As US President John F. Kennedy reminded the world: 'Those who make peaceful revolution impossible will make violent revolution inevitable.'

* 'Veerappan could have been a terrific commander: K. Vijay Kumar', *Times of India*, 21 May 2021.

17

BAL THACKERAY

Cartoonist Astray

Bal Thackeray was not meant to be a demagogue. The elements were so mixed in him that friends could stand up and say to all the world this was a gentle soul who found his fulfilment in a Sherlock Holmes-style pipe and a mug of beer. But he proved the elements wrong. He obliterated Bombay's history by changing its name and altering its face, and in the process, turned himself into Balasaheb Thackeray, an apostle of urban violence leading a lumpenproletariat mafia. Bal was agreeable, unblemished. Balasaheb was virulent, pestilential. There is no doubt that the Shiv Sena (name derived not from Lord Shiva, but from Shivaji Bhonsle, the warrior king who was crowned 'chhatrapati' of the Maratha Empire in 1674) grew beyond the stated purpose of its formation: ensuring preferential treatment for Maharashtrians over migrants in Bombay, India's premier city industrially, culturally, and aspirationally. The overnight appeal of the 'Maharashtrians First' platform saw the Shiv Sena grow into a bullying force of rowdies with enough political power to unleash violence with impunity. It went on to share power in Delhi as well as Maharashtra, yet retained its capacity to break the law and feel patriotic about it. From digging up cricket pitches to prevent Pakistan playing in India, to offering ₹2 lakh as reward to Hindu families that produced five children, the Sena set its own agenda in defiance of democracy's checks and balances.

As much as 80 per cent of its 18 MPs in the 2014 Parliament had figured in criminal cases. The profile of a Shiv Sena MP came into view in 2017 when Ravindra Gaikwad hit a 60-year-old Air India official with his slippers 25 times, as he claimed. The reason was that he was not given a business class seat. The official's plea that it was a flight with no business class made no impression on the honourable MP. As the entire country outraged, Air India was joined by other airlines in blacklisting Gaikwad. At no time did the man express any regret because the boss of his party, Uddhav Thackeray, backed him. It was soon discovered that Gaikwad was a habitual offender. Dissatisfied with the food provided by a Muslim caterer in Delhi's Maharashtra Sadan one day, he forcefully stuffed food into the caterer's mouth. It also came to light that Gaikwad previously faced charges ranging from rioting to criminal intimidation. That Uddhav Thackeray did not wince at such excesses showed how political power had influenced the outlook of the Thackerays. Unlike his son, Bal Thackeray was exposed, until he was in his 30s, to normal middle-class life and its existential problems. He had established a name as a cartoonist and built up a standing of his own unrelated to politics. He had friends and colleagues who had no association with sectarian ideals or agitational movements. Uddhav did not have the benefit of a freewheeling unaffiliated period in his adult life. The life he experienced was rooted in a political landscape where he saw his father sitting on a throne and a dispersed army of fighters ready to carry out his every command. Inherited power gave Uddhav the toughness of Thackeray the politician, without the softness of Thackeray the man, the middle-classer, the office-going journalist.

Perhaps it was fortuitous that Bal Thackeray's personality evolved in an atmosphere sandwiched between political forwardness and economic backwardness. His father, Keshav, was too busy with fighting superstition, writing books, and agitating for Maharashtra to think about the family's daily bread. Some bread came and that was enough. His unusualness was reflected in the alterations his very name went through. Great grandfather and grandfather were known by the surname Dhodapkar because an ancestor was the kiladar (governor) of the Dhodap Fort under Maratha rulers. When Keshav was born, his father named him Keshav Panvelkar after the Maharashtrian practice of using the birthplace as surname, in this case Panvel. When he was taken to school for admission, however, he was enlisted under the name Keshav Sitaram Thakre; apparently the traditional family name was Thakre. After Keshav matured into a champion of multiple causes, he changed the spelling of his surname to that of the British novelist he admired, William Makepeace Thackeray, who, to his delight, was an Anglo-Indian born in Calcutta. For all that, Keshav Thackeray, became known as Prabhodankar Thackeray, after the fortnightly publication he started with the title *Prabhodan* (Enlighten).

Keshav Prabhodankar Thackeray turned out to be one of the busiest activists of the independence era. He began as a crusader for social reform. A prolific writer, he used his books and pamphlets as well as stage plays and street demonstrations to fight dowry and untouchability and child marriages and casteist customs. He often resorted to risky ways to take his cause forward. According to one story, he was a teenager when he gate-crashed the venue of a 65-year-old's marriage to a 12-year-old girl and demanded that the ceremony be abandoned. When he was ignored, he set the tent on fire. He also arranged love marriages and inter-caste marriages by the dozen. In the 1950s, he became one of the militant leaders of the Samyukta Maharashtra agitation for the creation of the separate linguistic state of Maharashtra. Keshav Thackeray was a Hindutva-vadi, but in a class by himself. He denounced Brahminism and opposed religious rituals, his concept becoming known as Bahujan-vadi Hindutva. He launched the idea of celebrating Navratri without Brahmin control and encouraged Dalits to perform poojas. Clearly he was a man well ahead of his time.

No sign of his father's idealism-driven zealotry was visible in Bal Thackeray as he grew up, started a family of his own, and struggled to keep it afloat. He led a quiet life, so quiet that his mid-life transformation into an agent provocateur looked like a historical accident. The ground for that transformation was laid when unusual developments shook the *Free Press Journal* (FPJ), the newspaper where Thackeray worked for a decade as a cartoonist. Following the death of its legendary founder editor, S. Sadanand, the institution had gone into the hands of A.B. Nair, a small-time newsprint agent in Bombay who found himself sitting on a fortune when the Norwegian paper company which he represented abandoned its stocks and withdrew from India in the wake of the Second World War. He became a shareholder in FPJ in lieu of newsprint payments due from the always cash-strapped Sadanand. When control of the paper passed into his hands after Sadanand, Nair, who had only a primary school education, proudly put his name as editor in the imprint line. Under his editorship, the FPJ once carried a soap company advertisement as the lead news story of the day. The agency handling the soap account had talked to Editor Nair and Nair had thought it would be a feather in his cap to carry a lead story other papers would not. The agency knew what it was doing and managed to place the soap story after the editorial staff had finished the page. When the paper appeared the next morning, the staff was outraged. They received angry phone calls from readers, some of them well-known citizens. Unable to live with the scandal, half a dozen senior editorial hands resigned, Thackeray among them. Encouraged by the public reaction and supported by some influential political circles, they started a new daily which, they hoped, would become the new favourite of FPJ readers. The paper was professionally competent and attracted a measure of popular support. But the promoters quickly discovered that editorial competence was not enough to run a paper. None of them knew anything about management or finance. The paper closed. The valiant journalists were now left to fend for themselves. Thackeray was caught in a bad situation because cartoonists had far less openings than reporters and sub-editors. With a growing family, his needs were more urgent, too. It was becoming yet another case of desperate situations leading to desperate action. The stage was set for the historical accident that would transform Thackeray.

The early years of Independence was a golden age of Indian cartooning with the likes of Shankar and R.K. Laxman and Abu and Kutty and O.V. Vijayan at full gallop. Shankar added a classic edge to it by starting *Shankar's Weekly* in 1948, essentially a political satirical publication that drew inspiration from *Punch*. He closed it down when Emergency was proclaimed in 1975. (It was a measure of the importance Shankar and *Shankar's Weekly* had achieved that Prime Minister Indira Gandhi wrote to him, miffed no doubt by the closure of the weekly, saying that 'you are the best judge'.) Thackeray was counted among the top cartoonists of his time, though he was overshadowed by Laxman, who not only was based in the same city but also had the main newspaper of the city as his platform. Unlike Laxman, however, Thackeray secretly nursed the ambition to start a publication of his own, something along the lines of *Shankar's Weekly*. With his colleague from the FPJ, P.K. Ravindranath, he held discussions on how to go about it. They even produced a dummy or two, unbeknown to others. With the FPJ road coming to a dead-end and their alternative newspaper closing down, Thackeray went back to the idea of a magazine of his own. He had no money and no support base, other than his brother, Srikant, and his FPJ friend, Ravindranath. But he was jobless. With no option but to take the plunge, he launched his cherished dream and called it *Marmik* (essence, straight from the heart). It contained cartoons and articles on contemporary issues, just as *Shankar's Weekly* had. It struggled on. One issue carried by chance an article contributed by an unknown reader detailing how senior positions in big companies like Glaxo were monopolised by South Indians at the cost of local Maharashtrians. It was the first time a South Indian vs Maharashtrian approach had been adapted to measure current affairs. The article caused a sensation.

All of a sudden, in the big city of Bombay, a sociopolitical issue was born. Along with it a new Thackeray was born, and a new Bombay.

Before anyone sensed what was happening, some bashing of heads and smashing of shops occurred, the victims being Malayali narial-paniwallahs on Shivaji Park beach and Udupi hoteliers in suburban zones. There was no sign of the law-enforcement authorities taking note of this. But two powerful entities did and their unofficial backing proved decisive in the muscular growth of the Shiv Sena. These were the Bombay Pradesh Congress Committee (BPCC), which had an enemy to destroy, and the city's industrial lobby which had inimical forces to tame. Both tasks called for unconventional handling that respectable entities such as the Congress Party and the industry organisations could not be associated with. They found Thackeray and his Senanis a convenience.

BPCC was headed then by S.K. Patil, a no-nonsense task master. As it happened, the MP from North Bombay was V.K. Krishna Menon who achieved extraordinary popularity with no help from the BPCC. It did not take long for Patil to detest Menon. Bombay was his territory and here was Menon, an import from Delhi, strutting about as though he owned it. After an initial period of support, Patil decided to banish the outsider from his territory and Shiv Sena became Patil's weapon. Krishna Menon was built up as a non-Maharashtrian usurper. It was a tailor-made issue for the Shiv Sena to take up. Campaigns were mounted against Menon until he was defeated in the elections. He left Bombay humiliated. For the powerful industry lobby in the city, the thorn in their side was trade unionism. Some of the most militant trade union leaders made Bombay their battleground and gave hell to business leaders and industrialists who showed reluctance in agreeing to trade union demands. Thackeray's Sena stalwarts happily took on the trade unions. Workers on strike found Sena soldiers surrounding them with threats. What was considered unfeasible till then, the taming of Bombay's mighty unions, became feasible. With patronage coming from both political and business godfathers, Thackeray grew into a godfather in his own right with a freedom of action that extended beyond constitutional boundaries.

The emergence of the assertive Marathi Manoos was different from the rise of linguistic forces in Telugu and Tamil territories. Potti Sriramulu had to starve himself to death for Telugu speakers to have a state of their own; in time his memory was mocked when the Telugu state was cut into two antagonistic halves. The Dravidian movement needed nothing more than the articulation of Tamil pride by C.N. Annadurai; popular elections took care of the rest. By contrast, the Shiv Sena grew through militancy, opportunistically taking advantage of the political and business power wielders of the time. That suited Thackeray's ambitions. But it also produced challenges that compromised his position. The Shiv Sena's primary purpose was to promote Marathi pride and establish Marathi rights over Bombay. This was achieved rapidly, to the extent of renaming the city as Mumbai and developing a sports complex, a natya mandir, a school, a road, and a chowk named after Prabodhankar Thackeray. Maharashtrian identity acquired a new status at the state and national levels. But what does an organisation do after achieving its stated objective? Mahatma Gandhi asked that the Indian National Congress be disbanded after it had achieved its objective of independence. But his associates did not because they wanted to convert the goodwill of the independence movement into political capital. Their success was short-lived. The Congress as a party deteriorated into mutually warring factions, then into a dynastic hegemony, and then into a shadow of its past. For Thackeray, too, there was no question of dispersing the Shiv Sena, a political machine that had taken him to the summits of power. He could have developed it into a movement to raise Maharashtrian cultural pride to new heights as the Dravida parties had done in Tamil country, but that required a level of cerebral sophistication such as Annadurai possessed. Thackeray took the easy way out. He joined the communal crowd and converted what was a linguistic platform into a religious one.

Linguistic causes had limited voter appeal while religion's scope was vast. This was put on record some three decades later by a former Shiv Sena MP, Bharat Kumar Raut. He did so when a book *Samrat: How the Shiv Sena Changed Mumbai Forever* (2014) by Sujata Anandan came out saying harsh things about Thackeray's approach to building up the Sena. It said that Thackeray wanted to build an army of musclemen without education so they would obey orders without hesitation. 'One generation of Maharashtrians,' said the author, 'did turn out to be very mediocre because of this policy of Thackeray.' At the release of the book, Raut said: 'In 1985, Bal Thackeray realised that Marathi is a good cause for popularity, but it does not have elective merit. Then he realised that the bigger plank would be Hindutva. So it was a well-calculated move. He embraced Hindutva and won subsequent elections.' When Thackeray went into religion-based politics, he went into it wholesale. He went so far as to say that the concept of secular India should be abandoned and Hindutva should be constitutionally proclaimed as the country's official religion. He raised a special squad of cadres to participate in the demolition of the Babri Masjid. When Muslims in Mumbai retaliated, armed Shiv Sainiks took the lead in attacking Muslims. A virtual civil war engulfed Mumbai, Thackeray breaking all limits by egging on his troops. An inquiry commission later recorded that 'writings and directives issued by Shiv Sena pramukh Bal Thackeray' had whipped up communal frenzy. Some 900 people were killed and property estimated at around ₹9,000 crore destroyed. No case was filed and no action taken by the government. Clearly the authorities were too nervous to move against Thackeray. But their cautiousness was not enough to ensure peace. Rumours of arrest were enough for Mumbai to go into panic mode. Stock markets fell. Shopping areas downed shutters. People stocked up provisions. Some cabinet ministers resigned. Special constabulary took up battle stations. Fortunately, war did not break out. (Seven years later, state Home Minister Chhagan Bhujbal made an attempt to arrest Thackeray. Bhujbal had started out as a Shiv Sainik and hero worshipper of Thackeray, then fell out with him and joined rival parties. When he started moves against Thackeray, Mumbai went tense again. All Bhujbal could do was arrest Thackeray for a few minutes. The magistrate before whom he was produced dismissed the case as time-barred.) Thackeray's communal stridency persuaded admirers to call him Hindu Hridaysamrat.

Did Thackeray go violently extremist because the Hindutva space was already occupied and he had to force his way in? The BJP was on the ascendance in the 1990s under the leadership of A.B. Vajpayee. Mumbai and Maharashtra were key target areas for the party. The BJP's strategists knew that they needed Thackeray on their side. They were even prepared to accept him as the uncrowned king of the big city. But they never saw him as one of their own. He could be an ally, nothing more. It meant in effect that in the BJP's scheme of things the Shiv Sena chief could at best be a junior partner in the affairs of Hindutva politics. They gave him the paraphernalia of glamour and glory so that the junior status remained hidden.

There was also the outside world for Thackeray to cope with. Salman Rushdie made him a star in *The Moor's Last Sigh* (1995). Thackeray appears as Raman Fielding, a fundamentalist Hindu politician whose followers beat up anyone who opposes Hindu pre-eminence, especially Muslims. Despite the oddly mixed name, Raman Fielding's true identity was clear to all and the Maharashtra government lost no time in banning the novel. Pop king Michael Jackson was a different kind of problem and Thackeray personally steamrolled his way in to solve it. When the rock idol announced plans for a two-day visit to Mumbai in the winter of 1996, protests rose from some local circles. The Jackson kind of entertainment, said the protestors, was an affront to Marathi culture. The organisers, anxious to go ahead with the show in which they had invested heavily, made Jackson call on Thackeray in his house. There were reports that a dakshina of ₹4 crore was paid. What was known was that Thackeray issued a statement that was unequivocal.

'Jackson is a great artist...' he said. 'His movements are terrific. He represents certain values in America which India should not have any qualms in accepting.'* The Jackson show was a great success in Mumbai.

Whether a given subject tickled Maharashtrian pride or irked it, Thackeray's word was final. That extraordinary reach influenced his Hindutva as well. His was not an intellectually conceptualised Hindutva as was his father's Bahujan-vadi version. Prabhodankar Thackeray's aims were progressive; Bal Thackeray's were political and communal, yet different from the political and communal Hindutva of the BJP. This tightrope did not seem odd as long as it went on under the all-embracing shadow of Thackeray's supremacy. The situation changed after his passing. His son Uddhav's bid to take control of the Shiv Sena in 2012 faced resistance. Lacking his father's pre-eminence, Uddhav realised that his options were limited. He tried to achieve a measure of independence by criticising the BJP and engaging the BJP chief minister, Devendra Fadnavis, in wordy duels, even ridiculing Narendra Modi and threatening to fight elections solo. But when the moment of truth arrived, he forgot his complaints and teamed up with the BJP to fight the election. The dilemma of embracing Hindutva without embracing the BJP continued into the third generation as well. Uddhav's son, Aditya, tried to present a modernistic, English-educated profile but was at a loss to link it up with the Hindutva stance. In an interview, he said the Shiv Sena's Hindutva was different from the BJP's. But all he could offer by way of explanation was mumbo-jumbo. 'It is centrist, but it is right-wing centrist because we are pragmatic and we are talking of things like, say, nightlife, electric buses, and plastic pollution. You know, we are talking of something completely different.' The *Business Line* newspaper quoted an unnamed BJP leader who said that Aditya belonged to a nativist party that

---

* Suketu Mehta, *Maximum City: Bombay Lost and Found*, (New York: Random House), 2004, p. 66.

thrives on the narrow, parochial, and xenophobic platforms of 'Mae Marathi' and 'Marathi manoos first'. 'What can you say about the future of a party set up for the Marathi manoos whose GenNext cannot speak Marathi and writes poems in English?' So much for Bal Thackeray's efforts to graduate from the Marathi manoos to the Hindu manoos.

Even the Madrassi-bashing with which Bal Thackeray launched his political career was to some extent a put-on job. There were spicy coffee house theories that Thackeray had developed a personal grudge against South Indians because a Mysorean named R.K. Laxman rode above him in his own city. In fact, Thackeray had high regard for Laxman. He called the *Free Press Journal* news desk the Malayali Club and enjoyed referring to its members as Yandugundus. Yet some of them were his closest friends. FPJ's crime reporter, M.P. Iyer, was a Madrassi but celebrated for the brilliance of his colloquial Marathi. Every time he went by Thackeray's desk, it was Iyer's pleasure to shower friendly abuse on Thackeray which Thackeray enjoyed because of the picturesque Marathi Iyer used. Long after Thackeray became the power centre of Bombay and Iyer had become but a memory (he was waylaid and killed by a mafia gang), he paid a public tribute to Iyer and Sadanand and said they were models for journalists.

For all the problems he had with the BJP and the excesses he committed in the wake of the Babri Masjid demolition, Bal Thackeray's pre-eminence remained unchallenged. He seldom travelled outside his fortress in Bandra. The world came to meet him there. He used his acerbic cartoonist's language to express his views on current affairs. He proclaimed that the country was ruled by idiots (his word). No small achievement for a reticent man who struggled to make ends meet and who remained silent even among fellow journalists because he was not educated enough to be comfortable in English. With a sense of humour that was robustly provocative and with no hesitation using devastating power, he manipulated the accidents of circumstances that came his way and reached the top. A million people assembled to bid him farewell when he died in 2012. Panchatantra outlined a basic principle in life: 'What is not possible is impossible.' Bal Thackeray showed that what was not possible was possible.

(Disclaimer: I was a colleague of Bal Thackeray for a decade at the *Free Press Journal*, my desk adjacent to his. One of his private joys was to share with me ribald cartoons he drew strictly not for publication.)

18

HARSHAD MEHTA

White Collar Criminals

Criminals in India are creative. It may be that history's most celebrated villains are the gifts of the US—Chicago's Al Capone, New York's Sicilian Families. But that was because of the power commanded by American movies and books. Look behind the publicity and we see that the big-name gangsters of America were no more than run-of-the-mill killers, blackmailers, and looters. There was no artistry, no inventiveness in their operations. In India, even ordinary criminals have the imagination to become MLAs and ministers. The extraordinary ones develop ingeniously conceptualised careers that put them above politics. To this category belonged two of India's most gifted sons, Harshad Mehta and Abdul Karim Telgi. They were very different from stars of the ordinary world of crime such as Dawood Ibrahim and Chhota Shakeel who were criminal-criminals, not gentleman-criminals. In a class that did India proud were masters of the art such as Hasan Ali Khan, B. Ramalinga Raju, and the multiple genius who masterminded the examination fraud that came to be known as the Vyapam Scam in the closing years of the 20th century.

Hasan Ali Khan was a unique case because no one knew what he was all about. He was described as a businessman, but no one knew of any company, industry, factory, or business house that he headed. He was seen at racecourses but did he own a horse, or perhaps a stud farm? Actually, nobody paid any attention to him until one day he was found to have a Swiss bank account with deposits totalling $8 billion. In 2007, some of his properties were raided, but he was arrested only after four years and that too when the Supreme Court asked why he was not being interrogated. That was the first indication that Hasan Ali was not just Hasan Ali but some kind of a frontman for much bigger folk. Then bombs started bursting. Ranking leaders of the Congress Party, the Samajwadi Party, and the Nationalist Congress Party were named in published reports as close friends of Ali. The Swiss bank declared that claims and documentation about Ali's 8-billion-dollar deposits were false. The authorities went ahead and chargesheeted Ali for money laundering and hawala deals. Whose money? Whose hawala? No questions were raised and no answers came. That is the beauty of financial crimes in India. The principals may be named but are never brought before the law while the carriers and agents are sent to jail.

The Satyam Computer Services case was an exception. It saw the bosses getting the short end of the stick. But that was not the whole story. Incorporated in 1987, Satyam quickly earned recognition as a pioneer in the information technology outsourcing field. It offered a full spectrum of services from systems management and enterprise business solutions to infrastructure handling and software management. It had offices in 55 countries and more than 30,000 employees at its peak. It was listed in the New York Stock Exchange. It was founded and led by Byrraju Ramalinga Raju and his brother Ramu Raju, scions of a wealthy Hyderabad family. They turned it into a public company in 1992 and declared their core corporate purpose: 'To leverage information, knowledge, and technology to enhance human endeavour.' In 1997 the World Economic Forum selected Satyam as one of India's most remarkable entrepreneurial companies.

Somewhat suddenly, the company started nosediving in 2008. In December that year, a senior executive of the company turned whistle-blower and sent messages to a director of the company alleging wrongdoings at the chairman's level. Word spread quickly. Realising that he would be unable to defend himself, Chairman B. Ramalinga Raju made a virtue of necessity, admitted to committing fraud and resigned on 7 January 2009. Basically, the scandal involved fraudulent accounting aimed at inflating the company's bank balances and laundering money through several hundred companies. Satyam's auditors, the famed Pricewaterhouse Coopers, would subsequently be banned for two years by SEBI. Raju was arrested and jailed, but in ways that helped soften things for him. It was the state government that handled the police action: the arrest was made three days after Raju owned up to his crime. He spent 32 months in jail as an undertrial prisoner. Fortunately for him, he had two ailments during this period that necessitated his moving to a more comfortable hospital bed—first a heart attack and then a Hepatitis C infection. In April 2015, the Raju brothers were awarded a seven-year jail sentence and a fine of ₹5.5 crore. A month later they were granted bail by a special court in Hyderabad. The best takeaway from the Satyam–Raju scandal was the addition of a new word to the English vocabulary—Andhra-preneurship.

Just as Satyam was an ordinary accounting-fraud swindle, Vyapam was a typical bribery case. It became a landmark because of the brazenness with which it was carried out and the unexplained dead bodies strewn along its path. Vyapam was the short form for Vyavasayik Pariksha Mandal, the autonomous body authorised to conduct a series of entrance examinations in Madhya Pradesh. It became enmeshed in corruption from head to foot, not simple garden-variety bribery but defiant, all-embracing wickedness that covered everything from impersonation to murder. It became a vast enterprise because it involved thousands of appointments in government and outside based on qualifying examinations. The racket developed under the patronage of a full spectrum of officials and VIPs, from teachers to ministers to a reigning governor himself. The methods employed were bold-faced and insolent. Good students and the previous year's toppers would impersonate candidates and write examinations. Incompetent candidates would pay to be seated next to brilliant dummy candidates for extensive copying. Board officials would leak answers to select candidates. Practising doctors would pretend to be students and write examinations as proxies. An impersonating candidate would get a bribe of up to a lakh of rupees. A doctor writing examinations as a proxy would earn up to 40 lakh. The fake doctors who graduated and entered the medical profession through this channel were walking death traps. In 2017, the Supreme Court cancelled the degrees of 634 'doctors'. The number of those who got away was never known. Watching from afar, the *New York Times* described it as a 'corruption scandal of astounding proportions even by India's terrible standards'. As investigations and enquiries proceeded, many who were suspected to be informants fell dead. The number of reported deaths was between 23 and 40 although unofficial sources put it above 100. These included not only 'road accident' deaths but also custodial deaths. Among them was the son of the state governor. Many arrests were made and many were bailed out. Dignitaries of the government were widely believed to have been involved in the rackets. The first FIR was filed in 2000. In 2019, the CBI filed a chargesheet in one case against 26. The saga was assured a long life.

By accepted standards, Hasan Ali Khan and Ramalinga Raju and the Vyapam VIPs were well above conventional perpetrators of crime. They would have considered activities like robbery and extortion below their dignity. To that extent, they were intelligent felons. But there is a difference between intelligence and genius. The latter appellation rightfully belonged only to Harshad Mehta and Abdul Karim Telgi, pathfinders who dwelt in the higher realms of cognition. That they hit the headlines in the 1990s was perhaps natural; few decades have been more transformative for India. Economic liberalisation saw a resurgent India taking off in new directions. At the same time, disturbing sociopolitical forces burst forth with the demolition of the Babri Masjid in 1992. An unfamiliar India began to rise with an urge to compete with the best in the world and, simultaneously, with a penchant to see its fellow citizens only through the lens of religion, caste, and languages. It was the best of times, it was the worst of times; it was the spring of hope, it was the winter of despair. Sitting in their separate observation towers, Mehta and Telgi watched it all. They were not petty men given to emotions prompted by provincialism and dogma. Progress was their watchword and progress meant money. Both were convinced that money was their birthright. As wunderkinds, they spotted openings no one else did.

No two men could have been more different in background and temperament. Mehta was urbane and pushy. Telgi was rustic and withdrawn. Mehta had the verve of a Gujarati business mind. Telgi reflected the modesty of a backward Muslim from Belgaum. Born in Rajkot, Mehta followed his father to Bombay and then to Raipur as the family struggled to make ends meet. He returned to Bombay, and, while handling odd jobs, managed to get a BCom degree. Telgi, son of a porter, eked out a living by selling vegetables on trains passing through his native place. But he used his savings to attend an English-medium school and eventually got a BCom degree. Mehta, starting out as a despatch clerk in an insurance company, mixed with the shakers and movers of Bombay's business district. Telgi's innings began as a struggling travel agent in Bombay. Imagination soon started sending both men on similar trajectories. Mehta developed into a self-assured operator with the capacity to convince others about the worth of his ideas. He found routine brokering boring but discovered unconventional possibilities. Telgi's course was tougher. As a travel agent he had to procure various documents for his clients, from ID cards and marksheets to visas and birth certificates. He resorted to shortcuts, but some of the fake visas he issued landed him in jail in 1992. That became the turning point of his life.

When a stipulation was introduced in the 1990s that banks should invest a minimum amount in government bonds, Harshad Mehta's imagination took wing. The rule meant that money had to move from place to place. Mehta figured out ways for the money to move from one place to another through him. The bankers would be helped to meet their obligations and, by operating through him, make a profit on the sidelines. What made it worthwhile for him was that while the banks moved their moneys, some amount always stayed with him for short durations. During those interludes he would invest the money in shares and reap profits. Everything sounded proper. Then, out of the blue as it were, business journalist Sucheta Dalal quoted chapter and verse to show that Mehta's deals were full of holes. What stood revealed was a complicated arrangement that Mehta had worked out to channel money from the banking system to his transactions in the stock market. In April 1992, Sucheta wrote: 'The crucial mechanism was the ready forward (RF) deal. RF is in essence a secured short-term (typically 15 days) loan from one bank to another. Crudely put, the bank lends against government securities just as a pawn broker lends against jewellery. The borrowing bank actually sells the securities to the lending bank and buys them back at the end of the period of the loan, typically at a slightly higher price. It was this RF deal that Mehta and his accomplices used with great success to channel money from the banking system.' (*The Scam: Who Won, Who Lost, Who Got Away*, written by Sucheta Dalal and Debashish Basu remains the definitive record of the Harshad Mehta escapade.)

The going was good for Mehta while it lasted. His address changed to the patrician precinct of Worli Seaface where a 15,000-square-feet penthouse catered to his desires. His fleet of luxury limousines became the talk of the town because most of the brands he imported were unfamiliar to 1990s Bombay. The media lapped him up as the 'Big Bull'. A Delhi magazine put his face on the cover with the title 'Raging Bull'. Some called him the 'Amitabh Bachchan of the Stock Market'. But the house of cards crumbled when he was arrested in 1992, and charged with 72 criminal offences and 600 civil action suits. In 1999, he was sentenced to five years rigorous imprisonment. Between the first arrest and the final sentencing, he had tried to make a comeback as a market guru and even as a newspaper columnist. In June 1993, he created a sensation by saying that he had taken suitcases containing a crore of rupees to Prime Minister P.V. Narashimha Rao as a donation to the party. Rao denied it. In the end nothing worked for Mehta. Lodged in Thane Central Jail, he grew bald rapidly and developed health problems. He was moved to the civil hospital following chest pains and died there in 2001. He was 47. Death did not strip him of his mantle. His dexterous ways of juggling rules continued to win admirers in the Stock Market. Two Bollywood movies were based on his life, *Aankhein* (1993) and *Gafla* (2006). Most recently, there was a critically acclaimed series by filmmaker Hansal Mehta, *Scam 1992*. The name Harshad Mehta is unlikely to disappear from the collective memory of the business world in the foreseeable future.

Living a life very different from Harshad Mehta's and at a different social level, Abdul Karim Telgi experienced his epiphany in jail in 1992. A fellow prisoner was impressed by the initiative Telgi had shown in forging travel documents his clients needed. If you could make fake visas, he told young Telgi, you could as well make fake stamp papers. That was the first time Telgi paid attention to the role stamp papers played in the lives of Indians. He realised that this seldom noticed piece of official paper was playing a central role in practically every sphere of human activity. Financial deals, legal agreements, affidavits, power of attorney papers, contracts, declarations, wills and testaments, marriage certificates—there is hardly any human-to-human transaction that does not require stamped papers of various denominations and colours. There are also judicial and non-judicial stamp papers, court fee stamps, revenue stamps, notary stamps, insurance agency stamps, and stamps for freight bills and share transfer certificates. The authenticity of these papers is considered so vital that only a specially equipped government security press is authorised to print them. Their printing and distribution are handled with utmost care and safety precautions. Individuals who buy stamp papers have their names and other details entered on the paper each time.

Telgi was fascinated. Quick to grasp the possibilities stamp papers opened up, he went about the task of qualifying himself for the adventure. He acquired a vendor licence from the Bombay government. He then acquired a specialised, not-available-to-the-public stamp paper printing machine from, who else, but the Indian Security Printing Press in Nashik. The high-security establishment was not supposed to do any such thing, but Telgi had by now proved that he was special. For him, specialised technicians from the government press in Nashik set up the machinery and helped him get stocks of the special paper and inks, and even the security marks used exclusively by the Nashik establishment. What Telgi did was to duplicate the Government of India in his own way. Of course, he could not have done it alone. He not only acquired government employees of the Nashik press as his partners, he also had political leaders and police bosses actively assisting him, among them a Maharashtra home minister and a Bombay City police commissioner.

Telgi was very professional in running his industry. A network of about 350 agents ensured that the stamp papers reached designated officers such as brokerage firms and corporate headquarters. He also devised ways to create a scarcity of authentic stamp papers thereby creating a market for the duplicates that he supplied. The business spread to several parts of India and the profits poured in. Along with Telgi, hundreds of his associates and helpers from the political, bureaucratic, and police worlds prospered. The good days would have continued but for a chance discovery by a Bangalore police officer who was apparently not part of the network. He looked into the case of two men who were transporting stamp papers in the old business district of the city and were arrested on a tip-off. He discovered fake stamp papers worth about ₹9 crore. One thing led to another and Telgi was in jail in 2001. But the man's support system was so reliable that he continued his operations from prison using mobile phones. He did it so cleverly that the police could not catch him or stop him. Ironically, the High Court convicted two prison officials for supplying mobile phones to prisoner Telgi. Even a narco test failed to gather any information from him. When he was drugged, he told a police officer years later, he was fully aware of his surroundings and the questions that were being asked. Other reports claimed that he had mentioned top political leaders as being his associates. Nothing came of the interrogations or the fresh inquiry the CBI subsequently conducted. Some police officials who had been arrested on charges of being Telgi's accomplices were set free for want of evidence. Telgi himself was sentenced to various terms of imprisonment on various charges. When it was running, the Telgi empire seemed to have hundreds of people pushing it forward. When it stopped running, Telgi was alone. He stayed in prison, but his former police friends and political partners ensured that he had all the basic comforts he needed. They could do little about his poor health. He had many problems including diabetes, hypertension, and AIDS. On top all that, 16 years in Bangalore's Parappana Agrahara Central Prison took its toll. Although his friends had ensured proper medical attention, enforced prison life only added to his problems. In October 2017, he was moved to Victoria Hospital following multiple organ failure and meningitis. He died there, aged 56.

But he had a kind of last laugh a year after his death. On 31 December 2018, the Nashik sessions court abated charges against him. The dictionary meaning of the term 'abate' is to quash (a writ or action), put an end to (a nuisance). The dead Telgi must no doubt have felt relieved that charges against him were quashed and he was saved from nuisance. His co-accused, too, were acquitted for want of solid evidence. Among them were officers of the railways' security and parcel divisions. The verdict reminded some people who knew Telgi of the philosopher in him. He never maligned others, they said. He was always friendly, always had a smile on his face. When he was transferred to Bangalore Central Jail, Telgi admitted his guilt and said: 'I am the only breadwinner in my family. I am suffering from various ailments that have no cure.' On his way to jail, he told an investigating official: 'Money is very bad, sir. It makes a man as well as destroys him.' It did not destroy Abdul Karim Telgi. It made him a man tall enough to become a footnote in history.

19

RAGHURAJ PRATAP SINGH AND JANARDHANA REDDY

Money, la-la-la!

Adult franchise made Indian democracy dependent on money and crime. Canvassing votes among largely disadvantaged adults meant addressing the realities that dominated their lives—poverty and religion. Money helped manipulate both. Where uncertainties reared their heads or rivals gained strength, nothing proved more effective than a gangster's helping hand. India rapidly emerged as a democracy where a high-calibre Election Commission was routinely outmanoeuvred by wily financiers and resourceful criminals.

When Indira Gandhi split the Congress in 1969 and found herself in need of big money to put muscle into her half of the party, she initiated policies that eventually made crony capitalists powerful enough to influence the appointment of cabinet ministers and the framing of budgets. Telephone conversations exposing how fixers fixed such things shook the nation in 2002 (the Radia Tapes) and again in 2016 (the Essar Tapes). Conditions in India were reminiscent of what the Andrews Sisters described in a classic hit of the 1940s, although nobody paid attention to the solution suggested in the lyric itself. 'La-la-la' sang the popular Andrews trio. 'Money is the root of all evil/ Won't contaminate myself with it/ Take it away, take it away, take it away.' Why were they confident that they wouldn't contaminate themselves with it? Because they saw the value of what they had been given them for free. 'I got the one I love/ I got the moon and stars above/ I got my youth and health/ What do I want with wealth?' How innocent were the 1940s.

Innocence can be foolishness in public affairs. Liquor being an essential commodity in human society, Prohibition in America in 1920 provided an opportunity for criminal gangs to take over its distribution. Al Capone was best at it because he was ruthless; he would beat people to death with baseball bats. The growth of 'organised crime' was a direct result of Prohibition. The Indian experience was exactly the same. Prohibition brought organised crime syndicates to Bombay.

With Indira Gandhi herself misusing power, elected representative saw the illegal and the unethical as legitimate exercises of democracy. Uttar Pradesh's Raghuraj Pratap Singh (brand name, Raja Bhaiya) and Karnataka's Janardhana Reddy became symbols of the new culture. Raja Bhaiya turned to politics when he turned 20, holding janta darbars at his sprawling home in Kunda in Pratapgarh district. It was in effect a court of law where villagers, their heads bowed and knees shaking, would have their problems settled by the rules of instant justice. The reputation for ruthlessness established by the darbars was reinforced when the Bhaiya started collecting taxes from the people in his 'kingdom'. A Muslim boy, back home after education in Bombay, refused to pay this extra-legal tax. Raja Bhaiya's storm troopers set fire to homes in his village, raped some Muslim girls, then cut off their limbs and threw them into a river; the Bombay-returned boy was tied to a jeep and dragged around the roads.

In the feudal, lawless hinterland of UP, home of a 'kill-or-be-killed culture' as *India Today* magazine once put it, Raja Bhaiya emerged as a virtual king. When he stood for election, no one dared to speak against him. Those who did in the early days mysteriously disappeared. Legends grew about a pool—some called it a lake—in his Kunda compound. It was a fact that he kept pet crocodiles in the pool. It was a fact that terror-struck villagers used to whisper about Raja Bhaiya's enemies being fed to the crocodiles. But no one could come up with any conclusive proof. Chief Minister Mayawati once had the pool emptied and dug up. A few hundred skeletons were discovered. Did that prove anything? The Bhaiya himself said in an interview: 'It's folklore and nothing else.'

UP's BJP Chief Minister Kalyan Singh called Raja Bhaiya 'Kunda ke goonda'. Kalyan Singh then became the first chief minister to take the goonda into the state cabinet. Then Mulayam Singh Yadav's Samajawadi Party adopted him. Raja Bhaiya, facing cases of murder, kidnapping, assault, land grabbing, and possession of illegal weapons, such as AK-47s, became Minister for Programme Implementation (1997), Minister for Sports and Youth Welfare (1999), Minister for Food and Civil Supplies (2005), and senior minister in Akhilesh Singh Yadav's cabinet (2012). He had to abruptly quit the last posting following the murder of a DSP who had gone to investigate a fracas in Pratapgarh. The complaint filed by the DSP's wife said he was beaten up and then shot by Raja Bhaiya's henchmen. Raja Bhaiya professed innocence. He had done the same five years earlier when another DSP, assigned to investigate a case under the Prevention of Terrorism Act against Raja Bhaiya was killed in a road accident. Everyone knew about the accident in such detail that Raja Bhaiya had to be relieved of his arduous ministerial responsibilities, but only for a while. He was not arrested; and he went on to enjoy his leisure pursuits, horse riding, microlite aircrafts, foreign jaunts, and, when he had the time, admiring his pet crocodiles.

Janardhana Reddy, youngest of three brothers from Bellary, was also the most daring. In his 20s he became a chit fund agent and started a Kannada news daily. Both collapsed. But he realised that political connections were essential to get ahead in life. He formed a firm alliance with the Congress chief minister of Andhra Pradesh. In Karnataka he hobnobbed with the Congress first, then switched to the BJP, where he became a kingmaker.

Since the border town of Bellary was in India's richest iron ore region, Janardhana Reddy had a foot in the mining business, as a transport contractor and a labour supplier. In 2001 the skies—or should we say the earth—opened up for him. Unprecedented demand for iron ore came from China, in the throes of massive construction for the 2008 Olympics. Janardhana Reddy acquired a number of iron ore companies and began a round-the-clock operation of exporting ore through a port of Goa. Many of his licences and his transport operations were illegal. He even forcibly removed the border markers between Karnataka and Andhra Pradesh along with a tribal temple so that he could freely mine in both the states. With his friend as chief minister of Andhra Pradesh, there was no one to stop him. Locals whose farmland was taken over to make way for a helipad for the Reddys, and hutment dwellers who were asked to move elsewhere so that the area surrounding the Reddy mansion would look more gracious, had no choice but to obey. The Reddys did not have a crocodile pool, but reports occasionally appeared of people who drowned in knee-deep water. In five years, Janardhana Reddy's mining company reported a turnover of ₹3,000 crore.

But an unexpected problem cropped up. His income rose, according to published reports, to ₹5 crore a day. Spending that kind of money is not easy, even for politicians. Janardhana Reddy set his sights high, singlehandedly financing the formation of the first BJP government in southern India with the intention of making his older brother, Karunakara Reddy, the chief minister. He also spent heavily in Delhi with the undeclared—but not disowned—objective of making his chosen BJP leader the prime minister. Neither the chief ministership nor the prime ministership worked out the way he wanted. But the way he spent money to achieve his ends became a topic of envy.

Even after big-ticket expenses, there was too much left and more poured in; cash at the rate of 5 crore a day has a way of accumulating rather inconveniently. Routine acquisitions such as helicopters and Rolls-Royces tend to get boring after a while. Janardhana Reddy tried out new ways to spend money—custom-made tableware, gold bathroom fittings, and arrays of religious trinkets. Among the items the CBI took away when they raided his mansion were solid-gold idols that filled his puja room, gold utensils, 610 gold bangles, 35 of them diamond-encrusted, 300 pairs of earrings (75 of them diamonds), 1,200 gold rings of which 100 were set with diamonds, several bracelets, and platinum jewellery. According to an *India Today* report, he had an indoor swimming pool in which he would float and watch movies on a 70-mm screen. Gold thread was woven into his bespoke shirts which cost a lakh each. He wore a jewel-encrusted belt worth ₹13 lakh and carried a gold-plated Blackberry.

The magazine also referred to the local lore that Janardhana Reddy considered himself a reincarnation of the 14th century Vijayanagar king, Krishnadevaraya, and had himself crowned at a secret ceremony in Hampi, capital of the old empire. That would explain why he had a golden throne made to specifications, weighing 15 kilograms, monogrammed GJR in diamonds and costing ₹2.2 crore according to a CBI estimate. He had also donated a ₹43-crore crown to the Tirupati temple. Local talk in Bellary was that there were two identical crowns and one remained with Reddy after it had been used at the Hampi crowning. But Reddy was more down to earth than Krishnadevaraya. According to *India Today*: 'An estimated ₹5,000 crore was suspected to be salted away in tax havens including the Isle of Man.' Reddy was arrested in 2011 and taken to the central prison in Hyderabad. There he was served jail khichdi in a steel plate.

The Raja Bhaiyas and Janardhana Reddys were by no means exceptions. In 2009, 30 per cent of Lok Sabha members had criminal cases against them. In 2014, when Narendra Modi was seen as the harbinger of a new dawn, the criminally tainted accounted for 34 per cent of the Lok Sabha. According to studies by the National Election Watch and the Association for Democratic Reforms, candidates with criminal cases had 13 per cent chances of winning in the 2014 Lok Sabha election while the chances for candidates with a clean record was 5 per cent—an invitation for aspiring leaders of the country to start their careers with crime.

As irony would have it, leading legislators with criminal records claimed to be followers of RSS idealist, Nanaji Deshmukh. Addressing what he called his last political rally before withdrawing from public life, the widely respected Nanaji, then 62, said in Bihar in 1978 that party workers should retire from politics at the age of 60 and turn to social service, allowing younger people to come up. He did not see any of his colleagues in any state doing what he suggested. Instead, he saw them exploring every avenue to stay on in power and make money. He then published a pamphlet addressed to 'the country's elite'. The burden of his theme was that 'the so-called representatives of the people were shamelessly increasing their perks and perquisites'. Recalling that we had 543 MPs in the Lok Sabha, 245 in the Rajya Sabha and 5,269 MLAs in the various states, he warned: 'Let us not forget that monarchy became an object of hatred when misrule and the misuse of authority by the kings became unbearable with rulers spending the bulk of state revenues for their pleasures and enjoyments.'

Wise words, wasted words.

20

DAWOOD IBRAHIM

Most Wanted, Never Caught

For two hours and ten minutes in March 1993, bombs exploded at prominent landmarks across Bombay city, killing 257 people by an official count. A clutch of landmarks were smashed, changing the face of the city for ever. The Bombay Stock Exchange was reduced to a ruin. The iconic Air-India building at the southern end of Marine Drive and Sea Rock Hotel at the northern end of the city were mangled. The Plaza Cinema caught fire. So did Century Bazaar owned by the Birlas. There was no attempt by the perpetrators to remain anonymous; everyone knew that the underground mafia led by Dawood Ibrahim was seeking revenge for the demolition of Babri Masjid. Dawood entered the 'wanted' list in India and the US. Both countries labelled him 'the unapprehended mobster and drug dealer'. But it did not bother him: he had escaped to the UAE and then Pakistan where he was assured of safety.

Why do some countries provide protection to people other countries consider dangerous? Obviously the definitions of crime vary from society to society. This works to the advantage of gangsters. Dawood Ibrahim Kaskar was born in Khed, Ratnagiri. But he is identified with Dongri, a wretched Muslim ghetto in the wretched nucleus of Bombay. Life in Dongri centred round a market area called Thieves' Bazaar. It is Dongri's pride that Bombay's celebrated Mafia dons, Karim Lala and Haji Mastan, started out from its bristling, heartless dens. Their success turned Dongri into a legend of terrorism, murder on order, extortion, and drug trading. Liberal in its outlook, Dongri gave opportunities to small dons as well as big ones.

Dawood Ibrahim was the biggest of them all. No underworld figure attracted as much public attention. This was in spite of the absolute domination the other dons exerted in their prime. Karim Lala and Haji Mastan and Varadarajan Mudaliar exercised powers the prime ministers of the country could not.

Karim Lala was born Abdul Karim Sher Khan in the Kunar province of Afghanistan. He became King of the Docks in Bombay when Bombay was India's principal centre of international trade. Groups associated with him were known as the Afghan Mafia or Pathan Mafia because most of its members were ethnic Pashtuns from Afghanistan. They operated protection rackets and illegal gambling as well as the usual gangland businesses of gold smuggling and contract killings. Lala was the undisputed king of bootlegging and gambling in Bombay for as long as four decades beginning from the 1940s. Haji Mastan, with Tamil roots, was Bombay's first celebrity gangster. He was 8 years old when the family moved from Ramanathapuram in Tamil Nadu to Bombay where a cycle repair shop near Crawford Market became their source of livelihood. When he was about 18, Mastan became a porter in the Bombay Docks where mafia dons controlled most activities. He joined the gangs. Smuggling made him rich. He put a good bit of his money into film production, becoming an influence in Bollywood as well. His career ran parallel to that of Varadarajan Mudaliar aka Vardha Bhai. He too was a porter, though at Bombay's VT railway station. He found it easy to steal some of the cargo he was assigned to move. This made him rich and he expanded his activities to include extortion, kidnapping, and killing. Thanks to Morarji Desai's declaration of prohibition in the state, Bombay became India's principal centre of organised crime syndicates. Mafia chieftains wielded extraordinary power. When Vardha Bhai died in Tamil Nadu in 1988, Haji Mastan brought his body to Bombay in a chartered Indian Airlines plane for the last rites, as the dead man had wished. When the body arrived in Bombay, life came to a standstill in areas where South Indians were a notable presence, such as Matunga, Sion, Koliwada, and Dharavi. Amrish Puri's portrayal of a character called Varadarajan in *Mashaal* (1984) was just one of the tributes the film industry paid to the crime lord's memory.

In Dawood's case, crime was a family tradition. His father had laid the foundations of success in this field. Dawood Pere was a policeman. His understanding of policemanship was that it was meant to help entrepreneurs. Since gangsterism involved entrepreneurship of a high order, he developed close personal links with the gangsters of his time. That was how the Dawood empire came to include the kingdoms of Chhota Shakeel, Tiger Memon, Yakub Memon, Abu Salem, and Fazal Sheikh—the D-Company, as the media admiringly referred to them. A US Congressional report in 2015 said the D-Company was a 5,000-member criminal syndicate with strategic ties extending to the ISI, Lashkar-e-Taiba, and Al-Qaeda. Dawood won distinction when he became third on the FBI's list of the world's most wanted fugitives. They announced a reward of $25 million for his capture. India placed a similar reward separately. But neither the FBI nor India got anything for these efforts. Only Bollywood seemed to benefit with a clutch of movies, from *Shootout at Lokhandwala* (2007) to *Once Upon a Time in Mumbai* (2010). An outfit called Z-Company appeared in Salman Rushdie's 2018 novel, *The Golden House*. A shop selling casual clothing smartly named itself D-Company.

Clearly, Dawood Ibrahim was not just another criminal. His style was different and so was his presumed ambition. His very first crime marked him out as someone special. He waylaid a courier of none other than Haji Mastan, snatching a prize of goods worth $2,00,000. That hit made him popular with the police because the police had failed to grab Haji Mastan. The wealth Dawood amassed through his adventures was beyond imagination. Those were days when India's economy was in the doldrums and all kinds of restrictions were imposed on citizens. For Dawood, restriction meant opportunity. He benefited so much that at one point he bailed out Pakistan's Central Bank with a big loan. No other mafia don has shown such incredible clout.

Even after Dawood, the D-Company remained a presence in Bombay, active in smuggling, fixing cricket matches and extorting Bollywood stars. A US academic report described it as 'a transactional criminal organisation, a terrorist group and an economic actor' that remained 'both a national and regional security threat for South Asia'. The D-Company perhaps saw this as high praise.

Like any citizen, Dawood probably saw himself as working for the betterment of his family. He no doubt had his dreams, otherwise he would not have named his children in the M format—Mahruk, Moin, Maria, Mehreen. Wherever he lived, his residence was named White House. His life and work were significant enough to inspire journalist Hussain Zaidi to produce a series of books, among them: *Dongri to Dubai: Six Decades of the Mumbai Mafia* (2012) and *Byculla to Bangkok* (2014). The links Dawood established with Bollywood were durable. The role of the underworld in the Indian film industry became public when the inexperienced Sanjay Dutt was caught in its tentacles and jailed. His crime was association with Chhota Shakeel. Stars with no such association were also under pressure. Shah Rukh Khan said in an interview that he had been pressured by the mafia into acting in a particular movie. A photo of Anil Kapoor standing beside Dawood at a cricket match in Dubai was widely publicised.

Dawood's escape to safer shores did not put a stop to the legends associated with him. In February 2021, Parkar Chambers in Bombay's Nagpada area was attached by the government as property owned by Dawood. Ahmed Vazir Parkar's petition that the property was his, was rejected by the civil court. In 1996, tax authorities attached it for recovery of ₹40,51,77,942 due from Dawood for the assessment year 1990–1991. When Ahmed Parkar came to know of this in 2000, he objected. The court ruled that it was benami property owned by Dawood. The Income Tax Department told the court: 'Dawood Ibrahim Kaskar, main accused in the Bombay bomb blast case had forcibly acquired 23 properties in Bombay in the names of his family members, relatives, associates who did not have an independent source of income.' The court ruled that Ahmed Parkar was only a lessee of the building with no ownership rights over the property. In January 2021, the Narcotics Central Bureau apprehended Arif Bhujwala, a Dawood associate and 'one of the most-wanted drug lords of Mumbai' who had been on the run after his makeshift laboratory manufacturing drugs was raided. 'Dawood' was a name the echoes of which just wouldn't go away.

21

INDIRA GANDHI AND RAJIV GANDHI

Iblis Leads the Way

After a generation of lathi charges, firings, and imprisonment in the British Raj, was it wrong if Indians found freedom overwhelming? Freedom meant power. And power was magic. Overnight, as it were, a whole world of opportunities opened up. Many seniors saw it as a time to enjoy themselves after a lifetime of sacrifice. For younger elements, it was simply a chance to use their connections. Ambitions flowered; prosperity beckoned. Were the mysterious laws of a mysterious destiny also at work? The Urdu novelist and filmmaker, Ismat Chughtai, gave a peppery account of how she was taught the history of evolution during her college days in Aligarh.

'Kun fayakun,' God Almighty said, 'let there be light,' and the world came into existence. Then Hazrat Adam was created and the angels were asked to prostrate before him. The chief of the angels, Iblis, was bent upon rebellion. He refused to prostrate before an ordinary lump of clay. But he was given permission to lead human beings astray as long as the world lasted.

With the Almighty himself commissioning Iblis to mislead humans, what chance was there for political leaders, utterly human, to go straight? For a while after the republic started on its journey on 26 January 1950, the old values held. Confidence reigned among leaders. Jawaharlal Nehru's cabinets, India's first coalition governments, included stalwarts who would stand up to him. Nehru, despite his professed socialism, was bold enough—or rash enough—to accommodate known capitalist roaders like Morarji Desai and S.K. Patil in key portfolios. In the states he never felt threatened by local chieftains who ran their fiefdoms with a strong hand, such as Partap Singh Kairon in Punjab, D.P. Mishra in Madhya Pradesh and B.C. Roy in Bengal. Nehru's mass appeal was never dimmed by the contrarian policies many of his colleagues followed. It was his self-assurance and his faith in the people that helped him run a multiplex democracy reasonably well.

Ironic as it might seem, things started changing after Indira Gandhi became prime minister in 1966. She was no less popular than her father, but she lacked his self-confidence, a hangover of childhood trauma. It is part of the Indira lore that she grew up lonely and insecure at her father's mansion in Allahabad, resenting the way her mother was isolated for not being Westernised. She herself was a target of attack by her father's sister, Vijayalakshmi Pandit, who once called her 'ugly and stupid'. Whatever the reason, Indira used power in ways very different from her father's. She carved her own party out of the parent Congress, neutralised senior leaders perceived as rivals, got rid of Congress chieftains in the states who had their own independent stature, surrounded herself with loyal henchmen, and finally decided that she could completely trust only her immediate family. People seemed to accept it all. After her, Rajiv Gandhi was accepted as the rightful heir to the prime ministerial chair. After Rajiv, his widow was begged by emotionally agitated Congress leaders to become prime minister. Overcoming an initial attack of fear, Sonia seemed willing, but eventually chose to put a nominee on the chair while retaining overriding power and grooming her son, Rahul, for the prime ministership.

Perhaps the centuries-old experience of 565 princely states up until 1947 eased the way for the acceptance of family rule. The paterfamilias who established democracy's royal lines saw no contradiction between precept and practice. Hailed by their subjects, they went from strength to strength—the Karunanidhi family of Tamil Nadu, the Karunakaran family of Kerala, the Deve Gowda and Yeddyurappa families of Karnataka, the Rajasekhara Reddy family of Andhra, the Pawar and Thackeray families of Maharashtra, the Badal family of Punjab, the Chautala family of Haryana, the Abdullah family of Kashmir, the Mulayam Singh family of Uttar Pradesh, the Lalu Prasad family of Bihar. Biju Patnaik, internationalist hero of Orissa, sent his children abroad in the hope that they would not be defiled by politics. Yet, son Naveen, so foreign that he could not even speak the mother tongue, walked into the chief ministership of the state and remained unshakable.

At work was the simple principle recorded in the *Chandokya Upanishad:* 'He who knows the Supreme One becomes supreme himself.' The Supreme One in India was Indira Gandhi, followed by Rajiv Gandhi. Those who became Supreme by knowing them were Yashpal Kapur, R.K. Dhawan, M.O. Mathai, and Vincent George. All did well. V. George, winner of the 'Fastest Typist in Kerala' prize (120 words a minute), went to Delhi, landed a job in the Congress Party office, and rose to positions of power that made people call him King George. In March 2001, the CBI registered a case against him on charges of amassing wealth disproportionate to his known income sources. The agency said that since 1990, when George ceased to be a public servant, there had been a quantum jump in the assets of his wife and two children. His wife, Lilly, was a nurse in Kuwait who returned to Delhi when the Gulf War broke out. According to the CBI, she owned two firms which closed down in 1992. The agency said that even during his tenure as secretary to Rajiv Gandhi, in 1984–1990, he had received cash from foreign countries, especially the US—₹12.5 million in November 1991, ₹4.1 million in December 1991, ₹7 million in December 1992 and ₹2 million in March 1995. He paid ₹8.5 million by cheque for a house in Anand Niketan. He owned two shops at the World Trade Centre in Connaught Place. George countered the charges by saying that he bought everything with the earnings of his wife's two companies. But CBI said Lilliens Exports and Diana Agencies were active only in 1991–1992. George's supporters saw nothing improper in his affairs. As one of them put it: 'His brothers-in-law are well-off businessmen in the US. They own a hotel chain there. Most of the money came from them.'

The charges nonetheless were serious by any yardstick. But, as is the case with many serious matters, what should have happened did not happen. In fact, to the shock of many, the CBI filed a closure report in 2013. In a bigger shock, the trial court rejected the closure report and ordered a trial. But George went to the Delhi High Court and won a stay order. Noting that this happened during Narendra Modi's watch, political observers asked what was the CBI's advocate doing when Vincent George was arguing against the trial court's order. Months and years passed and the CBI did not even appeal.

Disappointing signals came from the wielders of power, whether it was the Congress or the BJP. If hope still persisted among citizens, it was due to the foundations laid by the early practitioners of democracy. Two factors stood out. Firstly, for all the feudal residue of history, the idea of the Constitution and the supremacy of the people had taken root in the psyche of citizens, especially the middle class; the idea was continuously refurbished by the efforts of the judiciary, civil society, and the media. Secondly, prosperity broke out.

When the economy opened up in the 1990s, initially many failed to comprehend its implications. The wise had always known about the potential of India. 'I am a short-term pessimist and long-term optimist,' J.R.D. Tata had said. In the midst of feeling tormented by the injustices and hypocrisies of India's ruling class, Nani Palkhivala never lost and opportunity to talk about 'my unquenchable confidence in the long-term future of India'. In 2005, private spending in India reached about $372 billion, accounting for more than 60 per cent of the GDP. Average household incomes were estimated to triple in the next two decades, making India the world's fifth largest consumer economy by 2025. An astonished world paused to acknowledge a new India.

While the real growth story began with liberalisation, entrepreneurs had started pushing their way through earlier. The so-called Old Money joined forces with a New Spirit to explore uncharted seas. Dhirubhai Ambani, a true rags-to-riches legend, created an equity cult in the Indian capital market that had been unimaginable. He ended up heading the country's largest private sector company. Along the way, he devised ways to manipulate the system of controls that prevailed then. In other words, he defied the law. What was perceived as illegal activities by him later won him praise.

New blood also began to make a difference. Ambani and Mittal, Tata and Birla, Mahindra and Godrej, Ruia and Dhoot—at least had business genes in them, hailing as they did from what were known as traditional business communities. Towards the 1980s, a new kind of kid came into town. No one noticed it when some unknown South Indians were found knocking at inhospitable doors in Delhi. Travelling to the national capital and spending days waiting for doors there to open meant considerable expense for them in time and money. But those dream-driven men had no choice because they needed nods of approval from Delhi to import badly needed equipment or get an operational licence. They persisted and somehow managed to get what they wanted. Suddenly, information technology, biochemicals, pharmaceutical research, and low-cost airlines became game-changers in India, and names like N.R. Narayana Murthy, Kiran Mazumdar-Shaw, Anji Reddy and G.R. Gopinath acquired the glow of business magic. (Recalling his early days at Infosys, Narayana Murthy put things graphically. 'Of the 21 years of my CEO-ship, about 11 years were lost in darkness. I used to make fifty visits to Delhi for small things. We did not have current account convertibility; we could not open offices. To import even a small thing, it required huge efforts.') It was the singlemindedness of the entrepreneurs and professionals that gave a new dimension to India's economic thrust. Once that thrust gathered momentum, politicians, parties, and bureaucrats vied with one another to claim credit.

Seven wealthy towns contend for Homer dead
Through which the living Homer begged his bread.

The Dalai Lama once said: 'In Chinese Parliament there is too much silence and in Indian Parliament there is too much noise.' In late-2010, Pranab Mukherjee hardly meant it as a compliment when he said 'our democracy has become too noisy'. He was referring to accusations and counter-accusations filling the political space and Parliament grinding to a noisy halt on each of that session's 23 working days. With the instrumentalities of Parliament becoming ineffective, democracy did begin to look rather over-ambitious for India—the exact opposite of the confidence that led to the erudite debates and the Constitution in 1950. The learned men who shaped those debates had set their sights high for India and India had risen to their expectations in the early phase of its journey. In a few years, we lost that India.

That would not have surprised Winston Churchill, who bore a grudge against India for demanding independence. When the Indian Independence Act was debated in the House of Commons in June 1947, Britain's ranking imperialist used wounding words to put a curse upon the new nation: 'Power will go to the hands of rascals, rogues, freebooters; all Indian leaders will be of low calibre and men of straw. They will have sweet tongues and silly hearts. They will fight among themselves for power and India will be lost in political squabbles.'

Everyone knew that the spell of the imperial curse needed to be broken. The problem was that nobody knew how to do it in the midst of personal ambitions and ideological hypocrisy.

22

RAHUL GANDHI

Growing Old vs Growing Up

Rahul Gandhi's problem was that he had to grow up with the world watching. To understand why it was a problem, we must remember Walt Disney's words. In the process of creating the angry Donald Duck and the easy-going Mickey Mouse, Disney must have acquired a good deal of pragmatic wisdom. 'Growing old is mandatory, growing up is optional,' he said. Both are easily handled if they happen in anonymity, as they do for most people. But Rahul belongs to the 1 per cent. He had to grow old and grow up with all of India watching. Naturally, many Indians thought that the mandatory part was happening while the optional was not. That is politics. You cannot be 100 per cent right even when you are 100 per cent right.

Birth and circumstances took his independence away. He could not walk into a shop or a garden or a friend's house without two black-shirted men in dark glasses shadowing him. But he did not allow that to stop him from doing what he wanted to. On a visit to Malabar, he took autorickshaws to Kalpetta and Kozhikode. No doubt he was aware of the public relations value of travelling in autos. He got into a fully photographed conversation with an auto driver, sitting on the front seat for the chat. In a Facebook Post, he noted: 'Got a chance to interact with Shareef V.V. an auto driver brother in Kalpetta. His concerns about the rising fuel prices need urgent redressal. Millions of hardworking people are suffering because of the central government's tax extortion.'

Rahul has developed a style that makes him look like the guy next door. Hence his sudden appearance one day at a tea stall in Kannur district, for instance, where he got into a conversation with a fellow customer who happened to be Advait Sumesh, all of nine years old. 'What is your ambition in life?' the visitor asked the local. 'I want to fly,' said the smart Kannurkaran to the Delhiwallah. 'My dream is to become a pilot.' Rising to the occasion, Rahul arranged for Advait and his father to go to the airport. There, Rahul took Advait inside his chartered aircraft. The boy was awestruck. Containing his excitement, he asked how this complex machine actually flew. The pilot explained as best he could. Rahul's post noted that it was his 'duty to create a society that will give him every opportunity to fly'. With his every-day, run-of-the-mill activities, the young Congressman makes a good impression on people who like the humility he projects.

He may have speech-writers, like all politicians do. But some of his remarks sound so natural they could just as well be his, and not a career writer's. You don't need a speech-writer to say: 'India is too big a country to be run by one person.' Or, 'We need to empower everybody. Not one person, not almost everybody, but everybody.' He speaks like an insider who understands intricacy. 'Congress is a funny party. It is the largest political organisation in the world, but does not a have a single rule. We create new rules every two minutes and then dump them.' He understood his India very well. 'It doesn't matter how much wisdom you have,' he said. 'If you don't have position, you have nothing. That's the tragedy of India.' But what exactly did he mean when he said: 'India is the Saudi Arabia of the 21st century'? Saudi Arabia has many faces, some of them reassuring, many of them intimidating. Not many Indians are likely to want their country to be Saudi Arabia.

Ultimately, though, Rahul has to live with the reality of his being the prince of a family that considers power as its ancestral right. He was amateurish to begin with, but he learned how to cope. Elected MP at the age of 34, he became general secretary of the Congress in 2007 and vice president from 2013 to 2017. During these dozen years, he made headlines by suddenly disappearing from public view without any explanation. Gossip filled the air. Most of the inferences centred around the possibility of romantic links abroad. (He admitted in 2004 that he had a Spanish girlfriend. In 2013, he said he might not get married at all.) The sudden and rather frequent absences spurred guessing games that had an edge of mockery. He was branded a part-time politician. He had gone to Bangkok, some would say. No, to Greece, others would claim. No, to Uttarakhand, yet another lot would proclaim. No, he was at a meditation camp, said others. In a rare instance, he went away after a proper announcement. In June 2017 he tweeted: 'Will be travelling to meet my grandmother and family for a few days. Looking forward to spending time with them.' That was fine, except that he was winging away when he was in the midst of a campaign for farmers' rights. Congressmen were frustrated by their leader's apparent lack of sensitivity and his proclivity to cut himself off when it pleased him to do so. His inept approach to leadership reached a climax in 2013 after the Manmohan Singh government issued an ordinance to save convicted legislators from disqualification. The vice president of the ruling party barged into a Congress press conference uninvited and said the ordinance was 'complete nonsense [which] should be torn up and thrown away'. He then proceeded to tear up a copy he had with him and threw it away. Then he dramatically left the scene. Never was a ruling prime minister so directly humiliated, and so publicly, by his own party. Inherited power was showing its freedom to be irresponsible.

In the second half of 2017, even as he was being persuaded to take up the presidentship of the party, Rahul Gandhi began to show signs that he was growing up. He visited the University of California, Berkeley in September that year. Preparations for a US 'think tank' tour had begun more than a year earlier. Initiated by the small but distinguished PhD class within the Congress, with men like Sam Pitroda and Shashi Tharoor at its helm, the tour was meant to engage innovators, thought leaders and policy-makers as part of a new conversation that the party wanted to start about the future of India and its position in the world. In the course of a two-week coast-to-coast tour, Rahul Gandhi interacted with policy intellectuals at the Atlantic Council and the Heritage Foundation as well as the US–India Business Council in addition to addressing students at Berkeley and Princeton. He spoke with maturity and understanding, acquitting himself as a leader of consequence. He faced tough questions from students and answered them candidly. A certain arrogance had crept into the Congress, he said. Narendra Modi was a good communicator and knew how to give a message to three or four different groups in a crowd, he said. Dynastic politics had become a feature of India, but many in the country such as Akhilesh Yadav, M.K. Stalin, and even Abhishek Bachchan, were similar, 'So don't go after me.'* He also warned that the idea of non-violence was under attack in India. He referred to mob lynchings and the murder of journalists, and said that 'the politics of polarisation is very dangerous'. The way he conducted himself, the ideas he spread, and the confidence with which he interacted with his free-thinking audience in the US, projected the image of a leader who had finally discovered himself and decided on what he wanted to do with his life. He became president of the party later that year and began focusing attention on the job with an energy that surprised everyone.

But Rahul's newfound enthusiasm was not enough to lift the Congress. It was a difficult time for the party and its new chief. Narendra Modi's first term was halfway through and the grammar of politics had changed. Committed Congress leaders had become frustrated that the party was unable to stand up to Modi. Priya Dutt,

* 'Why go after me? Rahul Gandhi says dynasts are a reality, BJP hits back', *Hindustan Times*, 12 September 2017.

daughter of film-stars Nargis and Sunil Dutt, spoke of a 'disconnect' between the leaders and the people. Satyavrat Chaturvedi, a cheerleader of the dynasty, called for a 'ruthless introspection'. Milind Deora, a highly rated new-gen leader and friend of Rahul Gandhi, drew attention to the party president's advisers who had no electoral experience and yet were calling the shots. He was careful to add that his 'comments [were] out of emotions of deep loyalty to the party'. Senior leader, Jairam Ramesh, came out with a creative comment. Narendra Modi and Amit Shah think differently, act differently, he said, and if the Congress did not become flexible in its approach, it would become irrelevant. 'We must recognise that India has changed, the Congress has to change. A collective efforts by party leaders to overcome the challenges is essential.' Rahul made what looked like bold moves to recast his backup team of advisers and various Congress committees. But when he ran into walls, he preferred to retract. And there were enough walls in the form of party veterans. When Jairam Ramesh said sultanates were gone, but 'we behave as if we are sultans still', veteran Sheila Dixit asked whether he wasn't part of the sultanate. In the critical 2019 elections, Dixit, 85 and a heart patient, manoeuvred to get the party's nomination to contest from Delhi. She lost. (Two months after the elections, she died.) Geriatric leaders refusing to retire was a problem the Congress did not know how to handle.

The 2019 election campaign saw Rahul Gandhi at his fighting best. He confronted the Modi phenomenon with a robustness that surprised even his admirers. He was eloquent, bold, and innovative, refusing to be provoked by Modi's offensive remarks about him. He criticised Modi and invented slogans like 'Chowkidar chor hai', but maintained civility in his personal conduct. When the results came, the Modi sweep was so massive that suspicions of manipulation spread across the country. Charges of EVM tampering were widespread, while the Election Commission was repeatedly caught taking partisan positions. But the results as announced were the final word and there was no avoiding it. The Congress won 52 seats across the country, not enough to qualify even as the principal opposition party. It was wiped out in Karnataka and Odisha as well as in Rajasthan, Madhya Pradesh, and Chhattisgarh, the three states it had won five months earlier. In UP's 80-seat assembly it won only Rae Bareli, Sonia Gandhi's seat. In Amethi, the family's traditional pocket borough, Rahul Gandhi himself was defeated by Smriti Irani, a BJP lightweight. In his traditional home base of Guna, and despite his royal status still recognised by the public there, Jyotiraditya Scindia lost. All this despite Priyanka Gandhi making her campaign debut in UP. Humiliation forced many Congress office bearers to resign. The cunning ones joined the BJP.

It was Rahul Gandhi's moment of truth. To his credit, he realised that nothing short of a complete overhaul would give the party a chance to survive. In an open letter to Congressmen, he said: 'Rebuilding the party requires hard decisions and numerous people will have to be made accountable for the failure of 2019.'* Leading from the front, he resigned from his position as party president and said that he was not open to re-appointment to that post. He had no intention of vanishing from the scene. He remained a committed Congress leader, speaking out whenever the occasion demanded. But he was clear in his mind that the dynastic tag had become untenable and that the first hard decision the party had to take was to find a non-Gandhi as its president. It was a notion the Congress was not familiar with. The result was confusion, but Rahul stood taller, his resolve undiminished.

There were brilliant young leaders in the Congress. There were also plotters and careerists. A period of internal tussles, of defection, and splits appeared natural for the party. Just as natural was the possibility of the party becoming a 21st century phoenix. The long-living bird of Greek mythology is known for its ability to obtain new life by rising from the ashes of its predecessor, a process of cyclical

* '"Accountability is critical for future growth of Congress": Rahul Gandhi tweets his resignation letter', *Times of India*, 3 July 2019.

regeneration. Rahul Gandhi opened the gates for the inevitabilities of history to play out. It did not take long for the scenario in the country to change. Narendra Modi had started off with a heroic profile after the country had become static under a complacent Congress government headed by an uninspiring Manmohan Singh. But the gap between Modi's oratory and his performance did not take long to come into view. With his second term, an impression of prime ministerial hauteur gained ground. As Modi adopted a distinctively divisive approach to governance, the expectations people had about him changed. Democracy seemed diminished. Those who tried to peep into the future saw that the Congress was a revivable platform, given its historic role in the freedom movement and in early years of nation-building. The question was whether a leadership would rise to make the party viable again.

23

AMITABH BACHCHAN

The Corporate Mess

Amitabh Bachchan surprised many by displaying a lack of business sense when he needed it. After all, he had qualified at Sherwood College in Nainital and then at the University of Delhi. After graduating, he had worked as a business executive in Kolkata. Despite all that, he made a mess of the company he founded, the Amitabh Bachchan Corporation Ltd., an entertainment-based venture that specialised in film production and event management. An event it managed in 1996, the Miss World pageant in Bangalore, brought to light the dismal financial realities of Bachchan's ventures. Even the workers of the pageant were not paid their salaries. All blame was put on the company's CEO, Sanjeev Gupta. But Gupta went on to become the CEO of Coca-Cola India.

Things were so bad for ABC Ltd. that Bachchan's son Abhishek left his studies at Boston University and came home. He tried to give whatever moral support he could to his father. Late one night, his father called him to his study and said, 'Movies are not working out, the business is not working out, nothing is working out.' Details of the discussion between father and son are not on record. But the father told an interviewer later: 'I spent many sleepless nights. One day I got up early in the morning and went directly to Yash Chopraji [successful producer; younger brother of B.R. Chopra, one of the leaders of the Hindi film industry] and told him that I was bankrupt. I had no films. My house and a small property in Delhi were attached. Yashji listened coolly and then offered me a roll in his film *Mohabbatein* [2000]. I then started doing commercials, television and films. And I am happy to say today that I have repaid by entire debt of ₹90 crore and am starting afresh.'* Published reports in 2021 estimated Bachchan's net worth at ₹2950 crore, and 'monthly income and salary' at upwards of ₹5 crore.

Most film-stars are happy being just film-stars. The money, fame, and glamour are a sufficient boost for them. A few get bitten by the business bug. Raj Kapoor got the better of the bug because he had a 2.2 acre plot in the heart of Chembur for RK Studios. He did face bankruptcy when *Mera Naam Joker* (1970) flopped. But he survived. His assets were probably managed by people who were fair to him.

The generational shift from Raj Kapoor's era to Amitabh Bachchan's era was two-faced. At one level, it showed a snobbish swing in favour of university doctorates. At another, it went crazy about getting involved in business. The filmic crowd was never known for its educational achievements. Perhaps that explained the rush for degrees in the Bachchan era. Pedigree-wise, Bachchan's parents were revered for academic distinction. Amitabh's father, Harivansh Rai Bachchan, a respected Hindi poet, was a PhD from Cambridge. His mother, Teji, was a social activist who taught psychology in college. Part of India's literary circuit, they were popular as singers at events. In husband's Hindi adaptation of *Macbeth*, wife played Lady Macbeth.

Unable—or unwilling—to go through the drill of university education, stars took the easy way out. The result was that Hindi filmdom saw an invasion by honorary doctorate holders. Shah Rukh Khan got a PhD from the University of Bedfordshire in 2009. Shabana Azmi got five PhD degrees. So did A.R. Rehman.

---

* 'Abhishek Bachchan on time when Amitabh Bachchan's company went bankrupt', *Indian Express*, 22 April 2021.

Sharmila Tagore, Preity Zinta, and Shilpa Shetty got doctorates from the UK. The best comment on this came from Amitabh Bachchan when he was offered a doctorate. He said: 'My father is the only Dr Bachchan there will be in the family.' That said, he went on to receive honorary doctorates from four universities.

While the academic grandeur of doctorates gave the stars an ego boost, the nuts and bolts of business success caught their attention in a more sustained manner. Nothing, after all, was better for the ego than money. Dilip Kumar would probably have found it difficult to grasp the structure of a corporate body with chairman and managing director and general manager and all that. But Shah Rukh Khan set up a company called Red Chillies to do business. He also became a co-owner of the Indian Premier League cricket team, Kolkata Knight Riders, one of the richest IPL teams with a brand value running into millions of rupees. Additionally, his brand endorsements brought him fabulous amounts. According to media reports, he charged ₹3.5 to ₹4 crore *per day* for an ad shoot. His first endorsement deal was in 1988 for Liberty Shoes. Then came Pepsi, Nokia, Dish TV, Big Basket, Byju's, and so on. Even so, he was ranked only fifth among celebrity endorsers. Earning more were Virat Kohli, Akshay Kumar, Deepika Padukone, and Ranveer Singh, in that order.

So who was more business-minded, Shah Rukh Khan or Amitabh Bachchan? Perhaps a story that went round the studios holds a clue. It seems that Bachchan was given ₹10 lakh for his guest appearance in Shah Rukh Khan's *Paheli* in 2005. Big B gracefully declined. A letter of thanks was enough, he said. Were sharp business minds at work?

Other stars were also in this super league. Ajay Devgn, apparently averse to hard work, invested substantially in solar projects in Gujarat. He also has a production house of his own. Suniel Shetty became the owner of the successful production house, Popcorn Entertainment. Salman Khan set up the Being Human brand and licensed it to a retail company selling fashion accessories and apparel.

He also entered the smartphone business with links to Chinese companies. Mithun Chakraborty, an early star-to-businessman trendsetter, owns the Monarch group of hotels. Preity Zinta, Bobby Deol, Malaika Arora, Hrithik Roshan are all stars with significant space in the business world. In this post-Raj Kapoor–Dilip Kumar age, it was no surprise that Amitabh Bachchan set up a corporation to do business. The only surprise was that he made a mess of it.

He made a mess of his attempt to get into politics as well. It is not uncommon to see film stars putting to political purpose their hold on the masses. Both fields depend on a common power base: mass appeal. Nowhere was this more evident than in Tamil Nadu where M.G. Ramachandran became an unbeatable politician. He was a Malayali with a Menon surname in his nomenclature, but he commanded Tamil emotions more mightily than any other leader. His death led to rioting by fans who refused to believe their idol was gone. For reasons yet to be analysed, Bachchan seemed unable to command a similar kind of loyalty in the late 90s.

It was his friendship with Rajiv Gandhi that made politics attractive to him. The Gandhis and the Bachchans were close from the time Harivansh Rai worked in Jawaharlal Nehru's foreign ministry as a Hindi Officer. Teji Bachchan became a close friend of Indira Gandhi around the same time. When Antonia (later Indianised to Sonia) Maino arrived in India as Rajiv's fiancée, it was Amitabh who went to the airport to receive her. And it was at the Bachchan residence that she stayed to let Teji teach her about Indian customs and traditions. Sonia was quoted in *Dharamyug* magazine as saying: 'Teji aunty is my second... no, my third mother. My first mother is in Italy and the other is Mrs Indira Gandhi, the third is Teji aunty. Amit and Bunty (Ajitabh Bachchan) are my brothers.'*

In 1984 Rajiv Gandhi succeeded in persuading his buddy Amitabh to join him in politics. He had to make an effort but

* Rasheed Kidwai, 'Amitabh Bachchan, Rajiv Gandhi and a tale of two families', *APB Live*, 11 October 2018.

eventually succeeded in making Amitabh contest election from Allahabad on a Congress ticket. He won. For the next few years, he was the face of the Youth Brigade that gave the Congress a new appeal. Then came Bofors. Both Rajiv and Amitabh were charged with receiving kickbacks in the purchase of howitzers from the Swedish Company AB Bofors during the 1980s and 1990s. The scandal brought the government down.

That was when Amitabh Bachchan started thinking that he had better put some distance between him and the Gandhis. It did not take him long to quit politics altogether. It helped cleanse his image, but it hurt the Bachchan–Gandhi friendship. The sense of hurt grew when Amitabh did not accept the proposal that he join the Congress to help Sonia. The Gandhis saw it as a betrayal. Bachchan, for his part, felt let down when he was in a financial mess and the Gandhis made no effort to help. Things got so bad that Jaya Bachchan publicly criticised the Gandhis by saying: 'Those who brought us into politics left us midway, when we were in a crisis. They are known to betray people.' Rahul Gandhi could not ignore that. He said: 'The Bachchan's are lying. They have changed loyalties. People know better about who betrayed whom. People also know who their loyalties are with.'* The parting of ways could not have been more rancorous.

Rahul referred to 'people' repeatedly in his remarks perhaps because he knew to what extent the Bachchans relied on what 'people' thought about them. Amitabh was born with the name of Inquilab Srivastava, a pointer to his father's commitment to the revolutionary history of India. Inquilab was changed to Amitabh because a poet friend of the father said that Amitabh meant 'the light that will never die'. Amitabh discarded the Srivastava surname and adopted Bachchan as his last name only after he became a film-star. It had been his father's pen name, and 'Bachchan' meant 'childlike' in Hindi.

---

* 'Bachchans full of lies says Rahul', *Times of India*, 13 October 2004.

Obviously, Amitabh was sensitive to the importance of tradition. He took pains to ensure that his pedigree was a source of strength. This was perhaps one of the factors that led to the criticism that 'he was high on power'. Shatrughan Sinha said he had withdrawn from several films ('and returned the signing amount') because Amitabh Bachchan featured in them. Political fixer, Amar Singh, who was close to Bachchan at one time and had claimed that he had helped when the star was bankrupt described Bachchan as 'greedy'. Others have suggested that even the projected unity of Bachchan family members was contrived. Daughter Shweta's relationship with her mother was anything but smooth. Bachchan's 'affair' with Rekha was never side-lined by the industry, or forgotten by the fans. The comely lady famously continued to wear sindoor and mangalsutra even after her beloved had moved on in other directions. Adding yet another layer to the complex story was the rivalry between Shweta and Aishwarya, the beauty queen whom brother Abhishek brought home as his wife. These were young ladies who were confused by too much money, too much fame, and too little maturity, proving that the glamour associated with filmdom can also be a curse.

Glamorous stars can be a cursed even when they propagate traditional Indian wisdom that does not gel with 'modernity'. During the pandemic, Bachchan posted a forwarded message on Twitter that carried an endorsement of traditional faith. It said: '5 pm; 22nd Mar, "Amavasya", darkest day of month; virus, bacteria, evil force of max potential & power! Clapping shankh vibrations reduce/destroy virus potency. Moon passing to new "nakshatra" Revati. Cumulative vibration betters blood circulation.' Twitter exploded with criticism of 'shameful superstitious propaganda' and 'unnecessary shit like this that makes no sense'. One comment exposed what many Indians saw as the double life of the rich. It said: 'He is not mad. His money is in Panama.' Bachchan later deleted his tweet.

The great irony of Bachchan's life may perhaps never be explained. Despite being the tallest hero of Bollywood in his time, he did not get the affection of the masses as heroes do. All he got was some respect. Was that a reflection of a generational shift or did it have something to do with his persona and its limited impact on the public?

Bachchan was known as a tight-fisted man who shied away from what has been described as social responsibility. When he realised this had adversely affected his image, he began programmes to help poverty-stricken farmers, and contributed substantially to relief funds in time of natural calamities. He became a United Nations ambassador for the girl child. In business, he appeared to have learned from his early blunders. In 2015, along with son Abhishek, he invested $2.5 lakh in Ziddu, a Singapore-based company. He also began investing actively in the stock market. Abhishek owned the professional kabaddi team, Jaipur Pink Panthers. When asked whether he was an actor or an entrepreneur, he once replied: 'Actor and sports fan. To run a business you have to love what you do. I love going to the movies, and that is possibly the biggest contribution to my becoming an actor. I am a huge kabaddi fan and football fan and that is the reason for me to get involved in the sport.'

Evidently, the horrible days of ABC Ltd were behind them and the Bachchans were in a new world. Their home was Jalsa, a two-storey bungalow in Juhu, a tony neighbourhood by the sea in north Mumbai. It was surrounded by green lawns on all four sides. They also owned parcels of agricultural land in Bhopal, Barabanki and Lucknow. The *Business Standard* reported in May 2021 that Bachchan bought a 5,184-square-feet apartment in Mumbai's Andheri for ₹31 crore. The duplex came with six car parks. The shrewd businessman he had become registered the property only after the government announced a 2 per cent waiver in stamp duty which reduced his stamp duty to ₹6.2 lakh. (Stamp duty rose to 5 per cent soon after.)

By now, Bachchan was a landlord of distinction. Apart from the duplex and Jalsa (where son Abhishek and family lived), the bungalow named Janak, right opposite Jalsa, was also acquired and turned into Bachchan's office. A kilometre away was the bungalow named Prateeksha, the first property Bachchan bought. He also owned another bungalow in Juhu named Vatsa which was leased to a bank. In 2013, he bought the 8,000-square-feet bungalow right behind Jalsa, extending the area of his home. Adding a spark of glitter to this privileged life, Jaya Bachchan 'gifted' a luxury flat in Paris to her husband. Abhishek and Aishwarya were owners of a luxury mansion in Dubai's Sanctuary Falls. In 2017, 'learned articles' appeared in some publications explaining the lessons entrepreneurs could learn from the 'Shahenshah of Bollywood'. Not bad for a man who could not even handle a Miss World pageant.

24

GIRISH KARNAD

Poet Manqué

Girish Karnad was India's Renaissance Man. Italians who invented that phrase defined Uomo Universale as a highly educated person, excellent philosopher, and also strong, handsome, and charismatic. Karnad was all of these. Additionally, he had a will strong enough to shape his career as he wished. Growing up in Dharwad, considered the intellectual capital of Karnataka, he had a yearning to go to England, the ultimate ambition of aspiring Indians in those days. But it was a dream the family could not afford. Young Girish devised ways to get a scholarship. Although his interest was in arts, he knew it was impossible to score high marks in arts while 100 out of 100 was possible in mathematics. Girish took up mathematics, mastered it, emerged as the top-scorer in his class, and thus qualified for the coveted Rhodes Scholarship.

But he had no suit to wear for his final interview. He had a dark-blue blazer given to him to wear as Karnataka University's representative at speaking events. He got trousers made in a matching blue, to 'approximate a suit', as he put it. But his problem was far from over. He wrote in his autobiography, *This Life at Play*:

> The candidates were to have dinner with the Committee on the evening before the interview. It was a formal, Western-style dinner, something I had never been part of or even seen. I brought a book of etiquette that described how to

> behave appropriately in different situations while moving in refined society. In those days, the train from Bombay to Delhi had a dining car in which Spencer & Co. supplied Western-style meals to those who wanted it. I sat in the dining car with my book of etiquette open in front of my plate, eating according to its instructions. 'The first course is soup. Use the rightmost spoon for it. Soup is only served once. You cannot ask for a second helping...' And so on. Over the course of a few meals between Bombay and Delhi, I did my best to learn how to eat like a gentleman.

The nostalgia with which he describes his first journey to England, on a ship of course, provides a commentary on popular aspirations of the time. 'What excitement! Aden!' That was the feeling of all Indians sailing to Europe. P&O (Peninsular & Oriental) ships were symbols of glamour from 1837 when its passenger operations began. Many Indians, especially Goans, were employed on those ships as kitchen and cabin crew. It was part of the lore that these crew members had their own reverse racism. They looked upon Indians as 'uncultured idiots' as Girish Karnad put it. Such realities of life did not detract from the excitement of seeing Aden, the first landfall after the ship left Bombay/Karachi. Today the capital of Yemen, Aden was part of India until 1937. When ships docked there, a kind of madness overtook Indians. They would rush out and 'do shopping' as if they had never shopped before. Things were not only dead cheap in Aden; all kinds of things not available elsewhere were on display at Aden's shops. When Girish said 'What excitement! Aden!' he was actually underplaying it. A few days later, another kind of excitement overtook him. What Indians considered the greatest achievement in life was now his. He went on: 'I stood against the railings on the deck. Tears of fulfilment welled in my eyes. England at last! All along the deck were Indians stuck to the rails, weeping tears of joy at having reached England.' In Karnad's case, though, the thrill of seeing England could not free him from the shackles of dreadful family events. Extraordinary were the irregularities in his family and the humiliations he faced as a consequence. His mother, Kuttabai, had to face the 'shameful fact' that she was unmarried when she came of age. When she did get married, her husband died after two years. She joined a nursing course in Belgaum. When accommodation became a problem, the doctor there said she could stay in his home. 'The doctor was handsome,' she recorded. 'Nearly six feet tall. Curly hair. Fair complexioned. With a gait that would attract anyone.'

To cut a long story short, Kuttabai spent five years in the doctor's house. 'It is true that they ultimately got married,' says Karnad. 'But what was the nature of their relationship during those five years? The very thought that our mother might have lived in sin with a married man—never mind that it was our father—was painful in the extreme.'

If Karnad's account of his parentage is devastating and heart-warming at once, his recollection of his childhood is literature. He describes 'the experience of total undiluted darkness' in words that are almost inspirational. Referring to the 10 years he spent without electricity in his home and the streets around it, he writes: 'We learned to taste the many shades of darkness... With the ability to instantly turn on a flood of bright, shadeless light, we have lost a certain delicate and ambiguous relationship we had with light and dark. When there is no evidence of light within the darkness surrounding us, the irises pick out floating slivers of light and weave them into changeable amorphous forms. That quality of total darkness, that takes us to the brink of blindness, also has a close relationship with complete silence.' He goes on to say that 'the other element we have lost along with the world of complete darkness is an abundance of stories'.

Karnad recollects a past that served his emergence as a storyteller of eminence. Growing up in Sirsi where there was no electricity, he found Yakshagana performances as the best way to spend his leisure time. Occasionally a film was screened in town and that too served as an inspirational experience. 'But otherwise the only entertainment was stories,' he recorded. 'It was a world full of stories. I learned all the puranas and history. What I learned about theatre was imbibed from the Havyaka community in Sirsi, from being with them, acting with them, and going to Yakshagana with them.'

For all his appreciation of British literature and theatre, and despite the windows that opened up for him with the Rhodes Scholarship and his election as Oxford Union president, Karnad stuck to his roots. The main reason must have been his success as a playwright. His plays were Indian, thematically and philosophically. His first play, *Yayati*, was published when he was still at Oxford. His second play, *Tughlaq*, was completed upon his return to India. It was *Tughlaq* that turned Karnad into a celebrity. *Hayavadana*, inspired by Thomas Mann's novel *Transposed Heads,* came in 1972, and *Nagamandala*, in which a myth takes over reality, in 1988.

What made Girish Karnad different from other literary heroes was his activism. That he held several posts of eminence was part of this. He headed the Nehru Centre in London and was a visiting professor at the University of Chicago in 1987–1988. He was at the forefront of protests against the murder of journalist Gauri Lankesh in 2018, despite medical problems that forced him to wear an oxygen tank on his lap with tubes going into his nostrils. That did not prevent him from wearing a placard round his neck that proclaimed 'Me too. Urban Naxal'. Author Amitav Ghosh described him as 'a very important public voice'. Karnad joined 600 other theatre personalities in 2019 to sign a public statement urging people not to vote for the BJP or its allies because the BJP put the idea of India under threat.

A confessional snippet brought the primal element in Girish Karnad to light in his own words. He recalled the time he watched David Lean's 1957 classic *The Bridge on the River Kwai.* As the movies progressed, Karnad felt that 'Someone was teaching a class on screen writing or, in a sense, playwriting. While watching the film, I found it difficult to breathe at times.'

Ebrahim Alkazi, the phenomenal theatre man of the 1950s

Bombay, also influenced Karnad. The technical precision of some of Alkazi's productions 'left me dazzled'. Citing the example of Swedish playwright Strindberg's *Miss Julie* directed by Alkazi, Karnad wrote: 'At one point Jean lit a cigarette. With the sound of the match being struck, the music stopped and the lights, which had been slowly fading, turned bright. These changes appeared to be controlled by the match being struck.'

Another, rather surprising, influence that materially affected Karnad's growth as a playwright was C. Rajagopalachari. This unusual politician who rose to become the last Governor-General of India (the post that colonial Britain called a Viceroy), wrote what he called concise versions of the Ramayana and Mahabharata. What attracted Karnad was how 'beautifully' C.R. narrated the important side stories in the epics. One of these stories featured Yayati as the hero. Karnad wrote: 'I was excited by the story of Yayati, where a son exchanges his youth with his father's old age. The situation was both dramatic and tragic.'

Yayati had already made headlines when Marathi writer V.S. Khandekar won the Jnanpith Award in 1974 for his novel bearing that name, originally published in 1959 (English version in 1978). It was a theme that excited writers. And it never bored readers and audiences. Karnad's rendering of it, in his own estimate, was a work of his juvenilia (written when he was only 22). It was subsequently modified to incorporate suggestions by noted theatre personalities. Karnad had no problem admitting that he was influenced by people like Ebrahim Alkazi, and his own unconventional thoughts, such as: If Yayati's son had been married, what would the wife do? Would she have accepted this unnatural arrangement? Karnad's play opens with a confrontation between Yayati and Chandralekha, not unlike Alkazi's young heroines come to life in *Antigone*. Imperceptibly influenced by C.R. and Alkazi, Karnad saw his pen moving. 'I did not feel as if I was writing a play. The characters came to life in front of me, and all I had to do was take down what they were saying to each other like I was a stenotypist. It was as if a spirit had entered me. Never again in my life did I experience this kind of loss of control while writing a play.'

Many great works of literature have had authors saying similar things. What made Karnad different was his own surprise at the impact *Yayati* made. He listed three things that nonplussed him: His writing it in Kannada while English was his aim, his turning to the puranas as source material, and his success as an accidental playwright. 'It had been my ambition since childhood to become a poet. With the arrival of this wretched play, I began to realise that I was not a poet but a playwright. I was greatly disappointed.'

It takes a poet to say that. While Karnad might have been disappointed at his not evolving into a versifier, aficionados were delighted at the playwright he evolved into. Erudition helped him to see things in a wide perspective. He observed how in the years following independence 'the presiding deity of Indian theatre was the English playwright, George Bernard Shaw'. The reasons were clear. 'Shaw's plays were all about middleclass family troubles.' P.K. Atre in Marathi and Kailasam in Kannada wrote plays in this tradition. 'To this "modern" sensibility of theatre, stories from the puranas or our folk literature were not only ridiculous but also politically regressive.' Recognising the influence exerted by Bernard Shaw's middle-class themes and Atre–Kailasam's modernity, Karnad still turned Puranic tales and folk stories into exciting theatre. For his very first play, he used the familiar Yayati theme.

Like all men of destiny, Karnad gave to the world more than he took from it. He was lucky to bloom in what was India's best time, the 1950s and 1960s. By the mid 1970s, unfamiliar political trends would begin to crush the spirit of India, turning the country into a collection of mutually suspicious little Indias. The blossoming years were inspirational. His generation was rich with creative minds that raised questions without pretending to answer them. It was indeed a nest of singing birds—Badal Sircar (born 1925) in Bengali, Mohan Rakesh (1925) in Hindi, Vijay Tendulkar (1928) in Marathi and in Kannada, B.V. Karanth (1929), U.R. Ananthamurthy (1932), and P. Lankesh (1935).

Two signature qualities helped Karnad shine. The first was his versatility, in acting, writing, cinema, drama, direction, and television. Lankesh was the only contemporary who showed similar ambidexterity, adding also poetry, fiction, and journalism to his repertoire. Yet Karnad soared higher because he made his plays go beyond Kannada to build for himself an international profile through leadership roles in Pune, Delhi, London, and Chicago.

Was *Tughlaq* Karnad's best play? It certainly was the most celebrated, appearing in Kannada in 1965, followed by performances in Hindi, Bengali, Marathi, and English. The play reflected disillusionment with Nehruvian dreams, thus giving it contemporary relevance. But it was Ebrahim Alkazi who turned *Tughlaq* into a spectacle of magisterial splendour by staging it at the ruins of Purana Qila in Delhi 1972. Ultimately, though, it was Karnad's boundless imagination that made him a playwright without parallel. Who else could think up a cobra making love to a woman on stage? Or a horse reciting the national anthem? Karnad was a man who was many men.

Eventually, those tubes going into his nostrils won the day. It was 'degenerative respiratory disorder' that brought those tubes into his life. What was degenerative expanded its reach until the familiar phrase 'multiple organ failure' became the decisive factor in his life. He was only 81 when the multiple failure took place and Karnad breathed his last at his home in Bangalore. The Karnataka government declared a holiday for schools and colleges. His last wish, according to family members, was that there should not be a funeral procession, no VIP should visit him, and no flowers should be placed on his body. Nevertheless, the government declared a three-day state mourning. Karnad must have protested loudly from wherever he was. In death as in life, Girish Karnad made himself an example for others to take note of.

25

NASEERUDDIN SHAH

Revels in Being Alone

What makes Naseeruddin Shah a greater actor and a greater man than idolised mascots such as Amitabh Bachchan? Why are Shankar Nag and Sunil Dutt remembered fondly although one had only a short life in the movies and the other was not one of Bollywood's greats? Movies represent a tricky world where the WYSIWYG principle does not work: What You See Is *Not* What You Get. What you see can indeed be misleading. M.G. Ramachandran and N.T. Rama Rao were not thinkers by any yardstick. One played the unprofound romantic hero in hit after hit while the other personified Lord Krishna in picture after picture. But both became chief ministers of their states. Jayalalithaa was a born politician who became an accidental film-star, but her ego wouldn't let a blade of grass grow in her wake, with the result that her dreams, whatever they were, her party, and her state collapsed when she died. Marquee names of Hindi filmdom, Lata Mangeshkar, Rekha, Dharmendra, Govinda, were sent to Parliament where they left a record of nothingness, a disgrace to the memory of Prithviraj and Nargis and other early MPs whose words, however few, carried weight in the House.

A defining quality of those who leave footprints behind them is passion. Most people do their jobs conscientiously, even efficiently. But not all are driven by the passion described in literature as a

Magnificent Obsession. Passion is the dividing line between the ordinary and the special. It was passion that made Homi Bhabha take the engineering tripos in Cambridge, then the mathematics tripos, and then decide to help his country become a modern nuclear power. It was passion that made Ebrahim Alkazi turn the National School of Drama into a wonder of India. It was P.K. Nair's passion that led to the birth of the National Film Archives in Pune, indeed to the very idea that films were archival material. In theatre, the outstanding pioneer was Prithviraj Kapoor. The man with the imperial voice was so obsessed with the theatre that he floated a travelling drama company, Prithvi Theatre, way back in 1944, meeting the expenses of the 150-member troupe with his earnings from films. Today, Prithvi Theatre is the most valuable theatrical venue in venue-rich Mumbai. The Kapoors kept the passion going. They and Prithvi Theatre had many advantages—filmic glamour, Mumbai connections, a connoisseur crowd to draw from. K.V. Subbanna had nothing when he adamantly chose his small Karnataka village of Heggodu as the site of his theatre-film-publishing institute, Ninasam, in 1949. But he had the magnificent obsession. It turned Heggodu into a renowned centre of the arts. Energy is sometimes mistaken for passion. Shah Rukh Khan is energy, Aamir Khan is passion. Sania Mirza is energy, Leander Paes is passion. In fact, passion may not even be accompanied by energy. Narayana Murthy and Bill Gates do not display high-strung energy in their slow talking style. But the passion is unmissable.

Passion comes in different shapes. With only an eight-year difference between them, Amitabh Bachchan and Naseeruddin Shah were participants in the same Indira/Modi span of Indian history. Bachchan was involved in some blunders that were business-oriented; he withdrew into a corner of his own. Naseeruddin displayed an intellectual dimension rare among film stars of his time. And he dared to put it in black and white for the world to accept or discard. There are autobiographies written by many film stars, from Dilip Kumar's *The Substance and the Shadow* to Vyjayanthimala's

Bonding: A Memoir. Most of them are ghost-written excursions into self-praise. Naseeruddin Shah's *And Then One Day*: *A Memoir* is an exception. It bristles with wit and brazen candour.

Autobiographers usually tell us how good they are. Naseeruddin Shah tells us how bad he was—how conceited, arrogant, and selfish, how easily given to drugs and women, how awful to look at. When his brothers went to IIT and the Defence Academy, he became a drifter, watching movies and plays. He couldn't get along with his father any more than he could get along with his first daughter. By being open about such things, he makes weakness look like strength. No one is left in doubt about his natural fascination for acting and for memorising classical passages. While still in school he considered the possibility of becoming a professional actor 'in spite of the face I had'. A schoolteacher told him to read *Macbeth* and *Hamlet* because most people couldn't tell one from the other. He was quite impressive at school debates. 'My speeches, peppered with quotes from Shakespeare were well memorised, thoroughly rehearsed... I invariably blustered my way to some prize but seldom did I know what I was talking about.'

The ambition of middle-class parents to see their wards become doctors and engineers is rooted in traditional concepts of security and safety. The beaten track is comforting. When someone breaks the mould and strays into unpredictable areas like acting, fear grips the elders. The stage gripped Naseeruddin Shah when he was still a school boy ('It was the only place apart from the cricket field where I felt happy in my skin'). Everything that happened in his life was in one way or another shaped by this early fascination. Despite his memorising capabilities, N.S. was a flop in school. He was used to being 50th in a class of 50 and left school in shame, having failed in Class 9. But he was never upset by such things because he had developed a capacity to imagine that he was someone else. There is philosophical substance in his observation that pretending to be someone else could be a source of great solace for actors. 'It does seem like an aberration of behaviour to want to be someone else all the time, and I think it happens to people who, like me, can find no self-worth early in life and thus find fulfilment in hiding behind make-believe.' N.S. was surprised when he accidentally heard about a school that taught drama. He managed to get into the National School of Drama in its heyday under Ebrahim Alkazi. Then he came to hear about the Film and Television Institute in Pune and he managed to get admission there when Girish Karnad was its director. He has interesting comments on the two schools, the gist of it being that it was at the FTII that he learned the basics of acting and also received opportunities to break into films.

N.S. has a way with words. He needs only a sentence, sometimes just a few words, to sum up personalities and situations. Here's his portrait of his school director: 'Girish Karnad, Rhodes Scholar, towering intellectual, pioneer of the art film movement in Karnataka, committed theatre worker, the author of two authentic contemporary Indian theatre masterpieces, *Tughlaq* and *Hayavadana*, and all-round Cool Cat more known for his writing than his acting.' If that is too long, consider this self-assessment: 'I kept to myself, and stumbled upon that part of me which revels in being alone.' Or this conclusion: 'The utter fearlessness, the astounding physical and emotional agility with which he performed is a quality Shammi Kapoor shared with Hindi cinema's certified nutcase Mr Kishore Kumar.' You also come across throwaway phrases like 'beautiful waterfall of a voice'.

N.S. studied at Aligarh Muslim University because he couldn't get admission anywhere else. A chapter in his memoir is titled 'The Aligarh University absurdists'. He describes the university as 'a hotbed of communal conservatism if not downright fundamentalism'. When he arrived at his hostel, even as he was unpacking, senior students called him for namaz. He notes: 'I felt miffed at being compelled to pray when at the moment I had nothing to pray for.' That avowal, like everything N.S. said and did in the course of his career, showed that he grew up without thinking of what religion he was born into. The name proclaimed the religion, of course, and probably his father, Aley Mohammed Shah, and mother, Farrukh Sultana, were practising Muslims. It was not a close-knit family and the children grew up their own way. N.S.'s older brother, Zamiruddin Shah, joined the army and rose as high as Deputy Chief of Army Staff. In good time, Lieutenant General Shah wrote an informative autobiography titled *The Sarkari Mussalman* (2018). He also had a stint as vice chancellor of Aligarh Muslim University and the records say that it rose in international university rankings during that period. Neither family experience nor educational exposure made N.S. think or talk like a Muslim. He thought and talked like a citizen. The boldness with which he did that began pushing him into tight corners after India entered the Narendra Modi era. N.S. remained a free spirit and would not hold his tongue just because some people did not like what he said. He said poison had spread in Indian society, that law breakers enjoyed immunity, that in many areas the death of a cow was more important than the death of a police officer. He was trawled, called a traitor; an extremist sent him an air ticket to Pakistan. N.S. stood his ground and said: 'If they have the right to criticise, then I also have the same right. I am expressing concerns about the country I love, the country that is my home. How is that a crime?'

Naseeruddin could not see any sense in the idea that his rights as a citizen were in any way affected by his identity as Muslim. This was not an issue in India when he and others like him were contributing their best to the common culture of the land. Nor did the nation see him as a Muslim when it gave him three National Film Awards and the world pitched in with a Venice Film Festival Award. The Government of India gave him a Padma Shri and then a Padma Bhushan, acknowledging his contributions to Indian cinema and Indian culture.

Prodded by his civic sense, N.S. involved himself in the issues that affected the nation's progress from time to time. When the farmers' march rattled the Modi government in early 2021, he did not seek the safe way out by keeping quiet. He plunged into it with the declaration that 'Everyone must talk about the farmers' protests. In the end you will not hear the words of your enemies but the silence of your friends. If our farmers are sitting in protest in the bitter cold, we cannot turn a blind eye. Being silent is tantamount to supporting the oppressor.' This was when big names in the film industry were 'extremely silent' as Naseeruddin put it. 'They believe they may lose something if they speak up. When you have earned enough for seven generations, how much will you lose?'

That was not the bread-and-butter question it might have sounded like; it was an active mind raising basic issues about life. His civic sense got Naseeruddin involved in current affairs even when it was diplomatically unwise. He was unlike stars like Sachin Tendulkar who seemed to be unaware of anything except cricket. When the Citizenship Amendment Act controversy was raging, Tendulkar explained that he liked his vada pav with red chutney and a little bit of green chutney. Naseeruddin lacked such an easy conscience. He once said that people who watched Shah Rukh Khan and Salman Khan should not watch his movies. Following an incident of communal violence in 2018, he had no hesitation in admitting something that was new to him; he said that he felt unsafe in this new India and was worried about the safety of his children if they were caught in mob violence. Naseeruddin Shah, who as a college student did not even see himself as a Muslim, was forced by circumstances to turn full circle, throwing light on the reality of life in India.

Naseeruddin's 'fault' was that he expressed his opinions without pausing to think about their diplomatic implications. He was open in his criticism of celluloid gods such as Dilip Kumar and Rajesh Khanna. He said Khanna was a mediocre actor, though he later considered it prudent to apologise for that comment. Naseeruddin was not constricted by factors that were not of his making, such as religion. He said publicly once that he hoped his marriage to Ratna Pathak would set a precedent when it came to inter-faith marriages. He strongly opposed the term 'love jihad' saying that those who coined the phrase did not know the meaning of the word jihad. About his own family, he said 'we have never told our children that they belong to any particular religion'. When he was about to marry Ratna, his mother had asked him whether he would want his would-be wife to convert to his religion and he had said no. 'My mother who was uneducated, prayed five times a day, observed roza all her life said: "The things that have been taught to you in your childhood, how can that change? It is not right to change one's religion."' The way Naseeruddin asserted his Indianness and delegitimised the presumed importance of religious identity had a classic touch about it. He said: 'Why should I be afraid? I am in my own country. I am at my own home. Five generations of my family are buried in this land. My ancestors have been living here for the last three hundred years. If this does not make me a Hindustani, then what does?'

But this Hindustani was only too aware of the changes overtaking the substance of India. By 2017, he had seen enough to be concerned about what was happening to his India. 'Never before have pleas for peace been interpreted as cowardly or seditious,' he said. It had become 'us' and 'them'. He put things boldly when he wrote: 'The visible increase in the sight of saffron scarves and tilaks, as well as on the other side beards, hijabs and topis is cause for apprehension... Till the length of Sania Mirza's skirt causes more agitation than the lack of modern education and employment opportunities for our community, as long as we hesitate to condemn the sadistic madness of the ISIS, we only help reinforce the belief that we support violence and regression.' He drew attention to the fact that on a quiz show '...not one of the contestants could answer who had written "Saare jahan se achcha, Hindustan hamara". That it was a Muslim astonished not a few of them.' (Allama Iqbal, the poet, later change his ideological position and became an advocate of Islamic separateness.)

Naseeruddin Shah was frank enough—and bold enough—to say that a shifting of the sand occurred in Narendra Modi's time. In this new India, citizens began to be seen by the religion to which they belonged. It was the first time, Naseeruddin said, that he became aware of this religious identity. Many things were happening for the first time. People were being compartmentalised on the basis of their names. Assumptions overtook facts. The non-religious could not remain non-religious, the secular and liberal were not recognised as secular and liberal. A stamp was affixed on every forehead and it could be removed only by removing the forehead. Like millions of his countrymen, Hindus included, N.S. was being taught that Gandhi was dead, that Nehru was dead, that Ambedkar and Tagore and Lal Bahadur Shastri and K.R. Narayanan were all dead.

26

VARAVARA RAO

The Poet as Criminal

In biographical notes, Varavara Rao is mentioned as a poet. And rightly so. He began writing poems when he was 17 and quickly established himself in Telugu literature. His words are often too powerful to be brushed aside. Consider the opening lines of his poem, 'Words'.

> *Words, smothered in the folds of the self*
> *Must be stirred awake*
> *Made to amble and watch*
> *See if wings can bear aloft*
> *The crippled limbs*
> *And soar into the sky.*

Poetry lovers found him inspiring. All good poetry has that effect on readers. But good poetry also has the effect of scaring those in power. Across history, rulers have looked at poets with suspicion. The rulers of Varavara Rao's land were no exception. In 1973, when he was 33 years old, he was imprisoned for the first time. The charge: inciting violence through writings. That was governmental recognition of the power of Varavara Rao's poetry. Many writers in many languages, some of them militant in their lines, are ignored by law enforcers. But Varavara Rao was jailed several times—under the Emergency, for supporting the labour movement, for speaking on Kashmir, for being himself.

This was part of the turbulent—and short-lived—Naxalbari period of history. Radical communists in Siliguri's Naxalbari block found inspiration in Chinese-style communism and established the Communist Party of India (Marxist-Leninist) in 1969, the CPI-ML. The movement spread to other states, but its open radicalism created divisions in the domain of the Communist Party of India (Marxist), the CPI-M. Even as the CPI-M was challenged by the CPI-ML, armed peasants' struggle broke out in Andhra's Srikakulam area with Telugu writers deeply involved in the turmoil. Young writers attacked Arasam, the literary platform set up by the older writers, for not getting involved in the new 'revolution'. Varavara Rao was in the thick of the controversy as one of the organisers of Tirugubatu Kavulu (Association of Rebel Poets) which subsequently evolved into Viplava Rachayitala Sangham (Revolutionary Writers' Association).

Rao had started out in ways that were too run-of-the-mill to attract attention. After education in Chinna Pendyala in Warangal district, he took a post-graduate degree in Telugu literature from Osmania University in 1960, and became a lecturer at private colleges in Telangana. Sticking to a conventional career graph, he joined the central government's information ministry as a publications assistant. He switched between government jobs and teaching, finally becoming principal of the CKM College in Warangal. It was his literary work that made him stand out. As Shaoni Sarkar wrote in *The Hindu* (August 2020): 'Rao's poems in their fluidity exceed the pragmatism of commitment to any ideology. His works are not unwaveringly the revolutionary poetry of a lifelong Marxist. They go beyond that, forged in a larger crucible of sensibilities. In addition to his unique status as a poet, he was also a famous orator of the time, addressing hundreds of meetings all over the state. An activist all along, he founded the Saahithee Mithrulu (Friends of Literature) in 1966 with a literary journal of its own called *Srujana*. Popularity turned the quarterly into a monthly by 1970. Later, it was replaced by a new journal called *Arunatara*. He published

15 poetry collections beginning with *Chali Negallu* (Camp Fires) in 1968. He also edited several poetry anthologies. In 2008, an anthology under the title *Varavara Rao Kavitvam* (Varavara Rao's Poems) was published. His poems have been translated into English by D. Venkat Rao, professor at Hyderabad's English & Foreign Languages University.

Political commitment was an undisguised feature of Rao's poetry as well as his literary studies. A book that was received as a landmark in 1983 was a version of his PhD thesis 'Telangana Liberation Struggle and Telugu Novel: A Study Into Interconnection Between Society and Literature'. Such literary works were seen by the authorities as tantamount to subversive political activity. To make things worse, Varavara Rao had initiated an organisation named Virasam, meaning revolutionary writers' association. He also actively participated in Dalit politics and the movement for peasants' rights. These were presumed to be anti-establishment and he attracted the condemnatory description 'literary Naxalite'.

The BJP-led government that came to power in 2014 did not like Naxalites, literary or otherwise. Its policy was to fight all opponents to the finish. This brought a wide field of activity under its purview. In August 2018, the world saw a bunch of respected human rights campaigners being arrested, including Sudha Bharadwaj, Vernon Gonsalves, Gautam Navlakha, Arun Ferreira, and Varavara Rao, on terrorism-related charges. In January 2020, the central government abruptly transferred the inquiry from Pune police to the National Investigation Agency (NIA). In February 2020, orders were passed to move the investigation to the NIA's court in Mumbai. By the time he approached his second anniversary in the overcrowded Taloja jail in Mumbai, Rao's medical condition had deteriorated. He also tested positive for Covid-19. The situation was grave enough for the authorities to agree to transferring him urgently to a private hospital. The Bombay High Court granted him conditional bail on medical grounds in February 2021. Probably the court took into account little details like Rao found lying 'on a soiled bed soaked in urine with no one to attend to him'. He was frequently turning delirious.

It can be argued that literature as well as the revolutionary cause gained from Rao going to jail. The poet's imagination found inspiration in the ordeal. Penguin was able to publish a book under the title *Captive Imagination: Letters from Prison*. The gist of his message was that, in prison, waiting was a habit that turned into an addiction.

A day without toil
A night without love
A waiting on the shores of history.

A veteran of prisons, Rao did not become cynical in his letters. He noted: 'TV is switched on for prisoners in the morning. As the seconds flash past they bring to mind the beauty of birds flying across the morning sky. I wonder whether you have ever counted seconds for even five minutes. Except in love, there is no such waiting in this life, save in prison. The difference is this: In love waiting is intense, a longing filled with sweet desire. In prison waiting is a habit turning slowly into addiction. Often one begins to wait for the petty and the inconsequential. During sleepless nights the pain hidden behind words is not extinguished like the beedi that goes out when you speak. And regardless of the sympathy and the sharing of joy and sorrow, the prison remains pitch dark and empty of love.' And then a cry from the heart: 'Only those who have experienced it can comprehend that the waiting itself is punishment while one waits in prison for freedom.'

Prison, fights, suffering as an aspect of patriotism—these were parts of the philosophy that inspired the early generation of nationalists. The next generation saw writers as politicians and politicians as writers. Was Atal Bihari Vajpayee a poet first, or a politician first? What is Shashi Tharoor, a writer or a politician? In a way, it is good that writers are active as politicians. Writing requires an intellectual discipline which, if infused into politics, can only enrich politicians. That combination of talents has been all too rare in India, which explains why the euphoria of independence quickly gave way to problems and anxieties, making the 1960s a troublesome period for India. The air of self-confidence was shattered when the Chinese army made a mockery of India's defences in the North-East Frontier in October 1962. There was nothing to cheer about in everyday living conditions either. Even the well-to-do needed political and business connections to buy a motor car. Only two brands were available in India, Hindustan Ambassador, a poor imitation of Morris Oxford, and Fiat Padmini, a poor imitation of Italy which became more Padmini than Fiat. It did not matter whether the imitations were poor or not; citizens had to make a booking and then wait for a year and more to get the precious vehicle. When it finally arrived, even the rich could not avoid showing their excitement. It was also the age of The Permit, a little piece of paper on which a qualified doctor certified that you were an addict who needed liquor to retain a semblance of normality. Without The Permit you could not enter the Permit Room that posh hotels maintained. The India of the 60s tried its best to deserve the epithet V.S. Naipaul gave it: an area of darkness.

Into this whirlpool of desolate emotions gate-crashed the Naxalite movement, instantly providing ideological anchorage to activists such as Varavara Rao. That he attracted a wide support circle was proof that his writings and activities reflected popular feelings. His commitment, as strong as Che Guevara's, was tempered by his rationalism, as pragmatic as Fidel Castro's. Even as law-enforcers found dangerous radicalism in his work, there were judicial umpires who saw him as balanced. When he was arrested in 1973 on charges of inciting violence, the Andhra Pradesh High Court rebuked the government for failing to show that his writings had actually resulted in violence. After his arrest under the Emergency, the court ordered his release. The judgment asked the government not to resort to such actions against writers unless their writings had an immediate and direct bearing on physical action. Failing to get the message, the government raised a conspiracy case charging that all actions of revolutionaries were the direct consequences of a poem or speech by revolutionary activists. As many as 41 revolutionaries were named, among them Virasam leaders Cherabanda Raju, K.V. Ramana Reddy, and T. Madhusudana Rao. Known as the Secunderabad Conspiracy Case, this litigation dragged on for 15 years from 1974, ending in acquittal. Varavara Rao, denied bail several times, was released on conditional bail in 1975, only to be arrested again three months later. During the Emergency, he remained a prisoner under the stringent Maintenance of Internal Security Act. Curiously, he faced greater threat from mercenaries of landlords and anti-social elements who made several attempts to eliminate him. In Adilabad district, a police officer beat him in public in 1979.

Varavara Rao seemed to emerge stronger from each beating. As a thinker and poet, he had developed his philosophy on an intellectual foundation. The power of his conviction grew from his study of world history and people's struggles against their oppressors. An interview he gave to Ramu Ramanathan was published in 2016 under the title, 'The poet as revolutionary: Talking with Varavara Rao'. There was hardly a theme that was not discussed in this lengthy baring of the mind. He conceded that times were changing and people's movements were losing the momentum they once had. As he put it: 'If you look at the Spanish Civil War or the Naxalbari and Srikakulam struggles, you will see that intellectuals, writers and poets spearheaded the movement. Today, due to the impact of market forces and globalisation, intellectuals are separating themselves from people's movements.'

It can be argued that Naxalism and the Maoist movement in general did not meld into the Indian psyche in a meaningful way because of the 'kill philosophy' it advocated. Naxalbari, a small village in West Bengal, saw an armed uprising initiated by Charu Majumdar and Kanu Sanyal in 1967, along the classic textbook strategy of armed struggle against landlords by the landless. Majumdar propagated the 'annihilation line' a dictum for the assassination of class enemies such as landlords, university teachers, and police officers. A sober assessment was provided by Srinivasan Ramani when he said (*The Hindu*, 11 April 2021): 'The Maoist movement in India seemed headed in the same direction that several violent and failed insurgencies, inspired by the Chinese revolution, went—from the Shining Path in Peru to the Communist Party of the Philippines. There have been exceptions—the Nepali Maoists, for example, managed to partake in power after peacefully ending the civil war—but if the Indian Maoists' denunciation of these steps taken by their Nepali counterparts are any indication, such a step does not seem to be in the offing.' India is a country where Mahatma Gandhi continues to be a living presence. That could be one reason why a movement that called for ideology-driven landlord killing did not get very far.

'Maoist' became a favourite term for all politicians to condemn all opponents. The police also found the term convenient whenever they wanted to arrest a public figure. In August 2018, they picked up Varavara Rao along with Sudha Bhardwaj, Arun Ferreira, Gautam Navlakha, and Vernon Gonsalves on charges of Maoist connections and also links with the Bhima Koregaon unrest. (Site of a battle during the British raj, the village of Bhima Koregaon had become a symbol of Dalit assertion over caste Hindus.) The arrests attracted world attention. A consortium of more than 100 global intellectuals issued a call for their release. The *Washington Post* commented: 'The space for dissent has diminished in Modi's India where journalists, activists and members of NGOs have faced arrests and harassment.'

An intolerant government in an India that had gone overtly Hindutva had cut a sorry figure before the world. Sentiments against the government hardened when reports surfaced in July 2020 that Varavara Rao had contracted Covid-19 in prison. The United Nations special rapporteur for human rights defenders was among those who drew attention to his plight. The National Human Rights Commission also expressed outrage over the development and said all expenses of treatment would be borne by the state as he was an undertrial business. Rao's family, however, drew attention to the 'terrible conditions' at the state hospital where he was initially treated. Published reports at the time said that Rao was admitted to the hospital only after his family issued a statement and held an emergency press conference alleging that he was being denied proper medical attention despite his rapidly deteriorating condition. The statement was titled, 'Don't kill Varavara Rao in jail'.

27

RAJINIKANTH

How a Gaekwad Became a Tamil Icon

Tamil has a cultural heritage nurtured and stabilised by 2,000 years of tradition. Into this established landscape came a man who could only be called an outsider. He was born outside Tamil country, his mother tongue was Marathi, and he earned his livelihood as a bus conductor in Karnataka. Suddenly, as is its wont, destiny interfered. The bus conductor became a film actor, the Marathi man a Tamil man. Shivaji Rao Gaekwad was reborn as Rajinikanth, a phenomenon that changed people's perceptions about cinema and its heroes. There were heroes before him. But no one tried to imitate M.G.R., whereas imitating Rajinikanth became a fashion among the young and the old alike.

This was because of the way Rajinikanth turned himself into a complex mix of mannerisms. Even the simple act of lighting a cigarette had a Rajinikanth version that made it unforgettable. No one could flip a cigarette in the air and catch it on his lips the way this filmic acrobat could. In fact, this cigarette tossing became a trademark feat no one dared imitate. So was his way of twirling sunglasses. He did these things in a style that was his own. It seemed to justify the title his filmic admirers gave him—Style King.

In a revelatory mood once, the mannan said he got the cigarette twirling idea from Shatrughan Sinha. No one seemed to associate Shatrughan with the action. Even if his was the original act, Rajini worked on it and turned it into a brand of his own. He said he spent hours before the mirror, practising. The difficulty lay in the fact that the act had to synchronise with the dialogue. He persevered and was able to do things that seemed impossible—taking the burning end of a cigarette into his mouth and swinging it out, for example. He developed a signature walking style with folded arms going sideways. He created a world of his own that others watched with fascination.

Born in 1950, Rajini was just past 30 when a girl from the Ethiraj College for Women went to interview him for the college magazine. Her name was Latha. By the time the interview was over, unexpected sentiments took over. The person she was interviewing developed ideas of his own and in no time the two were married. They were blessed with two daughters, Soundarya and Aishwarya. When her turn came, Aishwarya brought another celebrity into the family by marrying Dhanush, a Tamil movie star. Ensconced at the top, Rajini was able to charge ₹50 crore for a movie, making him the second highest paid actor in Asia after Jackie Chan, the Hongkong actor and martial artist famous for his innovative stunts and comic timing. It took Rajini's net worth to ₹365 crore (according to published 2021 reports), making him one of the richest men in the country.

This is related to Tamil-style hero worship, say academic pundits. At a conference on democracy in the digital age, held in March 2020, P. Panbu Selvan and Brindha Duraisamy said that image worship had been deeply entrenched in Tamil culture for thousands of years. Heroes have been glorified and venerated as gods and goddesses. Tamil Nadu is a state where temples have been built for film-stars and rituals performed to their images. 'The convention of trusting protagonists began right from folklore, music, theatre to the digital cinema today. Film stars have been adulated on and off screen even in today's new age of techniques.' No television watcher in India could have missed visuals of frenzied fans pouring gallons of milk on their icon's three-storey-high cut-out to celebrate the release of a new movie.

In December 2016, *Business Standard* published an article written by Sai Manish titled 'Why are Tamils impulsive hero worshippers?' He wrote: 'Tamils have a proclivity to hero worship which often touches maniacal proportions manifesting itself in myriad ways often hinging on the irrational. There is something about the Tamil psyche that makes it receptive and susceptible to the influence of the personality cult.' Economic misery at the level of the masses added to the weaknesses of the psyche. The article said: 'The people of Tamil Nadu, living in miserable conditions, burdened by poverty and with little hope of a better future found succour in M.G.R.'s films. His charming ways and on-screen roles were an alternative world, an escape route for the Tamil people from the drudgery of daily existence.'

There are also psychological factors behind what has become an apparent speciality of the Tamil persona. As Sai Manish put it: 'Film-stars in Tamil Nadu have fan clubs with numbers that could put an English Premier League football club to shame.' Film stars go on to become political masters because 'Tamils over the years have looked at cine actors to get a glimpse of what they themselves may never achieve in life. The Tamil psyche feels empowered when an ordinary actor who looks like them performs extra-human antics on-screen. The association of one's own self-esteem with that of the film actor is rooted in the deep poverty the state was in until the early 1990s.'

Tamil Nadu was economically worse off than most other states. In urban areas, the population below the poverty line rose from 62 per cent to 72 per cent between 1963 and 1970. Even in the 1980s, almost half the state lived below the poverty line. A quarter of the state's rural population had less than ₹500 in assets. Many educated Tamils migrated to other states in search of jobs. But no other state witnessed the kind of hero worship Tamil film stars attracted. It was the state where when M.G.R. died, at least 30 people committed suicide and widespread violence broke out. Perhaps it was the Tamil tradition of seeing film stars in larger-than-life proportions that made Rajinikanth what he became.

While life's burdens made Rajini take up a bus conductor's job, turn into a carpenter, and work as a coolie at one stage, the actor's itch in him was never dulled. He had participated in plays in school. He watched Kannada plays in Bangalore whenever the bus conductor's job gave him time. He even acted in some Kannada plays. In 1973 he joined the Madras Film Institute to pursue a diploma in acting.

Then came K. Balachander, the filmmaker known for taking up unusual themes and turning them into unusual movies. Initially, Balachander thought that Rajinikanth was below par. When he was auditioned, Rajini tried to imitate Sivaji Ganesan's dramatic mannerisms and dialogue delivery style. Balachander rejected the novice and advised him to learn Tamil and to develop his own style. Rajinikanth took that advice to heart. When they met again, Balachander gave Rajini a small part in his upcoming film, *Apoorva Raagangal*. Several more films hit the screen with Rajinikanth appearing in small roles. He grew in stature slowly but steadily, the cigarette-flipping trick making a big hit in due course. Balachander put things in perspective when he said: 'Rajinikanth claims that I am his school. But I must admit this wasn't the Rajinikanth I introduced. He evolved on his own merits and strengths. I gave him an opportunity and unveiled him to the world. He went and conquered it.'

One of the uncanny qualities of stardom is its ability to bypass linguistic and regional boundaries and shine in ways that are its own. Tamil icon Rajinikanth teaming up with Hindi mascot Amitabh Bachchan was news in itself. Their movie *Andhaa Kanoon* went on to become a big hit. At one point, Rajini suddenly announced that he was quitting films. As the industry shuddered, he allowed friends to persuade him to stay on. There was a moment in his career when ambitions of a political nature overtook him. Perhaps the Tamil tradition of stars becoming political leaders was beckoning him. In December 2017, he publicly announced that he would launch a political party and 'contest all 234 Assembly seats in the state'. Rajini Makkal Mandram (people's forum) was floated amid speculation that he would promote the BJP–RSS cause in Tamil Nadu. 'Spiritual politics' is the term he used to indicate his ideology. Within weeks of announcing plans to enter politics, he put out a statement saying: 'With extreme sadness I say that I can't enter politics.' During those intervening weeks he had entered a hospital in Hyderabad with blood pressure problems. As it happened, Rajini had avoided the Dravidian politics of other Tamil Nadu leaders and preferred a 'national' approach. For that reason, his political influence was virtually nil in Tamil country. Perhaps it did not really matter because the influence exerted by his filmic personal was unequalled.

Rajinikanth was also active in areas outside films. He attracted national attention when he supported Anna Hazare's anti-corruption movement in 2011. He campaigned in support of organ donation. He has been a donor to charities. His simplicity has been a talking point; with no film-star pretensions, he goes about in a simple South Indian dhoti and with no attempt to hide his bald pate. He must be the only film-star in history who, if a movie of his fails, returns the signing amount to the producers. Fans in Chennai, used to seeing fleets of fancy cars maintained by movie idols, are impressed that Rajini has only a Toyota Innova, a Range Rover, and a Bentley. His life story was part of the curriculum prescribed by the Central Board of Secondary Education (CBSE). The chapter title was: 'From Conductor to Superstar'. Press reports quote him as once saying: 'Yesterday I was a conductor. Today I am a star. What I will be tomorrow only He knows.' That he was already part of the curriculum in schools showed that He had taken a decision. Arts editor and theatre designer, Sadanand Menon, struck the right notes when he wrote: 'Rajini represents the noir in Tamil Cinema. He represents the suppressed, dark other of Tamil society... The history of oppression of the Dravidian race, the sense of subjugation, the feeling of second-class citizenship, the complexes about being dark-skinned, of not really being part of the national mainstream, and a clear whiff of political and cultural marginalisation at that point in time, were all encapsulated in the character of Rajinikanth and his screen persona... With Rajini, Tamil cinema and by extension, Tamil society learned to be kosher with being "bad". It was no longer something that someone was going to make them feel guilty about.'* That was a vital point that threw light on the way a generation broke free of its hangovers. Sadanand Menon went further and said: 'Rajini taught Tamil society to abandon platitudes about Rama as Maryada Purushottam and accept the possibility of a Ravana or a Duryodhana actually being good... After four decades of chubby, fair-skinned heroes, this lean, mean anti-hero emerges as a version of updated masculinity... Rajini is the first of the "dark stars" of Tamil cinema, which itself becomes a signpost for celebration. The validation of Rajini's dark skin has, in itself, become a sub-cult in Tamil cinema.'

That was an analysis of the sociological as well as political implications of the Rajinikanth phenomenon. This was not just a filmic hero. Nor was he just a guy who developed mannerisms and showmanship that captivated people. He was a symbol of society's class divisions and a pace-setter who showed how pigeonholing could be confronted effectively.

Financial pigeonholing was something else. The way producers rated film-stars in money terms was, in its very nature, arbitrary. But market estimates had a way of enforcing their unwritten rules on everything, including remuneration to stars. In the early 2020s Karthi was rated at ₹8 crore per film, Vijay Sethupati at 8–10 crore and Sivakarthikeyan at 10–12 crore. In the bigger leagues, Dhanush charged ₹15 crore for a film, while Vikram rated himself at ₹20 crore. Suriya was at 20–22 crore, Kamala Haasan at 25–30 crore, Ajith at 40–50 crore and Vijay at 45–50 crore. Rajinikanth of course was above all of them in star value, so his charge of ₹60 crore was no surprise. Compared to Tamil, other South Indian languages flail

* Sadanand Menon, 'From rakshasa to Dalit icon', *Hindustan Times*, 1 August 2016.

way behind. Malayalam's number one star, Mohanlal, is at the 5–8 crore level, while Mammooty is at 4–5 crore. Kannada's Puneeth Rajkumar was rated at 5–5.5 crore per film. Rajinikanth's fees put him above Hindi heroes, too. Shah Rukh Khan used to charge ₹50 crore per picture, but he moved on to a 45 per cent profit-sharing pattern. Salman Khan was on the same track with a fee of ₹70–75 crore plus a share of the profit. Time was when the mention of a crore saw jaws dropping. Now, every Tom, Trick, and Joker wallows in crores.

There was nothing, it seemed, that Rajini couldn't pull off. The mass following he achieved wherever Tamil prevailed was not the mass following film-stars normally achieve with their glamorous looks and their seductiveness. It was not easy for a man with a very bald head and a very dark skin to be considered seductive. If he did not have the Shah Rukh Khan looks, he did not have the Salman Khan body either. Rajinikanth had only his histrionics to rely on. Fortunately for him, and for the cinematic art, his histrionics were spectacular. They made him a force that mattered in cinema and beyond.

29

UMAR KHALID

Because of his Name

JNU, Delhi's glamour-tinged Jawaharlal Nehru University, had always held two opposing student unions, the BJP-led Akhil Bharatiya Vidyarthi Parishad, ABVP, and the leftist Democratic Students Union, DSU. The campus turned into a battleground in February 2016 when court-ordered capital punishment was meted out to Afzal Guru who had attacked the Indian Parliament in 2001. Students held a protest meeting in defiance of the university administration. Some in the audience, to the surprise of all present, raised anti-India slogans. They were found to be outsiders in masks, JNU students were among those who criticised the mischief by elements unconnected with the university. But the manner in which the government reacted made a bad situation worse. Students Union President Kanhaiya Kumar was arrested on charges of sedition. The way he was beaten up when he was being taken to prison shocked even those who were in no way connected with his cause. Classes came to a standstill as thousands of students and staff condemned the arrests. Protest meetings were held in several other campuses in the country. Five student leaders went into hiding. After 10 days Umar Khalid surfaced on his own and surrendered to the police.

With a BA, an MA, and an MPhil already in his bag, Umar Khalid was pursuing a PhD when he was rusticated from the university for one semester. He had to obtain a favourable order from the Delhi High Court to submit his PhD thesis. He got into a bigger controversy when he was charged with making provocative speeches at a famous meeting in Pune. This was the Elgaar Parishad (assembly for speaking aloud) rally held to mark the 200th anniversary of the Battle of Koregaon. Unusual importance was attached to this event because of the caste emotions involved. The battle in 1818 saw Dalit soldiers of the British army defeating the troops of the ruling Peshwa, a Brahmin. On 1 January every year, Ambedkarite Dalits gathered to commemorate the event at the Vijay Stambh. In 2018, the gathering erupted into violence, killing at least one. Right-wing Hindutva leaders were blamed in one FIR while another cited 'Leftist groups with Maoist links' as the culprits. The authorities pursued the latter, arresting 16 people, many of whom were not even present at the place where the incidents had occurred. Arrests continued in a planned manner, extending to 2019. Among those detained in the later rounds were well-known critics of the government, from Sudhir Dhawale and Rona Wilson to Sudha Bharadwaj, Varavara Rao, and Vernon Gonsalves. In 2020, Anand Teltumbde and Gautam Navlakha were arrested followed by anti-caste activist and Delhi University Professor Hany Babu Tharayil, all under anti-terror laws.

The specific charge levelled against Umar Khalid, along with Jignesh Mevani, then a Gujarat MLA, was of making 'provocative speeches creating communal disharmony' at the Elgaar Parishad. Umar Khalid was accused of saying that the battle of Bhima Koregaon had to be taken ahead. 'They had attacked. It is time to retaliate and we will fight this battle and we will win and this victory over new Peshwai will be the true homage to the martyrs of Bhima Koregaon battle.'* The special cell of the Delhi police said that, 'Khalid was one of the main conspirators of riots in which 53 persons died.'

* 'FIR against Mevani, Khalid in Bhima Koregaon violence', *Deccan Herald*, 4 January 2018.

To his credit, Umar Khalid refused to take these accusations lying down. In January 2021, he moved a plea in the Chief Metropolitan Magistrate's court in Delhi against what he called the vicious media campaign against him. The court said that the presumption of innocence should not be destroyed at the very threshold of the justice system through a media trial. One of the news items, the court said, started with the words 'Radical Islamist and Anti-Hindu Delhi riots accused Umar Khalid'. It portrayed the entirety of the Delhi riots as anti-Hindu. Khalid said there was a concerted effort to prejudice opinion against him in the case. He was being targeted, he said, in an attempt to exonerate the real accused who were closely associated with Prime Minister Modi.

This was another case that brought out the communal factor in all things Indian. Kanhaiya Kumar was an inspiring figure as he led the Azadi chorus at JNU in 2016. In September 2020, an article appeared under the by-line of Prashant Dixit that questioned Kumar's ideology. His comrade-in-arms, Umar Khalid, had been arrested in connection with the Delhi riots. Dixit said Kanhaiya was silent about this. 'Such silences enable the majority to push ahead with the narrative against any Muslim who lands in the crosshairs of the Narendra Modi government,' explained Dixit. Kanhaiya was one of the six leaders scheduled to speak at a meeting on Delhi police's handling of the February violence. He didn't show up. Dixit drew a picture as realistic as it was saddening. 'Today,' he said, 'Kanhaiya Kumar, a prized leader of the CPI, enjoys the freedom to build upon his political career; Umar Khalid stares at a long period in jail.' Saying that both Kanhaiya and Umar understood the stark difference in their fates, Dixit observed, 'This shows how, politically speaking, the Muslim identity in India has become "untouchable". You steer clear from being vocal for a "Muslim" because you fear being labelled as an "Islamist supporter". This enables the RSS–BJP narrative... to distance itself from the many Umar Khalids who are vocal, articulate and unflinching in their fight for the rights of India's Muslims, Dalits and Adivasis.' The final thrust must have given the former JNU hero pause. It was: 'By staying quiet on Umar, Kanhaiya's politics play into the hands of the RSS–BJP.'

Umar is the son of Syed Qasim Rasool Ilyas, a politician in his own right who was a member of the Student Islamic Movement of India (SIMI). The stated mission of SIMI was the 'liberation of India' by converting it into an Islamic nation. It was banned in 2001. As Umar hit the headlines, Ilyas said: 'I left SIMI in 1985, before my son Umar was born... My son is a tough man, not easy to break him.' Now a member of the All India Muslim Personal Law Board, Ilyas was of the view that his son was '...fighting to protect the constitutional values and for a better country. We have always stood with him.' He added: 'His ideology has become his worst enemy. He is a meritorious student. The country's media is slowly turning on him because he is a perfect fit: A Muslim face with views that don't gel with the state's opinion on things.'

Umar's mother, Sabiha Khanum, and sisters also came out in support of him. This was despite the fact that Umar was not in agreement with the Islamic ritualism followed by members of his family. 'Whether it was praying, fasting, or women in the family covering their heads, he was the only non-believer in our family, which angered me,' Ilyas said. But he stoutly defended the family. 'If you are branding my communist son a traitor because of my past, it is worse than targeting. Even the home minister of the country has put branding on him... All because of his name.'

Whether it was his name or his politics, Umar Khalid was under stricter restraints than ordinary prisoners. He said he was not allowed to talk to anyone, or to step out of his cell. The judge pulled up the jail staff for muting Umar's microphone when the case was going on. The undertrial should not be punished for putting forward his grievances, the judge said. Details of this kind described a basic reality: the government considered Umar Khalid an enemy of the state.

Those who knew him personally could never imagine him in that light. It was his intellectual vigour that impressed them and all those who came into contact with any aspect of his work. Sangeeta Dasgupta, associate professor at JNU, described him as 'one of the brightest students I have taught'. As she put it: 'His deep empathy for the marginalised would constantly emerge in the course of discussions. For him, the vision that he shared with many of his friends was "to transform every moment into a fight for the better". Poignant thoughts that today exist only in a utopian world. There is nothing unconstitutional about these thoughts. Please.'

Constitutionalities can be mutated into realpolitik, which is defined as 'a system of politics or principles based on practical rather than moral or ideological considerations'. In other words, practical considerations and moral considerations are worlds apart. The sensible, of course, go for what is practical, leaving it to the dreamers to stick with the moral.

A distinguishing feature of Umar Khalid was his ability to position himself and others within the political map of the country with a kind of precision that was difficult to fault. When the police arrested him in the wake of the Delhi riots in February 2020, it put him in the category of senior political leaders who had already been booked in connection with the case—CPM General Secretary Sitaram Yechury, Swaraj Abhiyan leader Yogendra Yadav, economist Jayati Ghosh, Delhi University professor Apoorvanand, and documentary filmmaker Rahul Roy. Khalid said the Delhi police had a predetermined theory and they wanted to vindicate it by sidelining the facts. He described the Delhi police investigation as 'a narrative-based investigation, not a fact-based investigation'. Referring to a newspaper describing him as 'gunehgar' (criminal), he told the court: 'This is not even a media trial. A trial presupposes that you will be heard. This is an inquisition.'

His contrarian interpretation of government policies had captured headlines even during the February 2020 brouhaha over *Namaste Trump*. 'When Donald Trump comes to India on 24 February,' Khalid had said, 'we will say that the prime minister and the Government of India are trying to divide the country. They are destroying the values of Mahatma Gandhi and the people of India are fighting against them. If those in power want to divide India, the people of India are ready to unite the country.' However, BJP leaders said Khalid was provoking people to protest ahead of Trump's visit. In the event, Trump's visit coincided with the riots in Delhi which led to the death of 50 people. A BJP leader, Amit Malviya, suggested that the riots had been pre-planned. He cited as evidence Umar Khalid's speech in Amravati on February 17 'where he exhorted a largely Muslim audience to come out on the streets in huge numbers when Trump arrives'. Malviya tweeted: 'Was the violence in Delhi planned weeks in advance by tukde-tukde gang?'

The general temper in Delhi started changing in 2014 with Narendra Modi's rise as prime minister. One of the climactic points was reached in 2018 with the arrests of Kabir Kala Manch (KKM) activists. This was a cultural organisation formed in Pune in the wake of the 1992 Gujarat riots. Students and young professionals were the organisers and their principal activity was the presentation of protest poetry and plays in slums and streets. They were jailed on the charge that they were 'Maoists' and 'Naxalites'. In December 2020, when two KKM members challenged their arrest in the Bombay High Court, the National Investigation Agency said that the reason for arresting them was that they sang songs criticising Prime Minister Modi and mocking his radio lecture *Mann ki Baat.* The names of arrested men released by KKM told their own tale: Meeran Hyder, PhD student at Jamia Millia, Asif Iqbal Tanha and Shifa ur Rehman of Jamia Millia, Siddique Kappan. The name of Stan Swamy was added later. This was an 83-year-old Jesuit priest working for the welfare of tribals in Jharkhand. Afflicted by Parkinson's, he could not sign his legal papers, and had to move the court to obtain permission for using a straw to drink water from a glass. The NIA took 20 days to respond to this plea.

It was clear that the climate was not favourable for detainees in general. One named Umar Khalid could only expect the worst. The assumption that those with Muslim names were not to be trusted was openly flaunted. The term 'love jihad' swept the nation, its communal overtones underlined by the word jihad. (Jihad means 'a holy war waged on behalf of Islam as a religious duty'. The implication was that a Muslim could fall in love with a non-Muslim only as Jihad, a religious duty. Young Muslims of the modern age were uncomfortable with this thesis.) Some who saw the danger of communalism in the phrase started a counter movement under the title 'India Love Project'. The courage and imagination the initiative demanded came from the journalist couple Priya Ramani and Samar Halarnkar with their friend, Niloufer Venkataraman. They curated love stories that transcended the boundaries of religion and social divides. Marriages that overcame conventional prejudices came to light—a Kashmiri Muslim marrying a Punjabi Hindu, a Syrian Christian man with a disability marrying someone three years older even after he proclaimed that he was an atheist and a communist. They celebrated interfaith, intercommunity marriages as a part of India's social tradition.

But in Narendra Modi's India they could only win a battle or two, not the war. In fact, no one could win the war. The 'right-wing Hindu nationalist party is power in Delhi' seems to have reduced the whole country into tukde-tukde gangs.

29

RANA AYYUB

'Muslim' and 'Woman'

The Gujarat riots of 2002 attracted world attention because the political leadership of the state headed by Narendra Modi was seen to have condoned the killings of Muslims. For three days, the state government said and did nothing as armed gangs went around annihilating entire Muslim settlements. Subsequent statements by government spokesmen were no more than a formality; it did nothing to stop the killings which went on for three months. An official count recorded 1,044 deaths. The Concerned Citizens Tribunal put it at 1,926. Media outlets described the killings as 'state terrorism' rather than 'communal riots'.

Many books recorded the brutality. In 2002 itself, veteran journalist, Siddharth Varadarajan, published *Gujarat: The Making of a Tragedy.* Civil rights activist, Teesta Setalvad, wrote a chapter in Varadarajan's book titled 'When Guardians Betray: The Role of the Police'. Setalvad's own book was *Gujarat: Behind the Mirage.* Gujarat cadre IPS officer R.B. Sreekumar wrote: *Gujarat Behind The Curtain.* Manoj Mitta came out with *The Fiction of Fact Finding: Modi and Godhra.* Harsh Mander wrote *Between Memory and Forgetting: Massacre and the Modi Years in Gujarat.* Foreign scholars pitched in with their accounts of the anti-Muslim violence and of riot politics. One study was *Scarred: Experiments with Violence in Gujarat* by Dionne Bunsha, an Indian journalist settled in Canada.

The journalist Rana Ayyub approached the subject from an altogether different angle. She wrote what might be described as an undercover book. The world saw her *Gujarat Files: Anatomy of a Cover-up* as something unusual; the *New Yorker* magazine profiled her while *Time* magazine included her in its list of 10 journalists who faced the maximum threat to their lives. The book was translated into 15 languages. The United Nations human rights division asked India to provide protection to her. But India seemed unlikely to oblige. After all, she had gone on record saying that 'an exploding Coronavirus crisis shows that Modi is not up to the task of leading India'.

Amid violence that was suspected to be officially endorsed, there was a fair amount of risk for those who ventured to check things out for themselves. It was doubly so in Rana's case: She was a woman and she was a Muslim. Experience had made her aware of what that meant. When she was a senior editor at *Tehelka*, she had said at a public function in Trivandrum: 'I personally have an added responsibility of proving my nationalism because I am Rana Ayyub.' But she wouldn't be deterred. Bent on reporting the ground reality in Gujarat, she went undercover for eight months, adopting the name Maithili Tyagi and posing as an American film student working on a documentary on Gujarat. Her investigation produced a report that won universal acclaim and a bunch of awards. But the Supreme Court of India thought otherwise. It considered the case when the Centre for Public Interest Litigation approached it seeking fresh investigation into the murder of the then Gujarat Home Minister Haren Pandya in 2003. The petition relied upon Rana Ayyub's *Gujarat Files*. The court said the book had no evidentiary value as it was 'nothing more than an opinion, lacking hard facts'. Suggesting that the book could possibly have been written out of political motivations, the court dismissed the petition and imposed a fine of ₹50,000 on the petitioners.

Rana also spent a good bit of time doing relief work, handing over parcels of daily necessities to people displaced by natural calamities and unnatural ones, such as a pandemic crisis exacerbated by government policy. She was a campaigner for relief funds for flood-affected people in Assam and Bihar, and for arranging rations for migrants on the move in the wake of the India's lockdown, the harshest in the world. The message she gave out wherever she went was: 'Your hate won't stop us from doing the right thing.'

It is tempting to imagine that Rana's determination may have something to do with the fact that she was born in the year George Orwell made immortal with his prophetically imagined 1948 novel, *1984*. Orwell configured a grave new world of doublethink, Big Brother, Newspeak and Thought Police. The India in which Rana grew up developed its own doublethink culture which forced her family in once-cosmopolitan Bombay to move to the Muslim-majority suburb of Deonar following the riots of 1992–1993. Some accounts say she was born and schooled in Srinagar, Kashmir (see starsunfolded.com). But no one disputes the fact that she grew up in Deonar–Bombay as a practising Muslim. Her father, Mohammed Ayyub Waqif, was a public school teacher and member of the Progressive Writers' Movement. He contributed occasionally to *Blitz*, the strident English weekly made famous by the owner-editor R.K. Karanjia's left leaning politics and his flair for tabloid journalism. Rana took to writing early on, becoming a reporter-writer for *Tehelk*a, then a popular investigative magazine. In 2019, she was engaged by the *Washington Post* as a contributing writer for its Global Opinion section. The 2020 Voices of Courage and Conscience Award was given to her by the Muslim Public Affairs Council of America. In a by-lined opinion piece in the *Washington Post* in November 2019, she recalled how the demolition of Babri Masjid 'changed the narrative of secularism in the world's largest democracy'. Until then 'we had a social identity, never a religious one'. The shift to the latter had a frightening edge to it, she said. After the Masjid demolition, '...our neighbour, a Sikh, came knocking nervously at our door. He said rioters were marching to our house to take me and my sister. I was 9, my elder sister 14. Hundreds of Muslim women were raped during that time. Within minutes we were whisked away through the back door on our neighbour's motorcycle with our heads covered. We were taken to a locality of Sikhs where my sister and I took refuge in a house for two months. We had no means of communicating with our family... From that point on, we were Muslims, outsiders, invaders. When we returned home, nothing was the same. Our neighbours were no longer just our neighbours—they were Hindus now. The next month, my family—like thousands of other Muslim families—moved to a Muslim ghetto.'

With experiences of that kind, it would have been natural to be intimidated. But Ayyub was ever conscious of her rights as an Indian citizen. She did not request special considerations; she wouldn't settle for differentiated consideration either. Calling herself a practising Muslim, she wrote: 'I believe I can continue to be liberal and secular while being proud of my faith.' It could not have been easy in an environment that often made a mockery of liberalism and secularism. When Rana's father and brother applied for credit cards, they were refused, apparently under instructions from above. There were also journalists and social commentators who did not hesitate to condemn her personally. A well-regarded columnist went so far as to call her a 'vile person' and a 'moral leper' who has 'the empathy of a door knob'. Perhaps Rana had more reasons than were apparent to tell a panel at the London School of Economics in 2019 that 'the government is not taking any steps to make journalism in India safer'.

Rana's journalism won resourceful enemies who used the internet to make her seem bigoted and worse. One post made her look like a supporter of child rapists ('Do they have no human rights?' she was supposed to have asked), and as a communalist who said the 'Hindutva government' was keen to 'hang Muslims in large numbers'. The incongruity of such posts was as obvious as the intention behind them. Yet, a tweet was a tweet and its ability to influence minds was transcendental. 'The troll posted my phone number, my house address,' she said. 'If this is the depth of their hatred, what will stop them from coming into my house as a mob and kill me. It was an on-line lynch mob.' Threats drove her closer to her god. In October 2020, she said in a post: 'My safe place. Prayer at the Hazrat Nizamuddin Auliya Dargah this afternoon. Sheer bliss.' She was drowned in an internet attack by critics who abused her for her religiosity.

A casual look at the messages sent to her brings home the extent of communal hatred in the air. Most of them addressed her in words that were unparliamentary. Many warned her to remember Gauri Lankesh, the Karnataka journalist who was shot dead in 2017 by people who did not like her opinions. Rana was acquainted with Gauri, and said: 'I remember three days before Gauri died, she posted on my Facebook wall when I was receiving a lot of hate, telling me that I shouldn't worry and that, these people won't do anything. Three days later she was killed, so there is always a sense of fear. What if online hate goes offline?'

The courage that was obvious in the public positions she took made Rana an unusual representative of her time. As Priya Ramani put it, Rana's 'no-filter critique of New India makes her impossible to ignore'. Priya revealed Rana's human side as well. 'She wants me to inform readers,' Priya wrote in a column, 'that she is single and looking for love, ideally something lasting.' It's the only space in her life where there's a void, she was quoted as saying. Priya added: 'Ayyub's writing may be grim, but her friends know she is full of joie de vivre.' Apparently no one took the hint.

Rana was alone in her moments of crisis, unlike Priya Ramani who had family and friends to support her. It was left to Priya to make up for it by writing in support of the beleaguered fellow writer. In a piece headlined 'The Impossible Rana Ayyub', she wrote: 'In a world where journalists are under siege, Ayyub's relentless critique, large public following and reporting chops makes hers a voice that's impossible to ignore.' The trolls and abusers were particularly incensed if Rana spoke about Kashmir, a topic that became more sensitive after the Modi government suddenly revoked Kashmir's special status and put its leaders in jail. Typical was her July 2020 comment that when it comes to Kashmir, 'There are no humanists, only convenient nationalists.' That it was a fair reading of the situation did not count. 'Every time I write or speak on Kashmir,' she said, 'the hate is unimaginable.' It could not have been easy for a woman in her 30s to stand up and challenge detractors and indeed dare them. Rana Ayyub also had to bear her minority status in mind. Anxiety and insomnia became medical problems for her in the wake of death threats and rape threats and threats to her family. At one point, she recorded symptoms of incipient paralysis: 'From having gone completely immobile on the right of my body to now taking baby steps in a span of four days, I'm hugely indebted to the Lilavati Hospital staff. You have given me a new lease of life.' Problems associated with her religion never left her: 'Friends question my journalistic credentials when I speak about attacks on Muslims. I am asked to detach myself from the story, not to speak of fascism and majoritarianism in India because it hurts the country's global standing.' It was always a dilemma trying to reconcile her religious identity with her national identity. She was always perceived as a Muslim and held answerable as a Muslim.

In the circumstances, it took courage to own up the articles of faith that guided Rana Ayyub in her life. She was as proud of her convictions as she was of her country. She would not have been controversial in the India of, say, Jayaprakash Narayan. Unfortunately, her India was the India of Amit Shah. She had to face the inevitable consequences. By facing them with grit and daring, she set an example; and she demonstrated how the worst of situations could be fought with judicious thought and action.

30

NAMBI NARAYANAN

Honour Restored

There was a time when the big powers of the world did not want small powers to become big. Vikram Sarabhai, founder of the Indian Space Research Organisation (ISRO), launched a programme for the development of atomic energy. He died mysteriously in his sleep. Homi Bhabha, known as the 'father of India's nuclear programme' wanted his country to develop nuclear weapons. He died in an air crash. In 1994, ISRO was on the cusp of an important breakthrough in rocket propulsion, aerospace engineer Nambi Narayanan's speciality field. He was suddenly stopped in his tracks by scandal, not death. Juicy stories broke out about Maldivian honey traps, police officers alternately amorous and ambitious, and scientists allegedly giving away top secrets for loads of cash. Nambi Narayanan, as one of the accused scientists, would later describe it as 'sordid drama... that a foreign agency was only too eager to prolong and propel, penetrating into such agencies as the Intelligence Bureau, taking some of the officials as pawns to scuttle India's inevitable march into space.'

What made foreign agencies turn murderous was the same thing that made Indian pioneers proud—the steady progress India had made towards developing a nuclear bomb. Raja Ramanna, who was part of the team behind the 1947 Pokhran-I atomic test, put it bluntly when he said that making a bomb '...for us was a matter of prestige that would justify our ancient past. As Indian scientists we were keen to show our Western counterparts, who thought little of us in those days, that we too could do it.' (Quoted in *Weapon of Peace* by Raj Chengappa.)

The plot-within-a-plot case burst into the headlines again in 2021 when the Supreme Court intervened to ask for a detailed inquiry. A three-member committee headed by the retired Supreme Court judge, D.K. Jain, had submitted a report on the role of erring police officials in the case. The apex court sealed the report and directed the Central Bureau of Investigation to probe further into the committee's findings. The court said the committee had found 'acts of omission and commission' by 'responsible officials' of Kerala Police. 'The report indicates something serious, thus appropriate action will have to be taken.' Nambi Narayanan (NN) said, 'The CBI probe is a great progress. It was a fabricated case and there is high-level conspiracy involved.'* The impression was widespread that N.N. was victimised for no fault of his. Public sympathy was on his side, as reflected in *Rocketry: The Nambi Effect*, a 2022 film starring R. Madhavan.

The first space research committee was set up in 1962. ISRO was formally inaugurated in 1969 and its first satellite, Aryabhata, launched in 1975. India's own Satellite Launch Vehicle was in operation by 1980. Several space systems have been launched for telecommunication, meteorology, disaster warning, and resource monitoring. The first Chandrayaan mission to the moon took off in 2008. Since then, many private companies also entered the field and the race was on to close the gap between the real and virtual worlds.

Satellite technology also means closing the gap between peace and war. Vikram Sarabhai understood this, hence the unusual interest he showed in developing certain professional contacts. Two specialists

* 'It was high-level plot, says Nambi Narayanan, hails ruling', *Times of India*, 16 April 2021.

he cultivated were Dadieu, the German rocket engineer associated with the V-2 that terrorised Britain during World War II, and Itokawa, the specialist for Japan's pencil rocket. This titbit is in the book *Ready to Fire* (Bloomsbury 2018) by Nambi Narayanan who worked with Sarabhai and looked up to him as his mentor. N.N. writes: 'With faith in the Japanese wisdom on onboard-control systems and the German mastery over fabrication, both not allowed by the US to be put to use in those countries, Sarabhai was trying to forge a deadly brotherhood. The US was ostensibly unhappy.'

Why would the US be interested in an Indian programme? The US was the leader of the post-war world which believed that nuclear power was too important to be trusted with anyone outside the big powers. For a newly independent country from Asia to try to break into the club was a no-no. The limits were tested when India collaborated with the Russians in procuring some advanced systems. Bhabha himself perhaps made it worse when he announced on All India Radio in October 1965 that India had the capability to make a nuclear bomb in 18 months.

The next year, Bhabha was dead in an air crash in the Alps. A half century later the *Times of India* published a story that began with the question: Was the CIA responsible for the Air India crash that killed Bhabha?* It quoted the transcript of a conversation in which a CIA officer said: 'We had trouble, you know, with India back in the 60s when they got uppity and started work on an atomic bomb... The thing is, they were getting into bed with the Russians.' Referring to Bhabha, he said, 'That one was dangerous, believe me.' When Sarabhai also died in a hotel room in December 1971 for no apparent reason, an associate in Ahmedabad was quoted as saying: 'Vikram had told me that he was being watched by both Americans and Russians.'

Critical projects Sarabhai had started continued to run into

* Srinivas Laxman, 'Operative spoke of CIA hand in 1966 crash: Report', *Times of India*, 30 July 2017.

obstacles placed by influential parties. ISRO was in need of cryogenic technology for the heavier satellite launch vehicles it planned. This technology helps achieve the extremely low temperatures needed to liquefy hydrogen for the propulsion of very heavy launch vehicles. Until the mid-1980s, only the US, France, Russia, and Japan had this technology. India, anxious to fast-track its programme, held discussions with France, Japan, and the US and finally struck a deal with the Russians to import some cryogenic engines. The US objected and circumstances forced the Russians to cancel agreements concerning technology transfer, and ISRO promptly decided to develop cryogenic knowhow on its own. That was in 1993. In 1994 the director of the cryogenic project, Nambi Narayanan, was arrested and thrown headlong into a scandal of sex, police, spies, and torture.

N.N. was ISRO's first scientist to develop a passion for cryogenics. His colleagues saw little merit in liquid engines. He felt so isolated that he even tried to resign. But he was a bit of a rocket engine himself. If he believed in a project, he would argue with his superiors, when provoked, in angry tones. 'I was known,' he admits in his book, 'for bulldozing through official barricades to achieve my goals which included the making of India's first big liquid propulsion system.' The goal was subverted by those who plotted to get him arrested. But his dream lived on, and India eventually developed cryogenic technology on its own.

Grounds for his ordeal were laid some time before N.N. became aware of them. It all started with a Kerala police officer eyeing a six-foot Maldivian woman in Trivandrum City. His attempts to seduce her were rudely spurned by the woman. The wounded male ego set out to get her tied up in legal knots using her foreigner status. He found an opportunity to file spying charges against her. In no time, multiple agencies jumped in with multiple motivations. The end result was that the scandal 'not only finished the careers of two exceptionally brilliant space scientists, but also put the country's cryogenic engine development on hold for more than 19 years' (Kumar Chellappan, *The Pioneer*, 8 December 2013). N.N.'s account of the persecution he went through fills us with equal parts pride and shame—pride at the man's integrity and courage, and shame that we have a police/intelligence system driven by personal ambitions and political corruption. His book, subtitled *How India and I Survived the ISRO Spy Case*, gives an insight into Sarabhai's vision and how his team of scientists became inspired by it. It makes us feel that we are a people who can achieve anything if only the dreamers are given a free hand. The next moment, however, we are forced to realise that we will never do well because of the dishonesty and crookedness of those who are in positions of power.

The morning after he was arrested, judgement was pronounced by the media—that Nambi Narayanan was a traitor who sold state secrets to Pakistan through two Maldivian women who acted as honey traps. Following the arrest, N.N. was at the mercy of the Kerala police, first, and then of the IB from Delhi. They lost no time subjecting him to their famous interrogation techniques. Blunt, no-nonsense questions were hurled: 'Why did you spy? Why did you give drawings to Pakistan?' Wild threats followed: 'Don't bullshit. If you confess, your life will be easy; otherwise we know how to make you confess.' Demoralising language was used to humiliate: 'You bastard, do you know what the charges are?'

The first body blow landed on him when they asked him to give the name of a Muslim friend of his and he, quite honestly, gave the name of his colleague A.P.J. Abdul Kalam. After striking him, they made him stand for 30 hours. When he asked for water, the answer was: 'You third-rate criminal, you want water?' The psychological pressure more than the physical torture had made Sasikumar, N.N.'s fellow scientist who had also been arrested, succumb. He told them what they asked him to say. N.N., astonishingly, held on. He recalls how he told himself, 'I cannot let down Sarabhai, my father, my gurus and myself.' As he puts it: 'I took deep breaths and stood my ground. I spoke, "You guys are committing a big crime, and you will be punished for it."' After those 30 hours of standing, he was allowed to sit down, but he declined.

N.N.'s book is an analysis of how the ISRO spy case affected him and his work, not a comprehensive study of the case itself. That could explain why he makes no references to reports that had come up at the time about Prime Minister Narasimha Rao's suspected interest in the case. According to published reports (example, 'Spies in the sky', *Outlook*, 3 July 1996), a Hyderabad-based company to which ISRO had given an engine manufacturing contract had business dealings with P.V. Narasimha Rao's son. It did raise eyebrows at the time when Prime Minister Rao made an unscheduled one-day trip to Trivandrum, followed by CBI chief K. Vijaya Rama Rao. With those visits, the tide suddenly turned. The CBI took over the case, asking the Kerala police and IB to stay away. Narasimha Rao's family interests prevailed over national interests. After a 17-month investigation, the CBI declared that the case was cooked up by interested parties in the police force for reasons of their internal rivalry. It wrote confidential letters to the central and Kerala governments recommending action against the officers concerned. The Chief Judicial Magistrate accepted the CBI report and absolved all the accused of all the charges. Prodded by its police brass, the Kerala government ordered further investigation into the case. N.N. challenged the order of the High Court but got a judgment that was too ambiguous to mean anything. With that, police officers started taking preliminary steps for 'further investigation'. N.N. went to the Supreme Court, this time with his fellow-accused from ISRO as joint petitioners. The judgment was delivered on 29 April 1998. It described the Kerala government's order a 'mala fide exercise of power... [which] does not comport with the known pattern of a responsible government bound by rule of law.' In its 2018 judgment, the Supreme Court described police treatment of N.N. as 'Psycho-Pathological'.

N.N. continued his battle. He moved petitions in the court seeking action against Kerala police officer's named by CBI for cooking up the spy case. He filed a suit in Trivandrum for ₹1 crore compensation, listing the Kerala government, the union government, and the police officers as respondents. Reinstated at the ISRO headquarters in Bangalore, N.N. presented himself at the chairman's room. 'You have a lot more to contribute,' said the chairman. N.N. replied: 'I've nothing more to contribute. I've got more than enough for all the contributions I have made.' ISRO had not lifted a finger in defence of its senior scientist, nor made any effort to tell the world that its specialists were clean. Nambi Narayanan lost his career and retained his honour.

31

DEVANGANA KALITA AND NATASHA NARWAL

Idol Breakers

Jamia Millia Islamia is, as the name proclaims, Islamic in its orientation and purpose. When it was established by Sir Syed Ahmad Khan in 1875, it was called Muhammadan Anglo-Oriental College. It became the Aligarh Muslim University in 1920. In 1925, Jamia moved to Delhi's Karol Bagh, and the following year to Okhla, then a nondescript south Delhi village. Its student hostels followed the common practice of promulgating their own rules and regulations for students. Jamia stipulated time schedules for women students to be back in their hostels. If they wished to stay out beyond 8 p.m., they needed to take permission from hostel wardens. The women who lived in the hostels responded to this rule in a defiant style. The restrictive regulations, they said, pointed to a perceived notion that woman needed to be protected. This, they said, was a CCTV-driven police concept of security. Such concepts and the ideas of safety emanating from them led to silencing women's right to mobility and liberation. They put women in a pinjra (cage) and it became necessary to break (tod) them. The resounding call for Pinjra Tod was born. The phrase grew into a movement, beyond the original objectives of ending curfews on women's movements and working for the prevention of sexual harassments. Now it included issues such as moral policing, and even inflated charges for hostel rooms for women. The challenge to 'patriarchal policies women face in their campuses' succeeded in persuading the University Grants Commission to take steps to protect women employees. Activists warned that 'hyper masculinity often masquerades as patriotism'. The Delhi Commission for Women asked colleges why curfew timings differed for men and women. From all corners echoes reverberated: 'I will break the cage and fly away/I will open my arms and fly away.'

Some critics said Pinjra Tod represented only Savarna interests. Others said this was criticism for the sake of criticism. Controversy did not prevent the arrest of two activists, Devangana Kalita and Natasha Narwal, from their homes. The police claimed the two were connected with the 2020 Delhi riots. Both students were PhD scholars at JNU and had opposed the Citizenship Amendment Act pushed through by Home Minister Amit Shah. This, and not the Delhi riots mentioned by the police, was assumed to be the real reason for the arrests. Booked under the stringent Unlawful Activities (Prevention) Act, both were given bail, then arrested again. Devangana, a student from Assam, had a BA in English, an MA in gender and development, an MA in history, and was pursuing an MPhil. She emerged as an example of how the educated and the enlightened were finding it difficult to contribute what they could to the India of today. In December 2020, Natasha had already been in jail for six months when her father Mahavir Narwal, a retired scientist, said: 'She will come back stronger. It is not right to dismiss every woman's independent views as radical. Most importantly, radical is not anti-national.'* That kind of conviction and will-power are stronger than Modi–Shah's muscle power.

Muscle power yielded to justice in June 2021 when a Delhi court ordered the release of Devangana, Natasha, and fellow student Asif Iqbal Tanha. The police tried to prevent the release on the plea that they needed time to verify the permanent addresses of

---

* Jyoti Yadav, 'Tale of 2 Indian fathers—one who stands by his daughter in jail, another who disowned his', *The Print*, 5 July 2020.

the accused. 'Do you follow this procedure in other cases as well?' the High Court asked the police. The students, as they came out of Tihar Jail, made their position clear by declaring that 'our fight will continue'.

Analyses by law students and other observers linked the arrests of Devangana and Natasha to the anti-Muslim activities the government was alleged to be engaged in. The riots Delhi witnessed in February 2021 were seen as an anti-Muslim offensive. Published reports said that homes and shops that were looted and torched belonged to Muslims. Of the 53 people killed, more than two-thirds were Muslims. An Amnesty International investigation went so far as to say that the Delhi Police were 'complicit and an active participant' in the violence. One of the survivors said the police told him: 'Even if we kill you, nothing will happen to us.'* The general impression was that the Delhi police were specifically targeting those who had objected to Amit Shah's pet project, the Citizenship Amendment Act (CAA).

Devangana Kalita was accused in as many as four FIRs relating to anti-CAA protests. This meant that she was a major offender in the home minister's books. However, when she was first arrested, the Duty Magistrate observed that there was 'no reason to maintain the charge... as they were merely protesting against CAA and NRC.' She was re-arrested under a new FIR with additional charges of murder, rioting, and criminal conspiracy. While months passed with Devangana and Natasha in jail, the police made no attempt to file an FIR against BJP leader Kapil Mishra whose speech was seen as the primary provocation for the violence in Delhi. There was no action against Union Minister Anurag Thakur either, although there was widely cirucalted footage of him chanting, 'shoot the traitors'.† Critics pointed out that 'disparate filing of FIRs' was 'a prima facie

* Parth Maniktala, 'What was the mysterious conspiracy of Delhi Police against Devangana Kalita?', *The Leaflet*, 2 September 2020.

† 'Anurag Thakur Leads Crowd to Chant "Shoot the Traitors"', *The Wire*, 27 January 2020.

violation of the right to equality' under law. The home minister did not seem to hear. His policy of suppressing dissenters went on.

Differences of opinion are a feature of democracy. But intolerance towards opposing philosophies is of recent origin. This was underlined by those who pointed out what they saw as the psychology that drove Home Minister Shah. Mahavir Narwal went on record with the statement that Delhi police (read Amit Shah) arrested activists out of fear. 'The world [read Amit Shah] is horrified by the idea of independent women.' He left something more for Amit Shah to think about when he said: 'When we were protesting against the Emergency, people viewed us as radicals. But how is that section of our history written now? I went to jail during aapatkal and my daughter went to jail during another aapatkal (dangerous times).' He went to jail again a few times to meet his daughter and was happy to note that 'she now teaches yoga to other inmates'. A police officer said: 'She doesn't get intimidated easily.'

Some court observations shed light on the realities of the situation. Rejecting Kalita's bail application, the lower court observed that Kalita was stated to have 'instigated common Muslims to protest against the CAA' and 'poisoned the mind of the Muslim community'. When the case went to the Delhi High Court in appeal, the police admitted that they did not have any videos of Kalita delivering hate speeches. Granting her bail, the Delhi High Court noted that Kalita had previously cooperated with the police and no prejudice would be caused to the investigation by her release.

Public opinion remained at variance with government opinion on Devangana Kalita and others who ploughed their own furrow. Just as the government saw her as an adversary, the general public appreciated her role in organising peaceful protests against the CAA; her basic argument was that the Act violated the fundamental principles of the Constitution. BJP supporters never responded directly to this charge. They went ahead with their plans irrespective of what others thought about them. The party's Delhi MLA, Kapil Mishra, knew that his pro-CAA rally in Jaffrabad in northeast

Delhi would lead to communal confrontations. He hastened it by giving a three-day ultimatum to Delhi police to get roads cleared of anti-CAA protestors. He then urged people to gather. In the violence that followed, 53 people were killed, most of them Muslims. Mishra's political influence saw to it that the Delhi police did not pursue any kind of inquiry into the riots. This is the same Mishra who had once described Narendra Modi as an ISI agent and later, seeing the way the wind was blowing, launched a campaign called 'My PM, My Pride'.*

Just as opportunistic was India's somersault over Pragya Singh Thakur, known reverentially as Sadhvi Pragya. In 2008, she was arrested on terror charges in a case pertaining to the Malegaon bombing that killed 10 people. In 2017, the NIA dropped the more serious charges against her and she was given bail. Two years later, she contested the general election from Bhopal against none other than Digvijay Singh who had been chief minister of the state. She won. She became a symbol of the 'simultaneously brazen but concealed, nebulous and mainstreamed, militant yet normalised' fringe element of Hindutva ideology, as the political scientist Christopher Jaffrelot put it. She was afflicted by breast cancer and she said it was cured with the use of cow urine and panchagavya. Doctors at Ram Manohar Lohia hospital at Lucknow said she underwent bilateral mastectomy and that both her breasts were surgically removed to cure the cancer. The truth hardly mattered, because in 2019 she was made part of the 21-member Parliamentary Consultative Committee on defence. Wearing that distinguished cap, she stood up in Parliament and said that Nathuram Godse, Mahatma Gandhi's assassin, was a patriot. Even her supporters found themselves unable to justify that stance and she was removed from the committee on defence.

There is no comparison between Kapil Mishra and Pragya Singh

---

* 'Rebel AAP lawmaker Kapil Mishra to launch "My PM, My Pride" campaign', *NDTV*, 6 November 2018.

Thakur on one side and Devangana Kalita and Natasha Narwal on the other. The tragedy is that the difference between the two sets of personalities has not been noticed. In the black-and-white set of ideas promoted in Narendra Modi's India, there is only one division: supporters of Modi and opponents of Modi. He made it very simple. 'Look at their clothes,' he said while speaking at an election rally. 'Those who are protesting violently against [the CAA] can be recognised by their clothes.' For the Prime Minister of India, there are only two types of people, and they are recognised by their religion.

That view does not sit well with today's young generation. Even Jamia Millia, a Muslim institution, encourages students to think beyond religion. Devangana and Natasha represent a new generation that wants to think about more than religion. Unfortunately, their scope is limited when the government of the country pursues a policy defined by Hindutva ideology. A majority of Indians see Hinduism and Hindutva as separate concepts. Hinduism is the most accommodative life philosophy known to mankind, unique in its universality. Hindutva is an attempt to politicise it. The attempt can succeed only at the cost of Hinduism as it has prevailed down the centuries. Hinduism will continue to prevail.

32

PRIYA RAMANI

Writer, Fighter

Indian journalism has never seen editors more powerful than M.J. Akbar and Tarun Tejpal. Talented innovators, they dreamed up new-style publications which overnight became industry models. But their careers ended in disgrace. Women employees rose to expose them as predators. The courage they showed and the details they revealed were not just sensational; they drew attention to the reality that, as the 20th century drew to a close, women in journalism, faced problems their predecessors had not.

It was journalism's loss that Akbar got side-lined. His creativity could turn something mundane into something heavenly. When India confronted Pakistan in Mohali in April 2011, Akbar rose to the occasion. He described how God could not oblige Afridi's prayer for help because he, God, was opening the batting for India. How God, on the day it mattered, was only human. How only when a god slips do you recognise how difficult it is to reach that pinnacle. 'The ascent of man is, after all, so much more fascinating than the descent of a god.'

On another occasion, he set the stage with idiomatic sparkle. 'Prime Ministers don't dine on humble pie,' he wrote. 'Manmohan Singh still cannot make up his mind whether he has been elected by the people of India or selected by Sonia Gandhi... You can tell a Salvation Army that there is no Army, but you can't suggest that there is no salvation. The Congress face of salvation is Rahul Gandhi, not Manmohan. The notional prime minister has more authority than the national prime minister... How long can a government last without governance?'* This was the man whose attention was diverted in ways that diminished his potential.

Akbar's nemesis was Priya Ramani and Tejpal's a former staffer at *Tehelka*. They belonged to the galaxy of gutsy women who began lighting up the Indian sky from the time of the independence movement. Kusum Nair (1919–1993) developed expertise in agricultural economy as well as women's issues and wrote acclaimed books such as *Blossoms in the Dust* (1961). Distinguished editorial positions were held by Fatima Zakaria, wife of the politician and Islamist, Rafiq Zakaria, and mother of Fareed Zakaria, a celebrity anchor in the US. Mrinal Pande, Anita Pratap, Githa Hariharan, and Chitra Subramaniam are some of the other women who distinguished themselves as internationally recognised writers and journalists.

This respectable world was messed up when Akbar and Tejpal began their escapades as assertive males. The *Tehelka* staffer who describes herself as a 'global women's rights reporter, yoga instructor and caffeine addict', graphically described her employer's predatory style. She wrote a lengthy letter to her colleagues, going into details of Tejpal's dexterity in keeping a hotel lift continuously going up and down without opening at any floor, thus giving him enough time to prey on her. The staffer was in her early 20s at the time and it took some courage to resist a boss and turn the matter into a tehelka (sensation).

Tejpal paid heavily for his libidinous excesses. Following the staffer's exposure, he offered to 'step down' for a few months from his top post at *Tehelka*. No one bought that line. In 2013, he was arrested, and, after six months in jail, released on bail. His case

* M.J. Akbar, 'Manmohan needs to assert his legitimate authority for better governance', *India Today*, 1 July 2011.

attracted special attention because he and *Tehelka* had expressed righteous indignation against sexual violators. When practice clashed with principles, he found himself friendless.

Akbar, smarter and politically experienced, faced no such trauma. He was essentially a power-seeker blessed with adjustable convictions for success in that area. He became a Congressman and friend of Rajiv Gandhi when the Congress ruled the waves. When the wind shifted, he had no difficulty becoming a BJP stalwart and Narendra Modi admirer. Modi, for his past, had no problem embracing a Muslim who, after the post-Godhra pogrom in Gujarat, had described Modi as worthy of the Nishan-e-Pakistan honour for destroying 'the idea of India'. When Priya accused Akbar of misconduct, he filed a defamation case against her, engaging 11 lawyers to lead the charge. Priya willy-nilly became an accused on bail. But she refused to be intimidated. Delivering a keynote address at the Goa Literature Festival in December 2019 she said: 'What does it mean to speak from the margins and about the margins? The last time I spoke the truth on a public platform, a powerful man slapped a criminal defamation case against me. I wonder what will happen today.'* She was clear about what needed to be done even in the face of threats. 'If we do not speak up against violence, injustice, fake news, and hate, we will lose this version of India and our children will never know what this country was like.' Priya sounded like a woman on a mission. She had seen enough to form opinions about the world around her. She discovered the importance of going public when most women instinctively preferred to keep a low profile. She said: 'I spoke because women before me spoke up. I spoke so people after me can speak up.' She said speaking up could be addictive as well as liberating. 'I believe we don't speak up enough.'

In 1994, Priya had worked as a journalist in *Asian Age*, a newspaper founded by Akbar. From the day she joined the paper,

* Tara Narayan, 'Speaking the truth is very liberating!', *Goan Observer*, 13 December 2019.

she began experiencing overtures from the editor. In the Goa speech she went into some details and described how she was offered alcohol and asked inappropriate questions. 'A predator,' she said, 'is more powerful than the prey.' Finding strength in the #MeToo movement catching on at the time, she said, 'It is unfortunate that women who experience sexual harassment at work places must now defend themselves in criminal proceedings to speak the truth.'

Most women are unable to defend themselves because social forces frown on women making a public show of the problems they face. Priya Ramani found the strength to take action because she had both courage and the backing of her friends and family. She understood the implications of her action; she said she did what she did 'at great personal cost'. The financial cost itself was heavy because she had to travel from Bangalore to Delhi every time a hearing came up. But her spirits were high because Bangalore had by then become her fortress of strength and safety. She had grown up as a typical Bombay-born Sindhi, a product of the famous Catholic institutions that made the city India's urbs prima in education. She was educated at the Convent of Jesus & Mary, the Cathedral School, and St. Xavier's College. As she progressed from *Asian Age* to Reuters to *Indian Express* to *Mint* to *Cosmopolitan* magazine, she found the love of her life in Bangalore. Samar Halarnkar can be described as a born-again man. With an MA from the University of Missouri, he had gained experience at *Times of India*, *Indian Express*, *Hindustan Times*, and *India Today*. Then wisdom dawned and he realised that journalism was a discardable vocation and that the only thing that mattered in life was cooking. He became a foodie, providing recipes and tips to readers of various publications. In 2020, he wrote a magazine article under the title 'The role of roast pork in my father's 88th year'. That was a tribute not just to roast pork but also to P.G. Halarnkar, Samar's father, who was the Commissioner of Police in Bangalore in the 1980s. Halarnkar Senior was an unusual kind of policeman, respecting those who crossed his path. He was in office for almost four years when the average tenure of commissioners was less than two. Perhaps roast pork was the secret. He died in January 2021, aged 88.

Samar Halarnkar was full of admiration for his wife when she came under what might be described as predator pressure. He wrote: 'She has always had a strong sense of right and wrong, black and white and she has never lacked courage.' Referring to Akbar's charge of defamation Halarnkar said: 'His intention is clear. To intimidate her and through her to intimidate the others who have spoken up, and to silence others who have not... He has access to a battery of powerful lawyers. There are 97 listed in the legal notice. She has one.'

With his journalistic background, Halarnkar was able to put things in perspective. 'No one ever spoke up against powerful men because the misuse of power and authority was considered normal,' he said. 'There was no redressal mechanism within media companies, no one took such complaints seriously and the only ones who stood to lose were the women.' Priya's experience was the best example of this abnormality.

The sense of right and wrong was strong enough in Priya to turn her into an activist journalist. Where misdeeds and injustice threatened to take over, she raised her voice regardless of who she was offending. This made her come out with reports others did not notice. Typical was a rather bizarre case that led to the jailing of an innocent person. In a July 2020 article she highlighted the story of Mohammed Amir Khan who was 'snatched from the street, tortured, made to sign blank sheets of paper and produced in a court only a week later'.* Aged 19 at the time of his arrest, Khan spent 14 years in jail. Then it was discovered that he was innocent. Priya narrates his story with empathy, making the reader feel the depth of the man's sense of hurt. Khan took to advocating the case for letters from prisoners and asked her to '...read [a prisoner's letter] alone. Close the doors. Read it three or four times to understand the

* Priya Ramani, 'How to read a letter from jail', *Bloomberg*, 8 July 2020.

true spirit of the letter.' Priya makes the reader aware of the need to look at prisoners with an understanding of their inner turmoil.

Was that a pointer to her own tumults? Her journalism reflected a fair bit of commitment—to the idealistic side of her profession as also to the ethical principles that guided her personally. The newspaper column she ran was called 'Rational Anthem', recalling the patriotic sentiments of the national anthem as well as the righteousness of rationalism. The hallmark of Priya's journalism, was professionalism on the one side and, on the other, commitment to the nation. It was serious journalism, seriously written. She said a possible second term for Modi would 'herald an age where Indianness would be sieved by religion and personal rights and freedoms would be curbed dramatically'. In a column in January 2021, she hailed Sneha Parthibaraja as 'the first Indian to win the right to have no caste or religion'. Unnoticed by most mainstream media, Parthibaraja, had fought for nearly 10 years to get a no-caste, no-religion certificate from a sub-collector in Tirupathur in Tamil Nadu. 'I never argued with officials,' she had said. 'I just waited and waited.' She was no doubt strengthened by what she saw in her own family. Her parents gave their three daughters names from three different religions—Sneha, Mumtaj, and Jennifer. It was left to Priya to bring this unusual family's story to public attention. Another case she made public was how a Haryana resident fought a court battle to get the right to write his name as Ravi Kumar Atheist on his Aadhar Card and other official documents. Ravi Kumar sported large 'Atheist' tattoos on his forearms and said it was his right to believe in the non-existence of God. She also brought out the story of fruitseller Selvakumar who named his three sons Sugadev, Rajaguru, and Bhagathsingh, after the freedom fighters who were hanged in 1931. All of a sudden, this forthright journalism was hijacked and turned into an inextricable part of personality politics. That the personality involved was a man who revelled in controversy as long as it promoted his political ambitions made the episode a sad one. It was one of the tragedies of the time that

Priya Ramani was reduced to an item associated with M.J. Akbar and his addiction.

But she did not remain just that. The importance of Priya's exposé of Akbar was proved when Akbar took legal action only against her, although her stand had encouraged others to come out with their 'Akbar story'. Ghazala Wahab's version of it gives a fair idea of the problems faced by these other women who came into contact with him. During her initial years, she said in an article in *The Wire*, she '...accepted everything as part of the office culture—Akbar's flirtation with young sub editors, his blatant favouritism and bawdy jokes.' Then one day '...his eyes fell on me. And my nightmare began.'

During the hearing of Akbar's defamation case, Priya's friend, Niloufer Venkataraman, told the court: 'After her job interview with Akbar, Ramani called me up late in the evening. She sounded upset and distraught. The interview had not gone as she expected. It was not conducted in the lobby of the coffee shop of the hotel where she was called for the interview. She was called to Akbar's room where they were alone.' She added that Priya had described 'the extremely uncomfortable details' of what had happened at the interview.

Some of the details were mentioned in her testimony before the court of the Additional Chief Metropolitan Magistrate. Describing her meeting at the Oberoi Hotel, she said: 'When I reached the lobby and looked around for Mr Akbar, I could not see him. Then I asked the reception to connect me to him. He asked me to come up to his room. I was silent and hesitant, he then asked me to come up.' She had gone to the hotel assuming that the interview would be at the 'coffee shop or lobby'. When he said come up, she was confused. 'I was 23 and not that confident to say, "No, I will wait for you in the lobby." I was hesitant, but went up.' And then she described the mood of the place. 'The room was small and enclosed. The bed was turned down for the night, there was a small two-seater sofa near the bed. It was a big window and I could see it was a sea-facing room... I was acutely aware that I was alone in this room with him.' In the very description of the trap laid for a woman, there was assertion of the dignity that women valued.

The experience of fighting a man of Akbar's standing must have had a traumatic effect on Priya. She braved it out because she realised that her story was part of contemporary history. She said that her move would empower women to understand their rights at the workplace. The court agreed. In February 2021, it acquitted Ramani with five observations that attracted attention: Women can't be punished for raising instances of sexual abuse; most often sexual harassment is committed behind closed doors and most women don't speak up for fear of the stigma; her disclosure was in the interest of the movement against anti-sexual harassment; society must understand the impact of sexual abuse on its victims; even a man of high social status can be a sexual harasser, and the right of reputation cannot be protected at the cost of the right to dignity. Ramani was the first woman in journalism to publicly accuse a boss of sexual harassment. Her moral courage and her ability to see herself as representative of a larger human predicament made her a symbol of her times.

33

DISHA RAVI

The Student as Activist

As women's colleges go, Mount Carmel in Bangalore has always been special. It is one of the earliest women's college in India, established before Independence. It was actually born in Trichur, Kerala in 1944 and was moved to Bangalore four years later, probably to escape the sweltering heat to a salutary sun.

From the start, the institution had a tendency to be innovative. It held a cultural festival every year, called Cul Ah. Some of its other national festivals were Cross Currents (focussed on business), Carpediem (management), and Manam (humanities). A galaxy of notables were shaped in its classrooms, among them Aparna Poppat, Deepika Padukone, Kiran Mazumdar-Shaw, Margaret Alva, Nirupama Rao.

And Disha Annappa Ravi. An activist student at an activist college, Disha moved into gear even as she was attending classes. She was one of the students attracted by the Swedish movement called School Strike for Climate, an international initiative that called for students to skip classes on Fridays and participate in activities that demanded action from political leaders favouring fossil fuel industry and renewal energy. The movement gained popularity under the name Fridays For Future (FFF). That was enough for the authorities in India to arrest Disha in February 2021 on charges of involvement in an online toolkit related to the Swedish environmental activist Greta Thunberg, as well as the farmers' protest that paralysed Delhi at the time. (A toolkit is a standard social justice communications and organising document providing, in this case, a list of ways to support the farmers' protest.) The government said that all those who used the toolkit fomented unrest in ways that amounted to sedition.

There was no escape for Disha from this kind of harrassment. She had to accept the reality that her India had slipped into a groove that no earlier generations could have envisioned. In fact, all kinds of other grooves had developed unexpectedly, shocking her own generation. In May 2021, a group of men in supposedly modern Karnataka were captured on video dunking themselves in cow dung to fight the 'bacteria' called Coronavirus. Milk was later used to wash down the dung. The action and the reactions it generated were summed up in a tweet by Congress MP Shashi Tharoor: 'Since the BJP is so obsessed with our image, reflect: For decades the world saw India as a land of snake-charmers and fakirs lying on nails. In the last 25 years, India became the home of doctors and computer geeks. Now we are a land where people drink cow urine and bathe in cow dung. Progress?' Tharoor was bombarded by a number of people who saw nothing wrong in cow-dung therapy.

There were many attendant issues that a climate activist such as Disha had to sidestep in order to focus on her main agenda. Within the FFF, there was a MAPA (Most Affected People and Areas) wing, which was Disha's area of special interest. MAPA in effect meant the developing world, otherwise known as the Global South, recognised as the area that bore the brunt of carbon emissions and climate change. Disha became involved in MAPA's mission for idealistic as well as personal reasons. She said: 'My motivation to join climate activism came from seeing my grandparents, who are farmers, struggle with the effects of the climate crisis. At that time I wasn't aware that what they were experiencing was the climate crisis because climate education is non-existent where I'm from.'*

* Hannah Ellis-Peterson, 'Disha Ravi: the climate activist who became the face of India's crackdown on dissent', *The Guardian*, 17 February 2021.

Bangalore is a modernistic metropolis and its colleges tend to promote a modernistic worldview. Disha was true to form when she said in September 2020: 'I'm striking because we are living through a climate crisis. Heavy rains and lax measures taken by governments have led to millions of people being displaced because of floods, particularly in India. My house was flooded last week. We are not just fighting for our future. We are fighting for our present. We, the people from the most affected areas, are going to change the conversation in climate negotiations and lead a just recovery plan that benefits people and not the pockets of our government.'

Disha told an American interviewer in 2020: 'In India protests are a part of life. There are a lot of protests on humanitarian issues and religious issues. Protests are very ingrained in Indian society.'

That is true, but just as ingrained is the intolerance from those in power. She told another interviewer: 'We live in a country where dissent is suppressed. We in FFF were labelled terrorists. Only a government that puts profit over people would consider asking for clean air, clean water, and a liveable planet, an act of terrorism.'

True to their own shabby form, the police came up with all kinds of allegations to justify her arrest. They said she was a 'key conspirator' who 'collaborated with pro-Khalistanis to spread disaffection against the Indian state'. International observers associated Disha's arrest with a larger pattern of intimidation of journalists and protestors. The *New York Times* described the arrest as part of a larger decline of internet freedom in India. NBC News reported that Disha had 'emerged as a symbol of the Indian government's crackdown on dissent'. Several Indian associations and leaders condemned Disha's arrest as 'unwarranted harassment and intimidation'. Tamil Nadu leader M.K. Stalin tweeted: 'Silencing critics of the government through authoritarian means is not the rule of law.' About 900 alumni of Mount Carmel College signed a protest condemning the arrest. But the wisest words came from sessions court judge Dharmendra Rana who, while granting her bail, said, 'Considering the scanty and sketchy evidence on record, I do not find any palpable reason for keeping the 22-year-old in custody. Citizens are conscience-keepers of government in any democratic nation. They cannot be put behind bars simply because they choose to disagree with the state policies. This 5,000 years old civilisation of ours has never been averse to ideas from varied quarters. The following couplet in Rig Veda embodies our cultural ethos expressing our respect for divergent opinions: *Let noble thoughts come from all directions*.'

The international attention Disha received carried its own message for the overzealous leaders of India. Noticing that residents stood defiantly alongside students on the streets of Bangalore, *The Guardian* said that the climate activist had become the face of India's crackdown on dissent. For Disha herself, the experience seemed to have an educative, and enlightening effect. 'Locked in my cell,' she said, 'I wondered when it became a crime to think the most basic elements of sustenance on this planet were as much mine as theirs.' Being locked in a cell seemed to bring out the philosopher in her. Noting that humanity had a short shelf-life, she said: 'We are inching closer to our own expiry.'

Splitting legal hairs on the issues the government raised vis-à-vis Disha can be a thankless job. What matters is that powerful elements in Indian government did not like her attitude of defiance and set out to punish her. They found it unacceptable that she corresponded online with citizens of other countries. (When did that become an offence?) They did not like foreign citizens criticising India's policy decisions. (Since when did that become actionable?) What the penalisation of a person like Disha Ravi showed was that the government in Delhi had rather suddenly become very sensitive to criticism, especially from people outside India.

After Narendra Modi's election as prime minister, terms like 'anti-national' began to be used widely against critics. In a democracy, no one ever becomes anti-national by criticising the government in power. In fact, a democracy can hardly be a democracy if no one criticises the government and its actions. Condemning criticism as contrary to the national interest is indicative of a sense of guilt in the minds of policymakers. That the Modi government had become touchy about criticism from abroad was a clear expression of guilt. Word spread even among universities that they must get government approval for 'international events on India's internal matters'.

Journalist Sidharth Bhatia put it in perspective when he wrote: 'In the past there have been the "tukde-tukde gang", allegedly planning to break India in many parts; Naxals, anyone who didn't subscribe to the rightist ideology; Khan Market gang, progressive elitists; Love Jihad, an imaginary plot by Muslim young men to trap innocent Hindu girls into marrying them; "presstitutes" which is how independent-minded journalists are described, and "terrorists" which was code for Muslims but now is applicable to Sikhs too. There is "termites" too, and all come from the fertile mind of the Sanghis, both official and freelance and immediately get the backing of the government.'*

No government support went to Disha Ravi because, while her smile flashed friendship to all, her eyes warned those who challenged her convictions. 'The face of India's crackdown on dissent,' is how *The Guardian* described her while reporting her arrest. She 'wears her heart on her sleeve,' the paper said. It also gave a thumbnail sketch of her approach: 'Whether it was coordinating environmental strikes, taking part in lake clean-up operations, organising tree-planting exercises or organising climate action workshops, Ravi was always there, and she was known for her deep knowledge of the issues. She was also the sole bread-winner of the family and juggled work at a company producing plant-based foods, alongside her activism.'

Her activism was by no means confined to her home state. She and the organisation she floated were involved in a variety of campaigns. They ranged from the protection of the Mollem forest area in Goa, an elephant conservation zone in Uttarakhand, the

* Sidharth Bhatia, 'The BJP has its own toolkit to go after dissidents which it uses ruthlessly', *The Wire*, 15 February 2021.

Aarey forest in Mumbai (home to the sprawling Aarey milk colony), the Raika forest in Jammu, and the Dumna nature park in Madhya Pradesh. There was not even a shadow of pro-Khalistani activity in any of these projects, but that did not prevent interested opponents from coming up with conspiracy theories. A group of 50 academics, artists, and writers released a joint statement supporting Disha and describing her arrest as 'completely atrocious' as former Environment Minister Jairam Ramesh put it. The farm union, Samyukta Kisan Morcha, issued an official statement condemning her arrest as 'atrocious'. The campaign against her took an ugly turn when tweets appeared claiming that her real name was Disha Ravi Joseph and that she was a Syrian Christian from Kerala. The intention must have been to suggest that being a 'Syrian Christian', she was less loyal to the ethos of India. The trick did not work because fact checkers came out quickly, saying that she was not a 'Joseph' of any kind. She was Disha Annappa Ravi, daughter of Ravi Annappa, an athletics coach, and Manjula Nanjiah, a homemaker. Both are traditional Kannadiga names.

Disha's work record and family background were too clear to be obfuscated. It was unclear why the cyber cell team of Delhi police had to go to Bangalore, pick her up from her home, and take her to Delhi. Perhaps they wanted to give a larger-than-real aura to the toolkit controversy, creating the impression that Disha was involved in activities aimed at weakening the Indian state. What the government in fact achieved was to create the impression that it was intolerant of criticism in areas where the egos of its top leaders were involved. Those egos were offended when public sympathy went to farmers protesting against three farm laws the Modi government enacted, in what was seen as a move to please powerful business circles. The government stood with the big lobbies. The small man with no network was crushed in the process.

Fighters like Disha Ravi were always on the side of the underdog. The importance of the causes she took up and the principled wars she fought attracted wide attention. So did most of the combatants who did similar work. In Bangalore itself, a teenager younger than Disha attracted attention with her involvement in unusual, but socially significant, work. Trisha Venkatesh, born and raised in California, had settled in Bangalore in her early teens. With experience in the Girl Scouts of America movement, she involved herself in organising awareness campaigns on the hazardous impact of smoking. She shipped more than 500 books and stationary items to an orphanage in Salem, Tamil Nadu. Her 'Girl Up' programme in Bangalore held workshops in schools, and spread information about gender-based violence and related topics. Similar activities were organised by other voluntary crusaders in other metropolitan areas of India.

A widely circulated publicity photograph of Disha shows her sitting on the steps of a college surrounded by placards, the causes dear to her sloganned on the boards. *We Won't Die of Old Age. We'll Die of Climate Change*, says one. *Green With Farmers* and *Fund Farmers, Not Coal* were other slogans carried by the roadside climate crusaders. Disha helped coordinate demonstrations and strikes in different parts of her city every Friday.

FFF was blunt in articulating its priorities. One formal statement said: 'It is our opinion that a free market would render the Indian farmer unable to bargain effectively against the multinational corporations who are sure to exploit this opportunity to capture and monopolise food production to the fullest.' It laid out a clear policy concept when it said: 'Opening up the farming sector to free market forces will most definitely worsen the situation not only for farmers but also for the middle and lower classes who will have to pay for the rise in food prices this policy is sure to cause. Additionally, it is likely to lead to further monocropping, loss of seed diversity, poor soil quality, less groundwater recharge, climate change and other environmental issues.'

Early in 2021, FFF organised a human chain to protest against the felling of 8,561 trees for road widening in Bangalore. Their demand was that 'the entire district of Bangalore have an integrated

Sustainable Development Plan which takes into account everything from ecology to industry, from suburban trains to better bus services'. Records show that Bangalore lost nearly 18,000 trees in nine years from 2008 in the name of development. The famous and protected grounds of the Indian Institute of Science were home to about 40 lakh trees until the 1980s. It now has less than 15 lakh. Bangalore's Corporation says it has planted 7 lakh trees between 2010 and 2015, green activists say that 'planting' is meaningless unless trees are 'nurtured to survive'.

It may be useful to remember that the Government of India was antagonistic to the FFF idea from the start. It had blocked the movement's website and filed an Unlawful Activities (Prevention) Act case against it. The case was later revoked. That is the way of power wielders. They are suspicious of grassroots initiatives that attract popular support. They are uncomfortable when they are not the centre of attraction. But they cannot blunt the spirit of knowledge-seekers, and the optimism of the young. These cherished treasures of India, cannot be extinguished by passing autocrats.

34

AMIT SHAH

Feared, Not Trusted

The portfolio of home minister, deemed to be not second to that of prime minister, has been held by some historical figures—C. Rajagopalachari, Govind Ballabh Pant, Lal Bahadur Shastri, Y.B. Chavan. Some inconsequential figures also sat in the chair, conveniently allowing the dominant prime minister to handle Home as well. Kasu Reddy, 1974–1977 and P.C. Sethi, 1982–1984, made it easy for Indira Gandhi in effect to dominate over them. Giani Zail Singh got the key portfolio by shamelessly displaying his sycophancy to 'Madam'. When he eventually became President of India in 1982, he disgraced himself and the country by saying that he would sweep Indira's courtyard if she asked him to do so.

The culture changed, as did the course of history, with Narendra Modi's rise in 2014. His second term, beginning in May 2019, saw Amit Shah becoming the home minister. Described by Reuters as 'the Iron Fist', Shah seemed to enjoy the reputation he built as a man to be feared rather than respected, the kind of guy you wouldn't want to run into on a dark street corner. That, it is possible to argue, is a desirable quality in a home minister.

Amit Anil Chandra Shah tended to make his associates apprehensive even as they recognised him as a master strategist. It was always so. Born in a Gujarati Vaishnav family of Baniyas, he watched his father managing a successful PVC pipe business.

He got a BSc in biochemistry and worked as a stockbroker for a while. But politics beckoned him. When he was only 18, he became prominent in the RSS and the ABVP. He formally joined the BJP in 1987 at the age of 23. It did not take him long to become the chief organiser of the party, credited for its victory in several state elections. He first met Narendra Modi in 1982, when Modi was an RSS pracharak. The chemistry between them has been the decisive influence in India's politics ever since.

Shah developed his own way of influencing events. He would study the logistics of a situation and work out a detailed strategy before taking action. This was evident in the first steps he took to gain influence. It was a time when the Congress held sway in all constituencies. The spirit of the independence movement was still alive and leaders were mostly unchallengeable in their strongholds. Modi–Shah set out to identify the second most influential leader in every village and persuade him to join the BJP. For traditional Congressmen who could not challenge their seniors, this was an opportunity to become senior themselves. Rural leaders who had lost elections for the post of Pradhan were condemned to remain neglected as also-rans. For them, what the BJP offered was as good as a new life. Some 8,000 of them, influential in their rural strongholds, saw new possibilities in the new party. The Congress's loss became the BJP's gain. Similar strategies succeeded in reducing the influence of the Congress in the powerful cooperatives and sports bodies of the states.

Above it all, a no-holds-barred Hindutva line became the imprint of the new leadership. Shah must have liked his reputation as 'a Hindu hardliner with uncompromising views'. The hardliner approach, shared by Narendra Modi, had led to what came to be known as the Gujarat pogrom in 2002. A train filled with Hindu pilgrims returning from Ayodhya had been set on fire in Godhra, a town known for Hindu–Muslim tension. In one coach, 59 people were burned to death. This was followed by two decisions taken by the state government under the newly elected Chief Minister

Narendra Modi. One was to put the 59 dead bodies on display. The other was to support a state-wide strike. The result was an explosion of mob fury leading to the death of nearly 2,000 people. The blood bath announced that India's democracy had entered an altogether new phase. Until then, national leaders had tried their best to prevent Hindu–Muslim differences from developing into confrontational politics. Now those very differences had become political capital to be exploited. Amit Shah was acknowledged as the micro-managing specialist in the new game. This was logical considering his record. In an unhelpful political climate in Uttar Pradesh in 2013, he had worked out a detailed, booth-based action plan that led to his winning 73 out of 80 seats. While the party's leadership crown sat firmly on Narendra Modi, Amit Shah controlled the strings as the BJP's uncrowned monarch.

That level of success was not reached easily. In fact, no home minister of India had a ride as and controversial as Amit Shah's. No home minister had such a record of arrest. Scandals spread around the so-called 'fake encounter cases' that made headlines in Gujarat in 2006 when Narendra Modi was the chief minister, Amit Shah home minister and D.G. Vanzara the police chief. In due course, Vanzara would earn his own footnote in history. He would be placed in judicial custody from 2007 on charges of participation in 'extrajudicial killings' while heading the anti-terrorist squad. He would receive bail only in 2015. But the political masters he served were generous in their appreciation. Thirteen years after his arrest, and nearly six years after his retirement, he was given a promotion by the Gujarat government.

The 'encounter' case that attracted the most attention was that of Sohrabuddin Sheikh, described by the CBI as a criminal on the wanted list. He and his wife, Kausar Bi, were seized by the Gujarat police's Anti-Terror Squad and taken to a farmhouse near Ahmedabad. From there, Vanzara took them away and had them shot. The police claimed they were terrorists with a plan to eliminate Narendra Modi. Tulsiram Prajapati, an associate of

Sohrabuddin, was also killed in a similar style. Apparently, Prajapati was an eyewitness to the killings of Sohrabuddin and his wife. The CBI named Amit Shah as the prime accused in the Prajapati case. The *Hindustan Times* reported that, 'Shah is facing a case of triple murder as the CBI has always held that Tulsi Prajapati fake encounter is linked with the Sohrabuddin fake encounter and is part of a larger conspiracy involving senior police officers and politicians of Gujarat and Rajasthan.' The paper attributed those words to 'a source in the agency'.

This was in 2006. In 2011, the Supreme Court told the CBI to take up the case. The agency named Amit Shah as the prime accused in the elimination of Prajapati. According to the CBI chargesheet, 'Shah and the police officials accused in the case first killed Sohrabuddin on 5 December 2005 because he could have become a crucial witness in the case.' (*India Today.*) Based on the CBI report, Amit Shah was arrested in July 2010. Three months later, he received bail. In 2018, all 22 accused in the Sohrabuddin and Prajapati cases were acquitted.

But questions raised by Ishrat Jahan's killing would not go away. A photograph published widely in 2004 showed four bodies lying on the street, one of them clad in salwar kameez. She was identified as Ishrat Jahan Raza, a 19-year-old. The police said they were Lashkar-e-Taiba terrorists involved in a plot to kill Narendra Modi. Several human rights organisations questioned that claim. Public sympathy was clearly in favour of Ishrat Jahan despite official attempts to present her as a terrorist. It was significant that police chief Vanzara wrote an open letter in which he implied that the political bosses, not the police, were responsible for what happened. 'I categorically state,' he said, 'that officers and men of the Crime Branch, ATS, and Border Range, during the period of 2002–2007, simply acted and performed their duties in compliance with a conscious policy of this government.' Actually, no such disclaimer was necessary because it was known to all that in the Ishrat Jahan case, as in the Prajapati case, political leaders were behind what happened, not policemen or civil servants. But formal inquiries never exposed them. A Metropolitan Magistrate who conducted an inquiry into the Ishrat Jahan case named Vanzara and others for 'the cold-blooded murder' of the girl and three others. A CBI court that was set up to inquire into the Sohrabuddin case in detail was headed by Justice B.H. Loya who died mysteriously. His immediate family members said that he had been offered ₹100 crore to give an order in favour of the prime accused. The general atmosphere and the evolution of several important cases seemed to work in favour of the home minister who enjoyed the collaborative confidence of the prime minister. There was a brazenness in the way Amit Shah pushed his political line. Indeed, it was reasonable to say that it was brazenness that took Amit Shah to the heights he reached.

Sometimes it also led to unseemly confrontations. One that was particularly embarrassing was a spat with the Shiv Sena's Uddhav Thackeray. Developed on a culture of collision politics, Shiv Sena is unused to yielding to others, and there could be no question of yielding when Uddhav Thackeray was the chief minister of the premier state of Maharashtra. When Amit Shah spoke in threatening terms about 'thrashing former allies', Uddhav said defiantly that 'one who will trounce Sena is yet to be born'. The Shiv Sena and BJP were allies in Delhi and in Maharashtra. Shah had spoken about the 'Modi wave' that swept the 2014 Lok Sabha elections. Thackeray said the Sena 'has seen enough waves in its journey'. To his allies, Amit Shah was not the Big Brother he wanted to be.

One quality that keeps Big Brothers big is their ability to ignore what is inconvenient to them. Amit Shah ignored his critics as if they did not exist. He proceeded to make his son, Jay, the most important man in the most important sport in India—cricket. Jay Shah, officially described as an 'Indian businessman', became secretary of the Board of Control for Cricket in India, the legendary BCCI. Then he became president of the Asian Cricket Council. Let no one belittle these harmless-sounding jobs. As joint secretary of the Gujarat Cricket Association, Jay Shah supervised the construction of the world's largest cricket stadium. The benefits offered by a mammoth project of that kind were neither small-scale nor confined to cricket. He drew additional benefit by naming it the Narendra Modi Stadium. (It was originally the Sardar Patel Stadium. And Sardar Patel was the acknowledged hero, in preference to Jawaharlal Nehru, of right-wing patriots. That Modi and the BJP braintrust thought it fit to discard Sardar Patel and enthrone Modi in his place told it is own tale.)

Jay Shah's support base had a way of pouncing upon critics with a show of aggression. This was in evidence when *The Wire* in October 2017 reported 'a dramatic increase' in Shah's business.* It listed examples such as his company's turnover increasing 16,000 times over in the year following Narendra Modi's rise. It also described how Jay Shah, whose business was chiefly stock trading, turned to windmill generation when he got a PSU loan for that unfamiliar business. Jay Shah responded to the report by filing a criminal defamation case and a civil suit for ₹100 crore.

The power of the home minister was clear to all. So was his unpopularity. A Mood of the Nation survey by *India Today* magazine showed that the number of those who considered his performance as 'good' fell from 50 per cent in August 2018 to 34 per cent in January 2019. His reputation as 'a winning leader of the party' was shattered after the BJP lost Madhya Pradesh, Chhattisgarh, and Rajasthan in one go to the Congress. Internally, too, there was restlessness. Mid-level leaders felt they received no encouragement from Amit Shah or Narendra Modi. Many political posts in the government lay vacant, suggesting a trust deficit between Modi–Shah and the second line of leaders. If the top leaders are less than confident about the next layers of leadership, something has to be wrong somewhere.

Actually Amit Shah's effectiveness as a leader was open to question. Within a year of Modi coming to power in Delhi, Shah's

---

* Rohini Singh, 'The Golden Touch of Jay Amit Shah', *The Wire*, 8 October 2017.

attempts to win in the Delhi Assembly elections failed badly. He could win only three of 70 seats available. Later that year, despite camping in Patna for three months, he lost the assembly elections to Lalu Yadav and Nitish Kumar. In 2018, he failed to form a government in Karnataka despite the governor making a mockery of his office with his efforts to help the BJP. In a prestige battle, he tried to defeat Ahmed Patel for a Rajya Sabha seat in Gujarat. Patel won. In the Delhi Assembly election in 2020, Shah went to the extent of campaigning on street corners. But he lost 62 of 70 seats. It was against such facts that base-line BJP workers were encouraged to look at 'Shah-ji as Sardar Patel the second'.

In fact, the Sardar was the opposite of Shah-ji. It was a people's campaign he organised in Surat's Bardoli taluka to save peasants from exploitation that earned Vallabhbhai Patel the title of Sardar. It is not easy to imagine Amit Shah organising a people's campaign, let alone for a popular cause. The Sardar was known as the Iron Man, a leader who used his iron-like strength for the betterment of the downtrodden. Amit Shah is known for his strength, but not for the way he uses it. The Sardar became a hero of history. Shah is a classical anti-hero. (Definition: a central character in a story who lacks conventional heroic attributes.) That will remain the defining perception of the man who filled the contentious Narendra Modi chapter in history with dubious footnotes of his own.

35

NARENDRA MODI

Ego Supreme

One fine morning, railway tickets and Air India's boarding passes began to be issued with Narendra Modi's photograph displayed on them. Additionally, the Civil Aviation Ministry instructed airlines to distribute to each passenger a note describing the achievements of the Modi government. This was something no Prime Minister of India or of any democracy had done before. The in-your-face publicity blast offended most citizens. An Air India passenger, a former Director General of Police, tweeted a photograph of the boarding pass with the comment: 'Wonder why we are wasting public money on this Election Commission which doesn't see, hear or speak...' An Air India official explained that the boarding passes were only carrying 'a third-party advertisement'. Following a Trinamool Congress complaint, Indian Railways stopped selling tickets that carried the Gujarat government's 'advertisements' of Modi's photograph. Clearly, Modi nurtured a desire to show that he was bigger than the circumstances that made him. There was substance in the argument that 'apakarshat bodh' or an inferiority complex had led him to go for symbols of high-quality life—Montblanc pens, Movado watches, Bulgari sunglasses. The young OBC leader, Alpesh Thakor, said in 2017 that he 'had heard' that Modi liked mushrooms from Taiwan that cost ₹80,000 a piece. *India Today* carried out a fact-check and said, yes, he liked mushrooms but the Himalayan Guchchi variety, which cost only ₹30,000 a kilogram.

Modi never tried to hide his perception of himself as the leading symbol of the nation. He told the *Times of India* in 2019: 'It is to BJP's credit that it has gone to the people in the name of the Modi government's track record, and unlike the previous governments, the party is not afraid to ask for votes in the name of its leader.' Although it presented a flattering estimate of himself, Modi got the facts slightly re-arranged. The Congress always asked for votes in the name of Jawaharlal Nehru, or of Indira Gandhi and, following an unexpected if short-lived shift in history, in the name of Narasimha Rao. It did not ask for votes directly in the name of Rahul Gandhi, but the fact that he was in the forefront of things and that Priyanka Gandhi, too, appeared in the forefront when the mood seized her showed that they were in fact asking for votes in the name of Gandhi.

Modi's concept of power was generally seen as self-centred and autocratic. He equated his progress and pre-eminence with the country's progress and pre-eminence. It was more than ego. It carried with it a sincere belief that he was the quintessence of the country, that the country's destiny was irrevocably intertwined with his destiny.

What was on display here was the phenomenon known as the cult of personality, the moment when 'a national leader tries to achieve, by using techniques of mass media propaganda, the big lie, using spectacle, the arts, patriotism and government-organised demonstrations and rallies to create an idealised, heroic and worshipful image of himself'. It was this cult of personality that led to Air India and Indian Railways issuing tickets with Modi's photograph on them. Instructions were given to Bharat Petroleum and Indian Oil to display pictures of Narendra Modi at retail petrol pumps ahead of the 2019 elections. These pictures are still displayed at many petrol stations although 2019 came and went. Perhaps they are still reeling under the threat held out that year, that 'those who refuse would have their supplies blocked'.

In an apparent attempt to create an atmosphere of tension,

state-owned oil companies asked the Consortium of Indian Petroleum Dealers (CIPD) to provide personal data of the employees of the companies it represented. They wanted to know details regarding marital status, name of guardian, religion, caste, and bank information. CIPD saw this as an attempt to profile them on caste/religion lines. 'It is a breach of privacy,' they said and warned of their intention to go to court. The position the oil companies took was that the government required the data for the Prime Minister's Skill Development Ministry. It was clear that there was an attempt to create a sense of fear among ordinary people as well as in the trades.

The personality factor was brought to the forefront. It occurred to no prime minister other than Modi that drama could be created by his doing a *sashtanga namaskar* on the steps of Parliament on his maiden visit as prime minister in May 2014. It was a gesture of accepting the paramountcy of Parliament. But it ended with the gesture. Modi made a convenience of Parliament in moments of crisis. He simply cancelled the winter session in 2020 citing Covid-19 as an excuse. This helped him avoid parliamentary scrutiny of some of his policy initiatives. As a critical commentator put it: 'Ambedkar felt that nobody could be as disdainful of the legislature as the British. Modi proved him wrong.'

Everything about Modi was showmanship, drama. The brouhaha over his education was typical. He could have said that circumstances did not allow him to go to university—and no one would have thought the less of him for that. Karunanidhi was Class 10-pass while Jayalalithaa was just a matriculate. Modi has once said that he was 'undereducated' and 'never went to college'. But he changed his stance later for reasons unknown. He said he had a BA from Delhi University (School of Opening Learning) and an MA in 'entire political science' from Gujarat University. The politics of these claims was laid open when Arun Jaitley and Amit Shah appeared before television cameras in May 2016 showing computer-generated mark sheets of Modi, a facility that was technologically not possible during Modi's presumed university days. RTI activist Neeraj Sharma's attempt to get full details (list of students, roll numbers, marks obtained) was blocked by Delhi University. Court cases followed, leading to various legal complications. Normally, DU publishes examination results in detail online. In 2017, Central Information Commissioner Acharyulu ordered DU to allow inspection of records. Acharyulu was divested of his charge of the HRD Ministry. The toing and froing turned it all into a farce with many saying that Modi was in fact an 8th standard pass (his 10th standard is disputed).

Even the World Yoga Day was used to dramatise Modi's persona. Photo shoots that day showed him performing yogasanas with ease and expertise, in sylvan surroundings, dressed in a black jogging tunic with a light shawl around his neck. He demonstrated various yoga postures, including bending back on a boulder and walking along a five-element-of-nature track. A very photogenic show, it went viral across the world. In addition to this, an animated yoga video was also aired with a cartoon character resembling Modi demonstrating various asanas. Reports later said that this was made by a private agency commissioned by the BJP's media cell. I&B minister, Rajyavardhan Rathore, tweeted that the videos and photos were shot by in-house PMO photographers. *IndiaScoops.com* reported that PMO sources unofficially confirmed that the exercise cost over ₹35 lakh 'which was donated or sponsored by a third party'. An RTI query revealed that the government had spent ₹15.87 crore in 2015 on SMS messages alone to promote Yoga Day. The Ayush Ministry spent more than ₹20 crore in 2018 for the fourth edition of International Yoga Day according to NDTV. Media reports said more than one lakh yoga people were gathered for demonstrations in Delhi alone. A spectacular mass yoga demonstration was staged at Raj Path in 2015 at a cost of ₹7.59 crore. Additionally, the Ministry of External Affairs spent ₹8 crore for promotion of the event across the world. There were reports that 36,000 yoga mats were procured from China at a cost of ₹1.02 crore. Why were yoga mats imported? Does their manufacture involve technology beyond India's reach?

Modi's India manufactured something no one else had thought of—woollen material of the highest quality with the Modi name woven into it with extraordinary dexterity. The blue bandgala he wore to receive Barack Obama had what appeared to be golden stripes on it. Actually, it was the name Narendra Damodardas Modi woven into the wool like stripes. *Hindustan Times* published a report with the heading 'Modi wears Modi'. Media reports speculated whether the design was crafted by Modi's trusted Ahmedabad-based firm, Jade Blue, or Mumbai-based designer, Troy Costa, which had designed Modi's ensemble for a US visit.

Described as the Modi Jacket, it was no different from what had come to be known around the world as the Nehru Jacket. But ideology-wise and personality-wise, Modi could not wear Nehru. So they tried to pass it off as the Modi Jacket. Bipin Chandra, managing director of Jade Blue Lifestyle Company, was aware of the embarrassment involved in using the term Modi Jacket for something everyone knew as Nehru Jacket. He had been making clothes for Modi since 1989. All he could say was: 'This was originally called Nehru Jackets. But what we make are Modi Jackets. It's a bit longer and more comfortable.' All good Indians were expected to be convinced by that explanation and not mistake Nehru Jackets for Modi Jackets. The role of ego in public life should never be underestimated. From Kashmir, Omar Abdullah pronounced the last word when he said: 'All my life I have known these jackets as Nehru Jackets and now I find they are labelled Modi Jackets. Clearly nothing existed in India before 2014.' A fabric designer commented: 'Modi is a bigger label than Gucci. Thus he is wearing his own brand.' Perhaps it was poetic justice. A man who liked to be remembered as a chaiwallah's son was now a brand ambassador. It is another story that Modi as prime minister was forced to feel politically guilty for showing his weakness for self-glory. He never wore the jacket again, stung by critics who accused him of 'megalomania and narcissism unparalleled'. A Modi fan saved the situation by buying the Modi-striped Modi jacket for ₹4.31 crore. But Modi won the political game of one-upmanship. No patriot calls the Nehru Jacket the Nehru Jacket any longer. Now it is always and everywhere the Modi Jacket. Nehru is dead. Alive and kicking in all directions is Modi, who has a 56-inch chest as testified famously by measurement expert Amit Shah. One day, perhaps, Jawaharlal Nehru University will be saved by renaming it Narendra Modi University.

In fact, there were too many things named after Nehru—22 colleges and universities, 119 navodaya vidyalayas, 16 stadiums, 12 parks and gardens, three museums, a port, cups in cricket, football and boat racing, a planetarium, a nagar, a dweep, even a chowk and a bus station. This was unfair. After all, Nehru was only an extension of the freedom movement. He did not think things through the way the buddhijeevi in Narendra Modi did. His books were full of the ideals and philosophy made famous by European thinkers. For Shudh Bharateeyatha, we will have to rely on the books Modiji will write one of these days.

Some anti-national conspiracy has prevented the world from knowing that Narendra Modi was in fact an author of many books. *Jyotipunj* (2008), *Social Harmony* (2012), *A Journey: Poems* (2014), *Abode of Love* (2018), *Exam Warriors* (2018), *Letters to Mother* (2020) are only some of the tomes written by this felicitous author. Evidently, he not only has a creative mind with a literary bend; he also has the time to sit back and look at the sky like poets do, deriving inspiration from the clouds that pass gently by. The books on Modi by admirers outnumber the books by him. They range from *Narendra Modi: Yes, He Can* (2012) by D.P. Singh and *Narendra Modi: The Game Changer* (2014) by Sudesh Verma to *Narendra Modi: The Architect of a Modern State* (2009) by M.V. Kamath and *Modi: The Making of a Prime Minister* (2014) by Vivian Fernandes.

So many books saying so many wonderful things about Modi must have been the reason for Prakash Javadekar, a BJP minister, to say that 'India's prestige has risen since Modi became prime minister.' Unfortunately, the outside world thought that India's prestige had collapsed. And it said as much. In December 2019, the *New Yorker* magazine wrote: 'Is the World's Largest Democracy Doomed? As Prime Minister Narendra Modi consolidates his power, dissenting voices were being quashed by disinformation, threats, and violence.' In 2015 a *Time* magazine cover had discussed the subject, 'Why Modi matters'. Four years later, in 2019, the same magazine ran a cover feature under the title 'India's Divider in Chief'. A *Financial Times* (London) story carried the headline 'India risks sliding into a second Emergency'. Even the leading daily of Israel, a country the Modi government admires, was unsparing. Said *Haaretz*: 'India under Modi is becoming a brutal authoritarian state'. It ran a story on how India's 'Hindu nationalists hijacked Gandhi'.

In a feature/article headlined 'India's democracy in decline,' the *Washington Post* wrote that 'the future of the world's largest democracy is looking increasingly less democratic'. It said Narendra Modi was the most dominant Indian leader in five decades, but added that the country's independent institutions have rarely appeared weaker. Without mincing words, it said: 'Much of the local mainstream media shies away from criticising the government. The judiciary seems reluctant to examine the constitutionality of major pieces of legislation. Government critics have faced intimidation, harassment and arrest. Academics who study democracy around the world recently put India in the category of nations moving toward autocracy.' International agencies of high standing have also found recent Indian moves unacceptable. The UN High Commissioner for Human Rights urged India to release arrested activists. The way the prestigious London magazine, *The Economist*, changed its views was dramatic. In 2010, it had run a cover story holding up India as a model to others. Its headline said: 'How India's Growth will outpace China's'. In 2020, its cover picture showed a lotus perched on a barbed-wire coil with the heading 'Intolerant India: How Modi is Endangering the World's Biggest Democracy'. No anti-Modi prejudice could have been the reason for this. When Modi began his reign in 2014, the magazine's cover story had trumpeted: 'Strongman. How Modi can unleash India.' Well, Modi could, but Modi didn't.

In 2018, the *New York Review of Books* prominently featured its review of two books: *How the BJP Wins: Inside India's Greatest Election Machine* by Prashant Jha (2017) and *When Crime Pays: Money and Muscle in Indian Politics* by Milan Vaishnav (2017). It drew attention to, 'Yogi Adityanath, a 45-year-old Hindu priest and founder of his own extreme-right Hindutva youth group with a penchant for bigoted vigilantism. His most vigorous initiative so far: repainting public buildings, walls and highway medians in bright pious orange.' Jha argues that the BJP's repeated victories are a result of 'discipline, focused leadership, deep pockets and ruthless tactics'. He also shows how Amit Shah's registration drive swelled the BJP's rolls to more than 100 million members, making it the world's largest political party. They were not 'members' in the usual sense of the term. RSS chief, Mohan Bhagwat, once said that he could mobilise his entire following in just three days whereas the Indian army would take six months.

Discipline helps the BJP as much as the lack of it weakens the Congress. Principles of the power game also are in favour of the BJP. As much as 80 per cent of all corporate political funding in Gujarat went to Modi's party. In the 1960s, the Congress received 32 times more in corporate donations than any other party. Academic studies such as *When Crime Pays* gives details of how money is used directly to buy votes. Vaishnav writes that a candidate's friend shelled out close to $2 million in a race for the Andhra Pradesh state assembly. Other candidates spent more, he was told. This was one reason why candidates standing for elections were either very wealthy or were criminals with access to big money. The rush of candidates continued because politicians, especially members of legislatures, could facilitate transactions with relative ease. A 2013 study cited by Vaishnav showed that the declared wealth of sitting legislators after a single term in office rose by an average of 222 per cent.*

* Milan Vaishnav, *When Crime Pays: Money and Muscle in Indian Politics*, (New Delhi: HarperCollins India), 2018, p. 144.

In six years of Modi government, India's GDP contracted for the first time in four years. Unemployment reached an all-time high. Private investment went down, as did exports. The government's spending capacity was also reduced. In February 2021, *The Economist* Intelligence Unit downgraded India from 27th in 2014 to 53rd on the Democracy Index. It called India a flawed democracy. It said the Modi government 'introduced a religious element to the conceptualisation of Indian citizenship' which led to 'undermining the secular basis of the Indian state'. But Modi seemed unconcerned by readings of this kind. His usual stance was to dismiss protestors as conspirators. Money continued to be the deciding factor in most issues. While observers saw signs of Indian democracy declining because of the greed for money, Indian politicians saw it as a factor that strengthened their game. What others considered cynical, Indian politicians perceived as practical. The BJP's ways might have been resented by many, but its hold on power enabled it to ignore them. The 21-day lockdown announced with four hours' notice in March 2020 was a disaster by all accounts. But Modi never expressed regret for the misery of millions that followed; power made him confident that there was no need for him to apologise to anyone about anything. The Modi saga made people in Karnataka recall a folk song popularised by Gururaj Hoskote. It was all about a mother's pride for her son.

> Instead of bearing ten children,
> I gave birth to one, a pearl;
> At 6 he hit his guru for trying
> to discipline him;
> At 9 he pushed a friend into
> the well;
> At 14 he robbed a neighbour
> of his jewellery;
> At 22 he went to jail for murder;
> At 42 my pearl became
> Mukhya Mantri.

BIBLIOGRAPHY

A.P.J. Abdul Kalam, *Turning Points: A Journey Through Challenges*, (New Delhi: HarperCollins India), 2012.

Dionne Bunsha, *Scarred: Experiments with Violence in Gujarat*, (New Delhi: Penguin India), 2006.

Girish Karnad, *This Life at Play*, (New Delhi: HarperCollins India), 2021.

Harsh Mander, *Between Memory and Forgetting: Massacre and the Modi Years in Gujarat*, (New Delhi: Yoda Press), 2019.

J.R.D. Tata, S.A. Sabavala and R.M. Lala (eds.), *Keynote: J.R.D. Tata—Excerpts from His Speeches and Chairman's Statements to Shareholders*, (Bombay: Tata Press Limited), 1986.

Jitender Bhargava, *The Descent of Air India*, (New Delhi: Bloomsbury India), 2013.

K.M. Panikkar, *A Survey of Indian History*, (Bombay: Asia Publishing House), 1947.

K. Vijay Kumar, *Veerappan: Chasing the Brigand*, (New Delhi: Rupa Publications), 2017.

Kusum Nair, *Blossoms in the Dust: The Human Element in Indian Development*, (London: Gerald Duckworth & Co), 1961.

M.K. Gandhi, *An Autobiography: The Story of My Experiments with Truth*, (Boston: Beacon Press), 1993.

M. Sivaram, *The Road to Delhi*, (Rutland, Vermont and Tokyo, Japan: Charles E. Tuttle Publishers), 1966.

Manohar Malgonkar, *The Men Who Killed Gandhi*, (New Delhi: Roli Books), 2008.

Manoj Mitta, *The Fiction of Fact Finding: Modi and Godhra*, (New Delhi: HarperCollins India), 2014.

Milan Vaishnav, *When Crime Pays: Money and Muscle in Indian Politics*, (New Delhi: HarperCollins India), 2018.

Nambi Narayanan, *Ready To Fire: How India and I Survived the ISRO Spy Case*, (New Delhi: Bloomsbury India), 2018.

Namita Devidayal, *The Sixth String of Vilayat Khan*, (New Delhi: Context), 2018.

Naseeruddin Shah, *And Then One Day: A Memoir*, (New Delhi: Penguin India), 2015.

Priya Ramani, 'The Impossible Rana Ayyub', *Mint Lounge*, 2 October 2020.

R.B. Sreekumar, *Gujarat Behind the Curtain*, (New Delhi: Pharos Media and Publishing Pvt Ltd), 2016.

R.K. Anand and Inderjit Badhwar (ed.), *Close Encounters with Niira Radia*, (New Delhi: Har Anand Publications), 2011.

Raj Chengappa, *Weapon of Peace*, (New Delhi: HarperCollins India), 2000.

Raj Thapar, *All These Years: A Memoir*, (New Delhi: Penguin India), 1991.

Rana Ayyub, *Gujarat Files: Anatomy of a Cover-up*, self-published, 2016.

Rasheed Kidwai, *24 Akbar Road: A Short History of the People Behind the Fall and Rise of the Congress*, (New Delhi: Hachette India), 2013.

Ravi Shankar, *Raga Mala: An Autobiography*, (New York: Welcome Rain Publishing), 1999.

S.A. Ayer, *Unto Him a Witness: The Story of Netaji Subhas Chandra Bose in East Asia*, (Bombay: Thacker & Co Ltd), 1951.

S. Hussain Zaidi, *Byculla to Bangkok: Mumbai's Maharashtrian Mobsters*, (New Delhi: HarperCollins India), 2014.

S. Hussain Zaidi, *Dongri to Dubai: Six Decades of the Mumbai Mafia*, (New Delhi: Roli Books), 2012.

Salman Rushdie, *The Moor's Last Sigh*, (London: Vintage UK), 1997.

Siddharth Varadarajan, *Gujarat: The Making of a Tragedy*, (New Delhi: Penguin India), 2002.

Sucheta Dalal and Debashish Basu, *The Scam: Who Won, Who Lost, Who Got Away*, (New Delhi: UBS Publishers Distributors), 1993.

Sujata Anandan, *Samrat: How the Shiv Sena Changed Mumbai Forever*, (New Delhi: HarperCollins India), 2014.

Swapan Kumar Bondyopadhyay, *An Unheard Melody: An Authorised Biography of Annapurna Devi*, (New Delhi: Roli Books), 2016.

Teesta Setalvad, *Gujarat: Behind the Mirage*, (The Book People), 2014.

The Air-India Art Collection.

Vaasanthi, *Amma: Jayalalithaa's Journey from Movie Star To Political Queen*, (New Delhi: Juggernaut Books), 2020.

Vajpayee: The Years That Changed India, 2020.

Varavara Rao, *Captive Imagination: Letters from Prison*, (New Delhi: Penguin India), 2010.

Vinayak Chaturvedi, 'Violence as Civility: V.D. Savarkar and the Mahatma's Assassination', *South Asian History and Culture*, Vol. 11(3), August 2020.